"Omi brings such amazing heart and soul to her cooking! Her joyful spirit resonates in every recipe, story, and photograph. A true light in this world, *Cooking con Omi* celebrates Puerto Rican cuisine in such an incredibly thoughtful, beautiful way."

—NYESHA ARRINGTON, chef, television personality, and restaurateur

"Omi's warmth and personal story are woven into every dish in *Cooking con Omi*. Her cooking lingers not just because of the flavors, but because each recipe tells a story—one baked with charm, heritage, and her own remarkable journey."

—DAVID BEGNAUD, CBS news contributor and host of *Beg-Knows America*

"From the moment I saw Omi, I was struck by how talented, personable, and genuinely awesome she is. What a pleasant surprise to discover that the honest, vibrant energy you see online and on TV is exactly the same in person. Needless to say, I am absolutely thrilled about *Cooking con Omi*. Experiencing Omi's way of celebrating Puerto Rican cuisine—and the island she so deeply loves—through her food is an absolute treat. I will devour every page and savor her essence in every dish and every word."

—ROSELYN SÁNCHEZ, actress and singer-songwriter

"The heart of *Cooking con Omi* is rooted in Omi's Puerto Rican heritage. Blended with her culinary vision, her cooking, and her essence, Omi is always authentic."

—IVY QUEEN, rapper, singer, and actress

"There are books that teach you how to cook and others that take you on a journey. *Cooking con Omi* does both with warmth and technique, and Omi fills her recipes with flavor and love for our culture. This book deserves a permanent place in every kitchen."

— RAÚL CORREA SOTO, chef and restaurateur of BACOA Finca + Fogón and Aldeana

Cooking *con Omi*

Cooking *con Omi*

A LOVE LETTER TO PUERTO RICAN HOME COOKING

OMI HOPPER

WITH CECILIA MOLINARI

PHOTOGRAPHY BY

BETH FULLER

TEN SPEED PRESS

California | New York

Contents

For Doña Gloria, mi abuelita, mi maestra, mi corazón.

Your hands taught me how to cook, but your love taught me why.

This book is for you, for every story you told while peeling plátanos, for every sofrito stirred with patience, and for the way you made magic out of simple ingredients and even simpler times.

I carry your wisdom in every recipe, and your spirit in every page.

2 TIMOTHY 1:5

Introduction

The first time I opened my eyes and took my first breath was at a hospital in Naguabo, on the east coast of the island of Puerto Rico. I'm the daughter of Alberto Hernández Opio and Consuelo Garcia Castro, and la Isla del Encanto is my home, my roots, my culture, my everything, and I'm a Boricua through and through.

The Taíno people, who likely inhabited the island starting in the sixth or seventh century, originally named this island Borikén (now Borinquén or Boriquén), which is where "Boricuas"—our nickname for Puerto Ricans—comes from. When Christopher Columbus arrived almost a thousand years later, he claimed the land in the name of Spain and decided to call it San Juan Bautista, after Saint John the Baptist. A few years later, once it became a Spanish colony, the island was renamed Puerto Rico, "rich port," due to the vast amount of gold found in its rivers. After the Spanish-American War in 1898, the island was ceded to the United States, which is when it officially became a US territory. By 1917, Puerto Ricans were granted US citizenship (though residents still can't vote in presidential elections), and in 1952, the island became a US commonwealth, which gave it a greater degree of autonomy—yet we lack full representation in the federal government to this day.

Despite its long and complex history, Puerto Rico has become a vibrant, flavorful cultural sancocho of Taíno, Spanish, African, and American ingredients that have influenced and contributed to the island's traditions, music, language, culture, and food. It has been home to renowned figures such as San Juan mayor Felisa Rincón de Gautier, aka Doña Fela, the first female mayor of a capital city in the Americas; the legendary Roberto

Clemente, one of the first Latin American baseball stars in the United States, and the greatest player of his time; beloved musicians, including Héctor Lavoe, El Gran Combo de Puerto Rico, Ricky Martin, José Feliciano, and Bad Bunny; and above everyone else, and at the heart of it all: my family.

Mi familia has gifted me with the cultural foundation, love, and legacy that has shaped every part of my journey and who I am today as a daughter, mother, wife, friend, and chef. As a true Boricua, I believe a good meal can solve any problem in life, just as much as I believe in Vicks (or, as we call it, Vaporú). Cooking isn't a task or a chore, but a memory-making experience. The kitchen is where I learned about my heritage, traditions, and the stories of my ancestors. And in my lifetime, it all starts with my maternal grandparents, Abuela Gloria and Abuelo Pedro.

My abuela was thirteen when my abuelo, fifteen, swept her off her feet. They were so head over heels in love that they decided to run away from home and start a life together. Although thirteen and fifteen sounds incredibly young to us nowadays, in the early twentieth century, it was quite common for teenagers to leave home and start a family, especially in rural areas.

My abuelos found a home and eventually began to have children, nine in total, including two who passed away at birth. With time and hard work, my abuelos managed to save enough money to purchase a house with a few acres of land, which we call a finca, in Parcelas Suárez, Loíza, a coastal town near San Juan. They came from very humble beginnings, but through their hard work, perseverance, and faith, they managed to build a good life and prosper.

My mami, Consuelo (aka Connie), my older brother, Carlos (or Junior, as I call him), and I moved so many times when I was a child that I lost track of all the neighborhoods we (temporarily) called home. But Abuelo Pedro and Abuela Gloria's house in Loíza was my constant—no matter where we were living, Mami always made it a point to visit her parents on the weekends and during every holiday, and I'm so grateful that she did. Amid the challenges and struggles we faced, that precious time in Loíza was a warm and soothing embrace that always uplifted my spirit.

My abuelos' house was always full of people, chatter, laughter, chisme, and a constant stream of love that came straight from my abuela's kitchen. While I busied myself making casitas de sábanas (bedsheet forts) in the living room, sneaking kittens and chicks into the house and pretending they were my pets, or playing hide-and-seek with my cousins, Abuela Gloria and her five daughters were usually in the kitchen preparing our next feast. From the outside, it probably looked like chaos. But they moved around the kitchen with such ease, talking, laughing, lowering their voices when the gossip got good, all while grabbing ingredients from the fridge, chopping, mashing, sautéing, stewing, and washing. And then they were done, and our next meal was served and the kitchen was clean. I loved watching them in action and yearned to be in that kitchen circle one day.

Unlike all the women in the family, my abuelito was more reserved, and most definitely old-school. When he wasn't busy keeping an eye on his daughters' prospective partners, he was either outside tending to the pigs or chickens or at the beach picking jueyes (crabs). On those days, he'd bring the jueyes back to the house and hand them over to my abuela, who would tell him to get cleaned up before our meal. Abuelo had built his own outside bathroom because my abuela wouldn't let him inside the house until he took off his dirty clothes. Meanwhile, Abuela and my tías would boil the jueyes in salted water, together with some guineos verdes (green bananas), and make what was basically the Puerto Rican version of a crab boil. I love jueyes, but when my tías would crack open their crabs and dip the guineo verde in the crab's brains, my cousins and I gasped in horror. We never got into that particular delicacy, but give me something filled with jueyes, like the Empanadas de yuca, coco y jueyes (page 91), and I'm your girl.

That three-bedroom house in Loíza represented peace, joy, and lightheartedness. It held every wonderful memory I have of those first eleven years of my life in Puerto Rico. It was also our safe space during times of trouble, including when the island was hit by the Category 5 Hurricane Hugo in 1989. After taking refuge with a family friend during the worst of the storm, Mami and I returned to find our apartment wrecked by the downpour and ravaging winds. Suddenly displaced, we silently climbed into Mami's Toyota Corolla and left what had once been our home in Daguao—then, halfway to Loíza, Mami's engine flooded with the rising water on the streets. Determined to reach my abuelos, we abandoned the car and hopped on a bus to complete the grueling, hours-long journey that on a normal day would have taken only forty-five minutes.

My seven-year-old brain found it hard to process the level of devastation around us. More than thirty thousand people, including Mami and me, were left homeless that day. Thankfully, the Loíza house was intact—a miracle given its proximity to the beach—so we stayed there until we got back on our feet. I will never forget the solidarity among the neighbors, everyone pitching in to help, including my abuelo, who had a well and a filter out back and was therefore able to provide the community with buckets of clean water. It took a long time for the island to recover from Hugo, but true to the spirit of my beloved Boricuas, no matter how many times we're knocked down, we rise from the rubble and move forward.

A few years later, Mami fell in love with José, my stepdad, whom I lovingly call Coop. After a devastating tragedy in his family, Coop and Mami decided to move to Rhode Island for a fresh start. Although I understood, I was gutted. Leaving meant that I would no longer have access to my abuelos, my dad, my tías and tíos, my cousins, that magical house—my happy place, my safe place.

We moved to the States when I was eleven, only a few months shy of finishing fifth grade. I didn't know a lick of English. At first, we stayed with my stepdad's sister, but by the time summer rolled around, they had rented a house of our own off Broad Street in Providence. By the end of that summer, between my time spent playing with the girls that lived across the street and the many TV shows I devoured, I was fluent in a brand-new language. Nevertheless, sixth grade was tough. Even though I could communicate, I still had a long way to go, so I was placed in ESL classes. To make matters worse, I also got bullied because of the way I dressed (Mami was very conservative about my clothing). I found solace in thinking that the situation was temporary, that we'd eventually return to my beloved island. As the months passed by, I grew so unhappy and homesick that Mami decided to send me back to Puerto Rico the following summer to be with my abuelos, a trip that became the standard every summer until I graduated high school.

During that first year we had been away, my grandparents had decided to sell the finca in Loíza and buy a plot of land in Río Grande, which meant saying goodbye to beach living and hello to the mountains. They found a place that was large enough to give their children a chance to build their own homes on the land that would one day be their own. My titi Marta was the first one to break ground, so she was living with my grandparents at the time and was the one who picked me up at the airport that first summer back.

Tears welled up in my eyes as we passed Loíza and continued down the highway, and eventually up a narrow road that led to the house on the mountain. It was all so unfamiliar, and all I wanted was my safe place. "You're going to love it," she said enthusiastically, but like any twelve-year-old, I didn't believe her. When we arrived, we walked past a large flamboyán tree in full bloom, through the marquesina (garage), and into the house. We crossed the living room, the dining room, and finally entered the kitchen, where I fell into my abuela's arms. Then, just beyond the kitchen, I noticed the terraza (terrace) overlooking the lush green mountain rolling down to the town below and, in the distance, a sliver of sand and the vast ocean. That's when I knew I was home.

I can replay each one of those summers in my mind vividly, like a movie. I went from a very strict household in Rhode Island to one that was stern when needed, but also allowed me to explore who I was becoming as a growing teenager. Titi Marta was my second mom, and she was the mother of my girl cousins, so it was easy to talk to her. She saw no harm in letting me do things like cut my hair, paint my nails, or get a new piercing, even though I knew I'd get an earful from Mami when I went back home. (¡Perdón, Mami!)

This was also when I truly began to take an interest in cooking. Even though my abuela rarely let me help, other than to mash some garlic in the pilón or grab her ingredients from the fridge, she did allow me to sit in the kitchen and watch her. I was so fascinated with the ease with which she cooked three or four dishes at once that I'd often bring my notebook and scribble notes about the ingredients, seasoning, and her techniques in hopes that I could capture some of her secrets on the page. I soon realized that food in her home wasn't just sustenance—it was an expression of love, like her Bacalao con viandas (page 76), which she made for my abuelo, who loved anything and everything with bacalao (preserved salted codfish). (In later years, she'd make the same dish for me anytime I visited, as it had become one of my all-time favorite dishes, too.) You'll find stories about Abuela's dishes, the aromas, and the way they moved my soul throughout this book, because she is my inspiration. I was in total awe of her—I wanted to be like Doña Gloria when I grew up.

Breakfast was freshly made every morning, lunch was home-cooked, and dinner always came with dessert. The jugos (juices), frituras, and feasts she prepared for special occasions (or our Sunday beach days) made a lifelong impact on me. She turned simple ingredients into love-filled delicacies that will forever live on in my heart and on my table.

No matter how many times we moved—we lived in nine different homes over the following seven years in Rhode Island—Mami always had a home-cooked meal on the table when I returned home from school in the afternoon. It was such a blessing—I still remember walking down the street toward our front door and smelling her habichuelas guisadas or pollo frito. Even though I didn't get to help her in the kitchen—because

Piraguas
latanutres
TiriJala

she would either be done by the time I got home, or she'd shoo me away from the stove if I got too close—we still had the chance to hang out during those early dinners. Sometimes she'd open up and tell me stories I'd quietly receive and treasure while watching her work her own magic in the kitchen.

My chance to try my hand at cooking finally arrived when I was sixteen. Mami had to have shoulder surgery, and my stepdad worked a full-time job, so I stepped up and proudly said, "Mami, don't worry, I'm going to cook." She looked at me sideways, but allowed it. That was the first time I ever made arroz blanco and habichuelas. I flew around the kitchen emulating my abuela Gloria and Mami, trying to remember their every move, the seasonings they used, the cook time. When I was finished, my habichuelas were pretty bland, and my white rice was so sticky it felt like fresh cement being poured on the plate. Mami took one bite and asked me to hang up my chef's hat that day. My time in the kitchen then was short-lived, but it wouldn't be the last attempt.

With time, I managed to adapt to life in Rhode Island, and by eighteen, I had friends, work that allowed me to pay some of the bills at home, my own car, and a plan to go to college. So, when Mami said she and my stepdad had decided to move back to Puerto Rico, I immediately said, "I'm not going." My longing for stability outweighed my family's disbelief at my choice. I needed to stay and see my plans through, even if that meant not returning to my beloved island. Hurt and worried, Mami expressed fear that I wasn't ready for such a big leap, but I reassured her that I had work experience, a sense of responsibility, an apartment to rent, and a plan. And so began my adulthood.

I was definitely on the struggle bus the following couple of years, working two jobs, studying, and fending for myself, but I felt accomplished and happy. Then came an unexpected turning point: Kradin Hopper. We met because he was a customer at the bank I worked at, and from the moment we started dating, I felt safe with him. One night, determined to impress this wonderful gentleman, I decided to cook for him. I set the ingredients on the kitchen counter of my tiny third-floor apartment and made pineapple pork chops and coconut rice, my first official presentable meal infused with the flavors that I knew and loved. It came out so well that he said if he was ever on death row, that was the meal he'd order. And I thought to myself—mission accomplished.

Kradin and I got married and became parents to four beautiful sons: Lil' Kradin, Zekiah, X'Avian, and Isaiah. As we raised our boys, the girl who couldn't cook a pot of rice turned into the woman who was always asked to bring the rice to friend and family gatherings and events. How's that for a plot twist?

I continued to find my groove in the kitchen, and my passion for cooking only grew stronger. But I only did it for fun, to see people's faces light up when they tried my food—which is a feeling I still find priceless to this day.

I spent ten years working my way up the corporate ladder at the bank, but when my fourth son, Isaiah, was born, something deep within me shifted. I yearned to stay home with my kids instead of working all the time just to spend it on a babysitter and miss out on so many of their milestones. Ever the supportive partner, Kradin said, "Don't worry, I got us. Do it." After close to a year of being at home with my babies, I got a call from a friend who was getting married—she wanted me to do her makeup. This led to my second career as a makeup artist, which flourished over the following ten years, as did my family.

Everything seemed to be on the right track until 2018, when Kradin was laid off and diagnosed with a degenerative bone disease, preventing him from finding new work. As the bills piled up, we ripped through our savings, and by 2020, we were experiencing such financial hardship that our church stepped in to cover our rent. Due to the Covid-19 pandemic, my makeup business was put on indefinite hold. My husband's disability payments hadn't kicked in yet, and I had just filed for unemployment, so those first couple of weeks of the pandemic were brutal. One day, I drove to the supermarket with thirty-five dollars to our name and, unable to keep it together any longer, I burst into tears. The future felt so grim that I just couldn't see a path forward. But my faith carried me. I gathered myself, masked up, and grabbed whatever I could buy with my thirty-five dollars. When I got home, I needed something that would lighten up my energy and take my mind off the bleak future, so I turned to what always made me happy: cooking.

I recorded myself making one of my everyday recipes, and I uploaded it as a story on my Instagram makeup account. Desperate to connect with the outside world and feel some sense of normalcy, I continued to cook, record, and upload these videos to my stories. Homesickness was hitting me hard, so the meals I was sharing on social media were the ones my abuela used to make, the ones that made me feel a little closer to my family in Puerto Rico, to home.

The response was immediate and enthusiastic, and it took me by surprise. Clearly, we were all going through it. Many people were losing loved ones or isolated and unable to see their friends or families, and I guess we all felt an aching need to bridge the distance. So, I continued cooking and posting stories, putting the teaching skills I'd honed in my makeup career to use by showing my viewers how to make simple Puerto Rican meals. I received a flood of DMs asking that I start a new profile exclusively for cooking content. I was still barely keeping myself afloat, and starting another page on Instagram felt daunting, so I decided to turn to TikTok. I was enthralled by those one-minute videos, especially Tabitha Brown's. Her cooking clips, like my own, carried a sense of love and nostalgia that spoke to me, and she inspired me to build up my TikTok profile with exclusively cooking content. I edited down the videos I had already posted on Instagram and repurposed them on TikTok, and Cooking con Omi was born.

In the following month, my number of followers shot up to ten thousand, then twenty thousand, then thirty thousand... I couldn't believe my eyes. As if that wasn't enough, I received a call from Univision's *¡Despierta América!* They wanted to feature me in a segment teaching viewers how to make a dish from home. What? I was going to be on an international TV network, on Don Francisco's channel no less? Once the shock wore off, I glammed myself up and shared my love for cooking with the show and its audience.

What no one knew at the time is that even as my star rose in the public eye, we were surviving off my unemployment. All those recipes posted during the height of the pandemic, including after I was on TV and my follower numbers skyrocketed, were made with groceries I purchased with food stamps. After the show aired, I received an enormous outpouring of love and support—so much that I had to turn off my phone to give myself some time to digest the moment. While experiencing one of the toughest

DIASPORICAN

times in my life, I was receiving a deluge of messages from strangers saying I had inspired them, that I had provided them with comfort when they needed it most.

Those strangers had no idea what they were doing for my family and me. During the previous couple of years, I had stopped dreaming, my faith had been challenged, I felt I couldn't catch my breath—and now I finally saw a ray of light, of hope, of purpose. I hadn't been looking to make money off this endeavor; my goal was to build community. I received inspiring messages from mothers and daughters who were reconnecting through my content, fathers who had lost their wives who were making meals with meaning for their children, and so many others who thanked me for reminding them of their Puerto Rican roots. The feedback was moving and incredibly humbling, and it filled me with purpose, allowing me to stand tall once again.

I didn't even consider the idea of turning Cooking con Omi into a business until later that year, when a friend basically told me to snap out of it. She helped me realize I was being given an opportunity to pivot, and she was right. But I was too scared to take the leap just yet, too scared to let go of what I had built over the last ten years. So I reopened my makeup studio and began to book clients again. Meanwhile, I continued to post recipes on my cooking channel, and on top of all the interviews, a wave of opportunities began to roll in—like the time I was flown to a hotel in Puerto Rico to do a promotion for Thanksgiving (thanks to my cousin), which allowed me to see my family after several years of not having the means to travel. As soon as I landed, I wanted to visit my abuelita, but she had fallen ill and was in the hospital. Because of all the necessary safety precautions in late 2020, my cousin had to sneak me into her hospital room, where I was able to see her for five minutes. I left feeling reenergized and with a clear path forward: I had to come back soon to see her. I couldn't wait another five years.

In January 2021, I received my first Cooking con Omi paycheck and I realized it was time to take the potential income source seriously, while holding on to my goal of building community and connection. My new business started to grow, and after years of being in the red, we were finally able once again to deposit money in our savings account. I partnered with brands and got invited to the Puerto Rican Day parade in New York, where I met some of my followers for the first time. Listening to their stories in person and realizing how my recipes had impacted their lives only helped my inspiration and conviction grow further. When I received a business grant that I had applied for earlier that year, I decided to use the money to jar and sell my sofrito online and in markets. It sold out the day after it was released, but I made sure to send a box to one of my tías in Puerto Rico and asked her to get it to my abuela. She was so proud and impressed—I couldn't wait to celebrate with her in person.

My husband, the boys, and I were scheduled to fly to Puerto Rico in August of that year, only a couple months after Mi Sofrito Fresquecito had hit the market. I was so excited, I kept hyping up my abuela during our calls: "Abuela, I'm coming to see you! ¡Te voy a ver!" And she'd smile big and reply, "Ay, deja que tú vengas pa'cá. Me voy a pintar la bemba colorá, vamos a cocinar y vamos a hacer ese sofrito que tú haces," promising to put on her red lipstick, and that we'd cook together and make my sofrito. My heart was full.

We landed in Puerto Rico during a huge storm that knocked out the power, a common occurrence on the island, so it took us a couple of days to settle into our rental. On the third day, as I was making plans to visit my abuela, I got a call from one of my aunts—my abuela had been hospitalized again, and her health was fragile. I was rushing out the door to see her when the phone rang again. "Omallys, tu abuelita acaba de fallecer."

I understood the words, "Your grandmother just passed away," but I just couldn't process what she was telling me. In disbelief, I hung up, jumped in the car, and began driving to the house in Río Grande, where one of my uncles and three of my aunts were waiting. On the way, I began to talk to God and to my abuela, asking, "How could you leave me? I came here to see you."

After the longest forty-five minutes of my life, I pulled into the driveway under the flamboyán tree that had been the bane of my abuelita's existence. Every summer, she'd task me with sweeping the bright red flowers and leaves this palo wouldn't stop shedding, and that became my yearly chore. When I arrived that day, the flamboyán tree was dry. I parked beneath it, and as I gathered my purse, I suddenly noticed a red flower quietly floating down from the tree and toward the car. I opened the car door and checked the ground, but there were no red petals in sight. I picked up that single red flower and, as I walked into Abuela's house through the same marquesina door I had crossed for the first time more than twenty-five years earlier, I thought to myself: *Cooking is the only thing that brings me joy, fills me with a sense of purpose, and has always connected me to my abuela Gloria*. That day, I decided to close my makeup studio and focus all my attention on Cooking con Omi. It was my way of honoring Abuela's legacy, her warmth, her way of expressing love through food, and I knew it would continue to make me feel close to her even though she was no longer physically present.

The following year, I was interviewed and picked to participate in season two of Gordon Ramsay's *Next Level Chef*. I firmly believe my abuela Gloria was there with me, guiding my hands as I cooked. I was one of the last people the producers contacted to fill one of their remaining open spots, which meant I only had three weeks to prepare before flying out to London to film. I watched season one around five times during those weeks, studying everyone's moves and strategies. I reached out to a few chef friends to learn some basic cooking methods and techniques, which I memorized. My husband, who doesn't cook at all, would head out to the store, buy a bunch of random ingredients, then come back, set them on the counter, and time me as I came up with dishes from scratch to test my skills. And on September 11, 2022, after doing my very last client's makeup for her wedding, I drove straight to the airport and embarked on this new adventure, feeling like I was closing one chapter and boldly opening another.

While most, if not all, of the show participants had some professional training in the kitchen, I had nothing but my family recipes and my intuition. I learned how to cook with ingredients I had never heard of, I learned how to plate, and I learned that the only way to get winning dishes is to truly stay authentic and cook from the heart. My first top dish came in episode seven, and it was my Bacalaítos (page 153) and my abuela's Caldo de pescado (page 86), which the show fancily called "Halibut Three Ways." Another winner was my Buñuelos sorpresa (page 196), which I had to bake instead of frying them the traditional way to stick to the baking challenge rules.

What carried me through to the semifinals, where I cooked my last dish on the show, was the spirit of my abuela nudging me forward and the awareness that I was representing mi gente, my beloved Puerto Rico, on national television. I wanted to show the world who we are. I wanted to showcase our food, our resilience, our spirit. And I wanted to show the community that faithfully followed me along my journey that if I could do this, if a Puerto Rican woman who learned to connect with family and friends through cooking could get this far, so could they.

I didn't win the title, but I won in every other way possible, including gaining new opportunities with brands, way more visibility, and new heartfelt connections—as well as the opportunity to write this cookbook. I may have more knowledge and exposure than I did before, but I still cook dishes that sing to my soul, and I continue to make intentional decisions to help lift us up as a people.

Cooking con Omi is my love letter to Puerto Rican cuisine. It is a collection of recipes that have been passed down through generations, each dish telling a story of love, resilience, and community. I hope to evoke a sense of nostalgia for those who are familiar with these flavors, and a sense of wonder for those who are experiencing them for the first time. Through this book, I share the warmth and richness of Puerto Rican food and I invite everyone to experience the magic that happens when cultures come together in the kitchen.

Puerto Ricans are like confetti—we're sprinkled all over the world. There are more of us living in other countries than on our island, and I know those of you living abroad yearn for our land, our beaches, our food, our warmth just as much as I do. This book is for you! Let's make sure our classic dishes aren't lost during our journeys away from home. Help me keep our vibrant, joyous, passionate culture, values, and traditions alive, no matter where we are. Mi gente, ustedes valen oro.

Cooking con Omi is more than just a collection of recipes. It's a tribute to my heritage, a bridge between cultures, and a culinary journey that shows the power of food in keeping tradition alive, from my heart to your table. For some of you, it will be a chance to discover Puerto Rico through these mouthwatering dishes; for others, it will be a way back home.

En tu cocina tú mandas
You're the boss in your kitchen

The traditional dishes I decided to share with you in this cookbook are my family classics. I'm well aware that although we call the dishes by the same name, each Puerto Rican family has their own special touch, technique, or secret ingredient—so my abuela's recipe may not be how your abuela used to make it, and that's okay. This is from my family to yours. And it's also from me to you.

Experimentation is one of the reasons I was drawn to the kitchen. I find immense joy in blending cultures through the universal language of food, and also bending and breaking the rules whenever possible. So aside from the classics, you will also find iterations of familiar recipes with unexpected twists and turns, or what I like to call "Omified" dishes. For example, I've taken a classic like bacalaítos (salted codfish fritters), replaced the bacalao with guava and cheese, and called them Guavalaítos (page 205). I love playing with techniques and flavors that sing to me—or simply putting ingredients together in a new way—because I like to have fun in the kitchen. That's a big part of the art of cooking: playfulness and joy.

When you start building a platform on social media, you are open to public opinion. As my videos received more and more views, I started getting asked why I didn't wear a hairnet or gloves or an apron, and my answer was simply: "En tu cocina tú mandas, pero en la mía mando yo." You're the boss in your kitchen, but I'm the boss in mine.

Funnily enough, what started as an innocent clapback became a genuinely empowering phrase: You have the freedom to have fun and experiment in your kitchen. When viewers ask me if they can replace a

certain ingredient or add something else, I now lovingly reply, "Of course—¡en tu cocina tú mandas!"

Cooking is a creative art in my eyes. This cookbook is here to guide you, to help you get your feet wet, and to show you how to use ingredients you may not normally cook with. The rest is up to you. If you want to follow my recipes to a tee, fantastic. If you want to experiment or add or take something out, go for it. If you want to take some shortcuts to make a recipe more doable, be my guest. I am not a baker, so why in the world would I sweat through making a simple cake from scratch when there's a box that calls for three ingredients, and I'm done? Nowadays, I have no problem buying premade biscuits and popping them in the oven or using prepackaged grated yuca instead of grating it myself. You'll see these suggestions in my recipes where possible because while I want us all to cook amazing food, I also know that time is a barrier.

When experimenting, remember that some trials may not come out the way you imagined—and that's okay, too. Just go back to the original recipe and try again. This is not a competition; it's meant to be a joyful, warm act of love. It's your kitchen, and you can do whatever you want in there. There's no judgment and no limit to your creativity, and I'm here for it. Cook with love, measure with your heart, lo que te diga tu corazón, porque ¡en tu cocina tú mandas!

Pa' que me entiendan
Glossary

For those of you who don't speak Spanish, here's a cheat sheet with some of my beloved catchphrases, which you will come across in my content on social media and throughout the book.

- **Bate que bate:** This is my way of saying "to beat" as in "beat the mixture."
- **Buenos días por la mañana, qué rico que estamos activos:** The closest translation is "Good morning, how beautiful that we're alive." The first time I said this phrase, I sang it in a little song I came up with while stuck in traffic one morning. I was being facetious, but everyone loved it, and now it's become my signature way to start the day.
- **En tu cocina tú mandas:** All I'm saying is, "You're the boss in your kitchen."
- **Eso es oro:** In other words, "That is solid gold."
- **Lo que te diga tu corazón, LQTDT♥:** This literally means "whatever your heart wants," and I use it a lot when measurements in a recipe aren't exact and you can add (or subtract) to your heart's desire. You'll also find the acronym in the ingredients list, next to "to taste," for the same reason.
- **No me mires con ese tono de voz:** I go back and forth using the phrase in Spanish and the English translation, "Don't look at me with that tone of voice," to basically emphasize that I know what I'm saying is raising eyebrows, but don't judge me.
- **Sal y pimienta se quieren casar:** This is a play on a nursery rhyme and basically means "Salt and pepper want to get married." I use it to imply you should add salt and pepper to your liking.
- **Ven pa'cá que te voy a enseñar:** This means "Come here and I'll teach you." I use this often in my videos, inspired by my abuela who used to say the same to me when I was in the kitchen yearning to learn from her (even though she never let me be her sous chef).

TOLEDO

En tu alacena
In your pantry

While you probably already have a pantry full of the basics that you turn to over and over, the elements in this section are must-haves in any respectable Puerto Rican kitchen. With the ingredients, tools, and recipes included here, you will be ready to whip up recipes from any chapter of this book that will speak to your heart and leave your guests begging for more.

The fresh ingredients have short descriptions to help you get a better sense of them before putting them to use. The packaged ingredients are intentionally set as a shopping list, so you can snap a quick picture and head to your supermarket to get started. I've also added the names in Spanish in case you're in Puerto Rico or somewhere else in Latin America eager to start cooking boricua cuisine.

Now check out the ingredients below, add whatever you're missing to your shopping list, and get to it, so we can start cooking!

El caldero y el pilón
Cookware essentials

The recipes in this cookbook don't require special utensils, but I can't go without mentioning two staple tools that you will find in any Puerto Rican kitchen: the caldero (aluminum pot) and the pilón (a wooden mortar and pestle). When I think of them, I get all the feels.

As a young girl, when I yearned to cook with my abuela, one of the only tasks she'd give me was to mash the garlic in her pilón. I did this with great pride, and once I was done, I felt an enormous sense of accomplishment. Aside from mashing garlic, you can also use your pilón to grind, crush, and blend ingredients for adobos, marinades, spices, herbs, and more. It requires some elbow grease, but the result will be more flavorful than using a food processor or blender, and the texture will be on point.

A caldero is the regular old aluminum pot with a lid—similar to a Dutch oven—that we use to cook our rice and beans, separately or together. I'm talking arroz blanco, habichuelas, arroz con gandules, the works. It is your reliable partner in the kitchen, a trusted companion that will help you cook each dish to perfection. When I made my first full meal for my now-husband, Kradin, it was in my trusty caldero. I would later make countless dishes in that same pot for my kids, and I still use it when cooking for our family. I honestly don't like to cook rice if it's not in my caldero. The one time I tried to do it in a fancy new pot was on Gordon Ramsay's *Next Level Chef*, and I failed miserably.

The pilón I have right now is older than me. Mami left it to me when she moved back to Puerto Rico. It has been seasoned with love for generations and I still use it to this day. The other piece Mami gave me before leaving was her beloved caldero, where she cooked endless meals for us over the years. She said, "Coge este caldero y este pilón y aprende, muchacha," or "Take this caldero and this pilón and learn, girl." Her words may sound gruff to the non-Boricua, but they were filled with love. And she was taking part in the age-old tradition of passing down these tools to the next generation.

I love my caldero so much, when followers started making fun of how old it looked in my videos, I felt the need to defend my battered soldier for having seen me through so many battles. So, I filmed a short video embracing my beat-up caldero, with lyrics I made up to the tune of the song "I Love My Boots" from *Dora the Explorer*.

So, trust me: If you already have these tools, don't let anyone make you think you have to run out and buy new ones, because those seasoned with love and time are better. But if you don't have a caldero or a pilón, I encourage you to buy them, cook with them, and start building your own traditions.

I love my caldero, my caldero and me.
It was passed down to me from my family tree.
People think I'm crazy and that it's not clean.
I love my caldero, my caldero and me.

312
Your Best Ally in Construction

Para darle sabor
Condiments, adobos, salsas

This is your sauce and condiment starter pack—the secret to the savory recipes in this cookbook, and almost all Puerto Rican dishes. The magic begins here.

To hit the classic Puerto Rican flavor profiles, you must first master your guiso, the base with which you will cook the rest of your ingredients. The guiso used to make anything from Habichuelas guisadas (page 100) to Sancocho (page 107) must include sofrito, mojo, sazón, and adobo.

In addition to our base flavors, I'm also including a few recipes for condiment add-ons to spice up any dish after it's cooked: Mantequilla criolla (page 42) is delicious on bread and is used to baste meat and to season Pavochón (page 220), so I highly recommend keeping it handy in your pantry.

Pique (page 43) and Omi's mayoketchup (page 38) are ideal for dipping the frituras featured in chapter 4, "De chinchorreo" (page 137). Once you get a taste, I'm sure you will find plenty of other dishes to use them with, too. Get creative, experiment, and enjoy!

Mi Sofrito Fresquecito

Every respectable Puerto Rican meal starts with sofrito. It is the base of our flavor DNA and a must-have in our kitchen. Although it's made with fresh ingredients, we do not consume it raw but rather soft-fry it, or sofreírlo, which is where its name "sofrito" comes from. I love the fact that a version of sofrito exists in practically every Latin American country. It may be called by a different name, but the concept is the same: It's the starter base that amps up the flavor of every dish you're about to cook.

This recipe calls for seven vegetables: onions, garlic, green bell peppers, red bell peppers, cilantro, culantro, and ají dulce. All except the last two are easy to find (see page 30). But if worse comes to worst, and you don't have access to culantro and/or ají dulce, you have my permission to make your sofrito without them. It will be missing some flavorful notes, but it'll do the job.

My abuela made her sofrito from scratch before every meal. And if you caught her in the process, she'd always smile and say, "Voy a cortar mi sofrito bien fresquecito." Although many of us use a food processor to make our sofrito, she liked to finely chop her sofrito ingredients with her trusty knife. And since she made it fresh before every dish, she had no need for olive oil, which we normally use to preserve it so we can use the same batch for a few days straight.

I kept all these tips and tricks in mind when I landed the grant that kick-started my sofrito business. When I posted my recipe for sofrito on social media, it immediately went viral, and I decided to scale the recipe so I could package and sell it online and in stores. In a matter of a few short months, Mi Sofrito Fresquecito, named in honor of my abuela's favorite phrase, hit the shelves and sold out in twenty-four hours.

If I don't have sofrito in the fridge, it's like my fridge is empty. I can't cook without it. And no, I don't chop it fresquecito before every cook; I use my food processor and I add oil. Pero, por favor, never ever use a blender. That will immediately make your sofrito way too watery. The goal is to see the fresh speckles of cilantro, culantro, ají dulce, garlic, and onion in every serving. Trust me, this is the number one recipe you'll come back to time and again, so keep it handy.

Mi Sofrito Fresquecito

Makes 3 cups

1 large yellow onion, roughly chopped

1 bunch cilantro with stems

1 bunch culantro (recao)

1 red bell pepper, roughly chopped

1 green bell pepper, roughly chopped

1 large head of garlic, peeled, or *LQTDT*♥

5 to 10 ajíes dulces (Puerto Rican sweet peppers), deseeded and roughly chopped

¼ cup/60ml extra-virgin olive oil

In a food processor, add the onion, cilantro, culantro, bell peppers, garlic, ajíes dulces, and olive oil. Placing the onion in the food processor first will provide you with enough water to help process the rest of the ingredients. Process the mixture until very finely chopped, resembling the consistency of chimichurri. Whatever you do, please don't try to process each vegetable individually, because it will change the flavor of your sofrito.

Pour the mixture into a large quart jar container and set aside.

Add ½ cup/120ml of water to the liquid that remains at the bottom of the food processor to create a sofrito juice, pour it into another jar, and reserve to make Mojo de Omi (recipe follows).

Store the sofrito in the fridge for up to 1 month, or freeze in ice cube trays for easier access. If you freeze in a completely sealed container, the sofrito can last for 3 to 6 months.

Omi Tip: Feel free to double this recipe if you have a larger family like mine, or if you'll be cooking larger quantities.

Mojo de Omi

Makes 1 cup

½ cup/120ml leftover sofrito juice (see above), or ¼ cup/60ml sofrito diluted in ¼ cup/60ml water

¼ cup/60ml lime juice (about 2 limes)

¼ cup/60ml white vinegar

1 tablespoon dried oregano

Kosher salt and freshly ground black pepper to taste, *LQTDT*♥

This mojo is super versatile. Add it to your guisos or use it as a marinade for chicken, pork, beef, or seafood. When using as a marinade, let the meat marinate for at least 30 minutes, or up to 24 hours for more intense flavor. You can also toss vegetables like bell peppers, onions, and zucchini in this mojo before grilling or roasting them or drizzle it over salads as a zesty dressing.

In a medium bowl or jar, add the leftover sofrito juice, lime juice, vinegar, and oregano and season with salt and pepper. Stir or shake well to combine all the ingredients.

Transfer the mojo to a clean, airtight container and store in the refrigerator for up to 1 week. The acidity from the lime juice and vinegar helps preserve the marinade, but it's best used fresh for optimal flavor.

If you want to make your mojo last longer, freeze in ice cube trays for easier access for up to 3 months.

Adobo

Adobo seasoning, a premixed dry spice blend, is perfect for marinating meats, poultry, and seafood. Simply rub the seasoning onto the protein and let it sit for at least 30 minutes before cooking. You can also sprinkle adobo on vegetables before roasting or grilling for added flavor. ¿Cuánto? La cantidad que te diga tú corazón.

Makes about 2½ cups

- ½ cup/70g garlic powder
- ½ cup/70g onion powder
- ½ cup/40g dried oregano
- 2 tablespoons ground cumin
- 2 tablespoons ground coriander
- 2 tablespoons white pepper
- 2 tablespoons freshly ground black pepper
- ½ cup/70g kosher salt
- 2 tablespoons paprika (optional, for color)
- 2 tablespoons turmeric (optional, for color)

In a large bowl, combine the garlic powder, onion powder, oregano, cumin, coriander, white pepper, black pepper, salt, and the paprika and turmeric, if using. Mix well to ensure all the spices are evenly distributed.

Transfer the adobo to an airtight container or multiple spice jars and store in a cool, dry place for up to 6 months.

Omi's mayoketchup

Use this magic pink sauce con to', with everything. Serve as a dipping sauce for French fries (page 127), Tostones (page 143), and yuca fries, or use it as a spread for sandwiches, burgers, or anywhere else your heart desires.

Makes 1¾ cups

- 1 cup/240g mayonnaise
- ½ cup/130g ketchup
- 2 garlic cloves, minced
- 1 tablespoon soy sauce
- 1 tablespoon lemon juice
- 1 tablespoon honey
- 1 to 2 teaspoons sriracha (adjust to taste, *LQTDT*♥)
- ¼ cup/10g finely chopped cilantro
- Kosher salt and freshly ground black pepper to taste, *LQTDT*♥

In a medium bowl, add the mayonnaise and ketchup and mix until well combined.

Add the garlic, soy sauce, lemon juice, honey, and sriracha and stir until all the ingredients are fully incorporated.

Fold in the cilantro, season with salt and pepper, and stir until combined.

Cover the bowl and refrigerate the mayoketchup for at least 30 minutes to allow the flavors to meld. I usually make and use this on the spot, but if you have any leftovers, it will keep for up to 1 week in the fridge.

Garlic paste and achiote oil

Makes 1¼ cups/300ml garlic paste and 1¾ cups/415ml achiote oil

Garlic Paste

2 cups/300g garlic cloves, peeled

2 cups/480ml avocado oil or vegetable oil, plus more as needed

1 teaspoon kosher salt

1 teaspoon dried thyme (optional)

1 teaspoon dried rosemary (optional)

Garlic-Infused Achiote Oil

1¾ cups/415ml oil left over from Garlic Paste, or avocado oil or vegetable oil

½ cup/55g achiote seeds (annatto seeds)

When you want garlic paste, simply grab a few of the garlic confit cloves and mash into a smooth paste in a pilón (mortar and pestle). This can be used in any dish that you'd like to infuse with a rich, garlicky flavor. I've combined the garlic paste recipe with the recipe for achiote oil, something I use to add color and flavor to rice, stews, and other dishes, with the garlic paste, since I make the achiote oil with the oil that's left over from infusing the garlic. Two recipes in one!

To make the garlic paste: Preheat the oven to 300°F/150°C.

Place the garlic cloves and the avocado oil in a small, oven-safe saucepan, ensuring the garlic is fully submerged in the oil. Add more oil if needed. Add the salt and the thyme and rosemary, if using.

Place the saucepan in the oven and bake, uncovered, for 45 minutes to 1 hour, until the garlic cloves are soft and tender. Remove from the oven and set aside to cool.

Once it's completely cool, drain the garlic cloves (reserving the oil) and transfer to a blender. Blend to a paste with ¼ cup/60ml of the oil, reserving the remaining 1¾ cups/415ml of the oil for the achiote oil.

Store the garlic paste in the refrigerator for up to 3 weeks, but do not freeze, as it will lose its flavor.

To make the achiote oil: In a saucepan over low heat, add the strained garlic-infused oil and the achiote seeds and cook, stirring occasionally, until the oil takes on a deep orange-red color, about 10 minutes. Be careful not to overheat or burn the seeds.

Remove from the heat and let cool slightly.

Strain the oil to remove the achiote seeds. Discard the achiote seeds and transfer the achiote oil to a clean jar or bottle. Store in a cool, dry spot on your countertop for up to 1 month.

Mi Sofrito Fresquecito,
page 37
Achiote oil,
page 39
Adobo,
page 38
Mantequilla criolla,
page 42

Pique,
page 43
Sazón,
page 43
Omi's mayoketchup,
page 38
Mojo de Omi,
page 37

Mantequilla criolla

Mantequilla criolla, a savory compound butter, is used to add richness and enhance the flavor of meats, seafood, and vegetables. I like using it to make Camarones al ajillo (page 119) and Pavochón (page 220), but it's also delicious spread on a fresh or toasted slice of bread.

Makes 2 cups

- 1 tablespoon extra-virgin olive oil
- 4 garlic cloves, minced
- 1 small onion, finely chopped
- 1 small green bell pepper, finely chopped
- 1 small red bell pepper, finely chopped
- 1 cup/220g (2 sticks) unsalted butter, softened
- 1 tablespoon chopped cilantro
- 1 tablespoon chopped parsley
- 1 teaspoon dried oregano
- 1 teaspoon ground cumin
- 1 teaspoon paprika
- ½ teaspoon kosher salt (adjust to taste, *LQTDT*♥)
- ½ teaspoon freshly ground black pepper

In a small skillet over medium heat, add the olive oil and heat until it shimmers. Add the garlic, onion, and bell peppers to the skillet and sauté until the vegetables are soft and the onions are translucent, 5 to 7 minutes. Remove from the heat and let cool slightly.

In a medium bowl, combine the softened butter with the sautéed vegetables. Add the cilantro, parsley, oregano, cumin, paprika, salt, and pepper. Mix well, until all ingredients are evenly incorporated.

Transfer the butter mixture onto a piece of plastic wrap or parchment paper. Shape it into a log (or your desired shape), wrap it tightly, and refrigerate for at least 1 hour, or until firm. Store butter in the refrigerator for up to 2 weeks, or freeze for up to 6 months.

Pique

This traditional vinegar-based Puerto Rican hot sauce is used as a condiment to add heat and tang to your favorite dishes, such as rice, beans, and meats, and to dip your frituras for an extra kick in every bite.

Makes 1½ cups

- 6 to 8 fresh hot peppers (habanero, Scotch bonnet, or ají caballero)
- 4 garlic cloves, thinly sliced
- 1 small onion, thinly sliced
- 1 tablespoon dried oregano
- 1 tablespoon black peppercorns
- 1 tablespoon kosher salt
- 2 bay leaves
- ¼ cup/6g fresh oregano, chopped (optional)
- 1 cup/240ml white vinegar

Cut your peppers and remove all the seeds. Slice or small dice all your vegetables.

In a large sterilized glass jar or bottle, add the hot peppers, garlic, onion, dried oregano, black peppercorns, salt, bay leaves, and fresh oregano, if using.

Pour the vinegar and ½ cup/120ml of water into the jar or bottle, ensuring all the ingredients are submerged. If needed, add more vinegar and water in a 2-to-1 ratio to cover the ingredients.

Seal the jar or bottle tightly with a lid and store the pique in a cool, dark place for at least 1 day and up to 1 week to allow the flavors to infuse. The longer it sits, the more intense the flavors will become.

After the pique has infused, you can strain out the solids or leave them in for continued flavor development. Store in the refrigerator for up to 6 months. The vinegar acts as a preservative, keeping the sauce fresh and flavorful.

Sazón

As a staple in most savory Puerto Rican dishes, this vibrant dry seasoning blend is used to add our signature color, warmth, and depth of flavor to meats, poultry, seafood, rice, beans, and stews.

Makes 1¾ cups

- ¼ cup/24g ground coriander
- ¼ cup/24g ground cumin
- ¼ cup/28g ground turmeric
- ¼ cup/24g ground achiote seeds (annatto seeds) or paprika (for color)
- ¼ cup/36g garlic powder
- ¼ cup/36g onion powder
- 2 tablespoons dried oregano
- 2 tablespoons kosher salt
- 1 tablespoon freshly ground black pepper

In a bowl, combine the coriander, cumin, turmeric, ground achiote or paprika, garlic powder, onion powder, oregano, salt, and pepper. Mix well to ensure all the spices are evenly distributed.

Transfer the sazón to an airtight container or spice jar and store in a cool, dry place for up to 6 months.

1

Los desayunos de abuela
Grandma's breakfasts

When I think of breakfast, my mind is instantly transported to my grandparents' country house, in the foothills of Río Grande, overlooking the northeastern coast of Puerto Rico. That's where I spent every summer from the ages of eleven to seventeen. I cherish those days for many reasons, but especially because it was my precious alone time with my abuela Gloria and my abuelo Pedro.

On any given morning, as night faded into dawn, the persistent, melodic chirp of los coquíes, Puerto Rico's famous tree frogs, gradually softened and gave way to the sound of the soft rustle of palm leaves and clicking of the cucubanos that drifted through my bedroom window. Somewhere in the distance, a rooster crowed, and brightly colored birds burst into exciting song, fluttering their wings to welcome the first rays of sunlight. But for me, the true mark that signaled the beginning of a new day was the rhythmic sound of my abuelo's machete harvesting the plantains and vegetables outside; the growing hum of guaguancó and boleros coming from my abuela's AM radio station; and the distinct, clean, fresh scent of Mistolín seeping through my door gap, all of which signaled it was time to get up and get moving.

By the time I crawled out of bed and headed toward the kitchen, my abuela had already hung the clothes to dry on the clothesline outside, swept and mopped the floors, and attacked the last speck of dust on every surface, leaving her home sparkling clean and ready for the day ahead. When she caught sight of me wandering into her kitchen, she'd greet me with a cheerful "¡Buenos días!," while giving me a bendición kiss on my still sleepy face, and eagerly ushering me to the dining table in the terraza, the gallery where we ate most of our meals. "Siéntate, mija, que te voy a dar una cremita," she'd say lovingly, telling me to sit down while she prepared a warm, comforting porridge. When Puerto Ricans say "cremita," we're usually referring to a cornmeal porridge, but in our house, a cremita also included avena (oatmeal), farina, and maizena (cornstarch) porridges because they all had that warm, comforting, creamy consistency.

While the main morning dish simmered on the stovetop, my abuela would shuffle from the kitchen to the gallery in her white Keds, capri pants, oversize shirt, and headscarf, setting the remaining breakfast staples on the table like a choreographed dance: a cup of cafecito con leche; a plate filled with freshly picked mangoes, carambola (star fruit), and guayaba; and another with our beloved, soft, pillowy, slightly sweet pan sobao, a bread that's kneaded and "massaged" to create its hallmark smooth texture. Every night, someone in our family would head downhill to the bakery and buy fresh loaves of pan sobao for the next day. Back when my mom and I lived in Puerto Rico, anytime we'd drive over to her parents' home, we'd make a pit stop at the panadería to get milk, jugo de china (orange juice), and bread for them. Nowadays, when I visit my mom in Río Grande, I keep the tradition alive and always stop to get the same milk, orange juice, and bread trio before heading uphill to her house.

Seeing this vibrant breakfast spread in front of me would make my stomach rumble like a barril de bomba. While my abuela continued to busy herself in the kitchen, I dug into my warm cremita, fresh fruit, buttered pan sobao, and hot cafecito con leche, gazing at the lush green mountains thick with palos de plátano, mango, and papaya trees. In between bites, I'd glance down to the clearing where the pigs, hens, and goats lived, then look up and catch a glimpse of Luquillo Beach's golden sand and the glistening Atlantic Ocean extending as far as the eye can see—my favorite view of all time. Those mornings were good for the soul, and more than that, they were a consistent routine. I loved taking part in Doña Gloria and Don Pedro's day-to-day life—it gave me peace. It was home.

When Mami and I moved to the United States, she kept some of those breakfast staples in our morning routine, but the island pace was ramped up and replaced by the need to get me to school on time. Without a minute to spare, her early-morning call usually consisted of a "Vente pa'ca y siéntate a comer!," urging me to sit down and eat my breakfast, and then an "Es que no te puedes ir a la escuela sin comer. Después estás ahí con hambre y . . ." and so on. As she continued to regañarme, telling me I had to eat breakfast so that I wouldn't starve at school, I'd quickly scoop the cremita into my mouth and sip my coffee before we headed out the door.

I get it now that I'm a parent—my morning routine with my husband and sons is also speedy with a focus on efficiency. Having to make it to school and work on time is not the same as having to do house chores throughout the day—the sense of urgency is threefold. Nevertheless, when my boys were small, I continued the tradition and always made them cremitas (page 56) for breakfast. In true Latina mom fashion, I believed that it would keep them healthy and make them grow stronger: "Esto te va hacer más fuertecito y te va a poner gordito, mi amor."

But as my kids got older, their breakfast requests began to shift: "Mami, can you make me pancakes?" Cremitas soon became a treat only enjoyed on special occasions, so I decided to start Omifying their American favorites. I figured I could keep the look and feel of their most-requested dishes while infusing them with Puerto Rican flavors. That's how the two French toast recipes in this chapter, Sándwich de tostadas francesas (page 62) and Caserola de tostadas francesas (page 65), were born.

Funnily enough, when we visit Puerto Rico as a family, the first thing my kids want when they wake up in the morning is—you guessed it—¡una cremita! But now they want *my* mom to make it for them. According to them, "You just don't make it like Abuela." And although I may act like I'm offended—"Are you kidding me right now?"—I secretly get it. No one will ever make cremitas like my abuela made them for me.

Cafecito
A cup of morning magic

I've been addicted to coffee since I was five years old. I know some of you may be clutching your pearls reading that, but actually, drinking café con leche (strong espresso-like coffee with scalded milk) in the morning is pretty common in Caribbean and Latin American countries, regardless of age. It's a tradition that reflects our cultural bond with the coffee bean and has been passed on from generation to generation.

Coffee was first introduced to Puerto Rico in 1736 during Spanish colonial rule. The plants were happy in the rich, moist soil of the mountains—so much so that by the late nineteenth century, Puerto Rico had become the world's seventh-largest producer of coffee. After this peak, production slowly declined as all eyes shifted to growing sugarcane instead. Thankfully, with the resurgence of more diverse agricultural practices, a response to the extreme isolation felt after Hurricane María hit the island in 2017, some growers have taken an interest in working the coffee fields and bringing back our precious beans. It gives me enormous joy to now see new Puerto Rican mom-and-pop coffee brands prospering in the markets and keeping our traditions alive.

As kids, we start off with a much lighter version of café con leche, which is usually made with more milk than coffee, and is always deliciously sweet. Then, as we grow older, our morning café con leche grows stronger, and we begin to add other servings of this warm elixir to the rest of our day, as with the classic post-meal pocillo, a single espresso shot, or cortadito, a shot of espresso cut with a dash of milk. When we need an afternoon pick-me-up, we may go for a café puya, a strong black coffee with no sugar, or a café aguao (or americano), a watered-down espresso shot for those who want the caffeine hit without the bold punch of flavor. But coffee isn't just for warming our hearts and giving us a burst of energy; it's part of the fabric of our culture and social life.

My parents separated when I was two years old, so for the first ten years of my life growing up in Puerto Rico, weekends were usually spent with my dad. What I remember most about that time was visiting family and friends, and the question that followed absolutely every greeting as we walked through the door: "¿Quieres una tacita de café?" Papi would take a cup of coffee at any time of day. Sometimes our hosts didn't even ask if he wanted a cup of coffee; they'd just bring it out as he sat down in the living room or at the dining table. Whether we were visiting a prima, a tía, or a friend, la tacita de café was always there. And this isn't just in my family; it's a Puerto Rican thing. Anytime you step into one of our homes, you will always be offered a cup of coffee, no matter the time, the season, or the day. It's inevitable. The rich aroma paves the way for stories, laughter, chismes, and heartfelt confessions; the cafecito, our faithful companion through it all.

When I think of my first-ever cafecito con leche as a child, I picture my abuela Gloria in the kitchen with the classic cloth coffee strainer we call el colador, or la media, which was once white but over time exhibits beautiful coffee stains from years of use. First, she'd add finely ground Café Crema coffee topped with a sprinkle of cinnamon and a pinch of salt to

enhance the flavor. Then she'd grab the kettle of water that had just reached a boil and pour the water into the colador, which was placed over a small pot. She'd dance along to Los Condes while she waited for the coffee to drip through the cloth strainer and into the pot.

Once the coffee was made, Abuela Gloria would turn to the milk. She'd place her favorite small saucepan on the burner next to the coffee, add milk, sugar, and cinnamon, and whisk it together with . . . a soup ladle. Yes, mi gente, she'd scoop the milk with the soup ladle, lift it high above the saucepan, and pour it back into her little olla in a steady stream, repeating the gentle, meditative process until the milk was warm and creamy. Then she'd stream the freshly brewed café into the milk, give it all a whirl with her ladle, and serve it in my green taza de mantequilla (butter cup).

I'm sure many of you who grew up on the island or spent time there as kids will remember the butter that came in a round, bright green plastic container with a side handle, which, once empty, was washed out and used as a cup. It's a childhood classic. As kids, my cousins and I always had our café con leche in that taza de mantequilla verde. I can't imagine it any other way. As soon as my abuela set that green plastic cup in front of me, I'd butter up a piece of pan sobao, dip it into my café con leche, and momentarily feel like I'd died and gone to heaven.

When my mom and I moved to the United States, I continued to have my morning cup of café con leche, even though I soon found out it was frowned upon for kids to drink coffee here. Years later, I kept the tradition going with my young sons, but as they grew older, they no longer wanted that warm cup of magic. It took me years to get my husband to even try coffee. Anytime I offered him una tacita in the morning, his go-to phrases were: "I don't like coffee. It tastes horrible. I don't know why people drink it." And I'd reply, "But what kind of coffee have you had? I'm telling you; I think you'd change your mind if you had a true Puerto Rican cup of coffee."

Fifteen years into our marriage—yes, fifteen!—he finally accepted a cup and has never looked back. Now he's the one making our café con leche in the morning, using a coffee maker. He may not do it exactly like my grandma, but at least I made a coffee lover out of him!

Café con leche

Makes 2 cups

- 2 tablespoons ground coffee (enough to fill your Moka pot filter)
- Pinch of kosher salt
- Pinch of ground cinnamon
- 1 cup/240ml whole milk, or *LQTDT*♥
- 1 tablespoon brown sugar, plus more to taste, *LQTDT*♥

Fill the bottom chamber of a 3-cup Moka stovetop espresso maker (aka La Greca) with water to just below the inside valve.

In the filter basket, add the ground coffee and sprinkle in the salt and cinnamon, which will bring out the coffee's richness and add warmth and depth of flavor.

Assemble the Moka pot and brew the coffee over medium heat for about 5 minutes, or until you hear the gentle bubbling sound turn into a loud gurgle or sputter. Remove the pot from the heat immediately and let it sit for 30 seconds as the coffee finishes brewing with the residual heat.

While the coffee is brewing, pour the milk into a microwave-safe cup, add the brown sugar, and heat it in the microwave for 1 to 1½ minutes, until warm.

Remove the milk from the microwave and froth using a handheld milk frother or whisk until it's light and airy.

Pour the hot brewed coffee into two favorite mugs, then slowly add the frothy milk on top.

Give it a gentle stir—or don't . . . ¡en tu cocina tú mandas! I like to leave a little foam on top for that classic café con leche vibe.

Maizena de coco

Coconut cornstarch porridge

Makes 4 servings

¼ cup/35g Maizena (cornstarch)

2 cups/480ml coconut milk

Granulated sugar to taste, *LQTDT*♥

Pinch of kosher salt

1 tablespoon salted butter

Splash of vanilla or almond extract, *LQTDT*♥

1 cinnamon stick

1 lime peel

Maizena, a milky, pudding-like porridge that's thickened with cornstarch, is delicious, but it's hard to get the right consistency—it takes constant stirring and a little elbow grease, but it is so worth it. The trick to avoiding a lumpy mess when making a maizena is to add and mix all the ingredients in the saucepan off the stove before cooking. (When I posted a reel explaining that on my social media, I was flooded with messages of gratitude for the tip.) Oftentimes, maizena is confused with the desserts tembleque and majarete. It makes sense since they differ by only a few ingredients and measurements, but if you want to know how to keep them straight, here's your cheat sheet: Maizena is a warm porridge, tembleque is a jiggly Jell-O–like coconut pudding, and majarete is a cold corn pudding. And just to mess with you a little—and because it's sooo good!—I decided to give this classic a twist by using coconut milk instead of regular milk, infusing it with a tembleque-like flavor that will confuse you in all the right ways.

In a small container, mix together the cornstarch and ¼ cup of the coconut milk, whisking to remove lumps.

In a saucepan, combine the cornstarch–coconut milk mixture, the remaining coconut milk, the sugar, salt, butter, vanilla extract, cinnamon stick, and lime peel. Set over medium-low heat and stir continuously with a whisk until the mixture thickens and has the consistency of pudding, 8 to 10 minutes. Discard the lime peel and cinnamon stick.

Serve in your favorite bowls and enjoy. ¡Buen provecho!

Maizena de coco, page 53

Cremita de maíz con frutitas del bosque, page 56

Avenita de especias,
page 57

Cremita de maíz con frutitas del bosque

Wild berry cornmeal porridge

This is the OG of cremitas. I tend to call all my porridges cremitas, but if you ask for a cremita in Puerto Rico, this cornmeal one is what you will get (minus the fruit topping—that's my addition). When I ladle this warm cremita into my bowl, I can't help but flash back to my abuela's kitchen and her small, worn saucepan, its metal dull from many years of use. I can see her setting the bowl of steaming cremita on the table and giving me a loving smile before disappearing back into the kitchen. If it was too hot, I'd pour in a touch of cold milk to help it reach the perfect temperature before sinking my spoon into that liquid gold—pure comfort for my heart.

Makes 4 servings

⅓ cup/45g cornmeal

2 cups/480ml whole milk

Splash of vanilla extract

1 cinnamon stick

Pinch of ground nutmeg

1 lemon peel

Pinch of kosher salt

Granulated sugar to taste, *LQTDT*♥

Mixed berries, for topping, *LQTDT*♥

Maple syrup, for topping (optional)

In a medium bowl, add the cornmeal and milk and mix until smooth.

In a medium saucepan, combine the cornmeal-milk mixture, vanilla extract, cinnamon stick, nutmeg, lemon peel, salt, and sugar. Place over medium-low heat and cook, stirring continuously to prevent lumps, for 3 to 4 minutes, until well combined and thickened slightly.

Reduce the heat to low and cook the mixture for another 10 to 15 minutes, continuing to stir often, until the porridge thickens to a silky texture that coats the back of a spoon and gently bubbles at the top. Discard the lemon peel and cinnamon stick.

Serve the porridge warm, topped with your choice of berries and a splash of maple syrup, if desired.

Avenita de especias

Spiced oatmeal

On any given morning, I love to have a thick, creamy bowl of avenita. I like to add warmth to this breakfast staple by bringing in some traditional Puerto Rican flavors. To do this, I infuse the milk with the same spices we use to make the drink coquito, or té de especias (spiced tea). I top it off with toasted coconut flakes and walnuts, making the whole dish a sweet embrace from the island.

Makes 4 servings

2 cups/480ml whole milk

1 tablespoon salted butter

½ cup/50g quick oats (see Tip)

1 cinnamon stick

Pinch of kosher salt

Pinch of ground cinnamon

Pinch of ground nutmeg

Pinch of ground cardamom

Splash of vanilla extract

Granulated sugar to taste, *LQTDT*♥

2 tablespoons unsweetened coconut flakes, for topping

1 tablespoon chopped walnuts, for topping

In a medium saucepan, combine the milk, butter, oats, cinnamon stick, salt, cinnamon, nutmeg, cardamom, vanilla extract, and sugar. Stir well, cover, and let cook over medium-low heat for 10 to 12 minutes, until the porridge has thickened.

While the oats are cooking, prepare the toppings: In a pan over medium heat, toast the coconut flakes and walnuts for 2 minutes, until fragrant. Remove from the heat and set aside until the porridge is ready. Discard the cinnamon stick.

Remove the cinnamon stick and transfer the avenita to a bowl and serve warm, topped with the toasted coconut flakes and walnuts.

Omi Tip: If using old-fashioned oats, soak them in water for 20 minutes, rinse, and drain before cooking.

Bananas Foster farina

There's nothing like heading to a panadería and ordering a bowl of warm farina to start the day—unless, of course, your abuelita makes it better! Farina porridge is usually grainier than the cremitas made with cornmeal or cornstarch, and I love them just the way they are. But when you try this creamy, decadent porridge infused with tropical flavor from banana and lime, you'll be doing a little dance in your seat. ¡Ay bendito! That hint of sweetness from the banana is everything.

Makes 4 servings

Farina

4 cups/950ml whole milk

Pinch of kosher salt

Pinch of ground nutmeg

Pinch of ground cinnamon

1 cinnamon stick

1 tablespoon unsalted butter

Splash of vanilla extract

Granulated sugar to taste, *LQTDT*♥

1 cup/130g farina

1 teaspoon lime zest

Bananas Foster Topping

3 tablespoons unsalted butter

3 ripe bananas, sliced

½ cup/100g brown sugar

Make the porridge: In a medium saucepan, combine the milk, salt, nutmeg, ground cinnamon, cinnamon stick, butter, vanilla extract, and granulated sugar. Set over medium heat and bring to a gentle boil, whisking often to prevent scalding.

Gradually add the farina, ¼ cup at a time, whisking to prevent lumps. Stir continuously until thickened and smooth, 10 to 13 minutes. Remove from the heat, discard the cinnamon stick, and stir in the lime zest.

Make the topping: In a medium pan over medium heat, add the butter and allow to melt and lightly brown. Then, add the sliced bananas and brown sugar, cover, and let cook for 2 to 3 minutes, until caramelized.

Serve the warm farina in bowls, topped with the caramelized banana.

Revoltillo con salchichas

Scrambled eggs and sausages

Growing up, my favorite breakfast staple was my abuelita's cremitas, but that didn't mean the revoltillo con salchichas didn't have a recurring role at the table. I wasn't into it as a breakfast—"Why are you serving me vegetables so early in the morning?"—yet those same peppers and onions I wholeheartedly rejected as a kid are now part of my go-to breakfast. I love my revoltillo with a side of buttered pan sobao to start my day (some things never change!), but many people also have it for lunch or dinner.

Makes 4 servings

4 or 5 large eggs

1 tablespoon Mi Sofrito Fresquecito (page 37)

1 teaspoon Sazón (page 43)

1 teaspoon garlic powder

Kosher salt and freshly ground black pepper to taste, *LQTDT*♥

2 tablespoons extra-virgin olive oil

One (4.6-ounce/136ml) can Vienna sausage (chicken or pork), drained (liquid reserved) and chopped

1 tablespoon salted butter

¼ cup/35g diced onion

¼ cup/40g diced red bell pepper

⅓ cup/35g shredded mozzarella cheese

Toast or cooked rice, for serving

In a medium bowl, beat the eggs until smooth. Stir in the sofrito, sazón, and garlic powder, salt, and pepper, and set aside.

In a large skillet over medium heat, add the olive oil and heat until it shimmers. Add the sausages and cook until they start to brown, 2 to 3 minutes.

Add the butter, onion, and bell pepper to the skillet and cook until the vegetables are tender and the onion is translucent, about 5 minutes. Then, add the reserved Vienna sausage liquid and cook for another 2 minutes, until the liquid is absorbed.

Pour the egg mixture into the skillet and scramble until the eggs are fully cooked, 7 to 8 minutes. Add the cheese and cook for 1 to 2 minutes, until melted.

Serve hot with a slice of your favorite toast (ideally pan sobao) or a side of rice.

Omi Tip: For fluffier eggs, add ¼ cup/60ml water to the egg mixture when beating. And remember: Do not throw away the Vienna sausage liquid (¡eso es oro!).

Sándwich de tostadas francesas con pasta de guayaba y queso

Guava and cheese French toast sandwich

There's a delightful Puerto Rican treat called pastelillos de guayaba y queso (guava and cheese–filled pastry pockets). Whenever I bring them home from the local spot in Rhode Island, my sons pounce on them like they're the last food on Earth. Once, my older kids were so quick to gobble them up that my youngest son was left empty-handed. Since his birthday was just around the corner, I made it up to him with this surprise guava and cheese French toast sandwich inspired by the pastelillo he missed out on. When he bit into it, he smiled so wide, I felt everything was right in the world.

Makes 4 servings

Cream Cheese Icing

½ cup/115g cream cheese, softened

¼ cup/30g powdered sugar

2 tablespoons heavy cream

1 teaspoon lemon zest

Cream Cheese Filling

One (8-ounce/225g) package cream cheese, softened

½ cup/60g powdered sugar

¼ cup/60ml whole milk

Guava Sauce

1 cup/300g cubed guava paste

1 tablespoon salted butter

French Toast

3 large eggs

1 cup/240ml whole milk

1 cup/240ml heavy cream

1 teaspoon ground cinnamon

1 teaspoon vanilla extract

8 slices Texas toast

2 tablespoons salted butter

Make the cream cheese icing: In a medium bowl with an electric or hand mixer, whip the cream cheese until smooth. Add the powdered sugar and continue to whip until fluffy, about 3 minutes. Add the heavy cream and lemon zest and whip until smooth, about 2 minutes. Set aside.

Make the cream cheese filling: In a medium bowl with an electric or hand mixer, whip the cream cheese until smooth, about 1 minute. Add the powdered sugar and milk and whip until fluffy, about 2 minutes. Set aside.

Make the guava sauce: In a small saucepan over medium-low heat, combine the guava paste, ¾ cup/180ml of water, and the butter. Cook, stirring occasionally, about 10 minutes, until the guava paste melts into a thick sauce. Cover the saucepan with a lid to keep warm and set aside.

Make the French toast: In a shallow bowl, whisk the eggs, milk, heavy cream, cinnamon, and vanilla extract until smooth. Set aside.

Grab four slices of the Texas toast. On each slice, spread about 1 tablespoon of the cream cheese filling and ½ tablespoon of the guava sauce (reserve the remaining guava sauce for serving). Cover with the remaining four slices of bread to make four sandwiches.

In a large pan over medium heat, melt ½ tablespoon of the butter. Dip one of the Texas toast sandwiches into the egg mixture, submerging for 1 to 2 seconds on each side. Transfer the dipped sandwich to the pan and cook until golden, about 2 minutes per side. Don't forget to tilt the sandwich sideways and cook the crusts until golden, too, about 1 minute more per side. Decrease the heat to low and cook for another minute on each side, until golden brown. Remove from the pan and set aside. Repeat this step with the remaining 3 sandwiches.

Place each French toast sandwich on a plate and drizzle with the cream cheese icing and remaining guava sauce, o lo que te diga tu corazón.

Omi Tip: Store the remaining cream cheese filling in a container in the refrigerator for up to 3 or 4 days.

PR

Caserola de tostadas francesas a la piña colada

Piña colada French toast casserole

This is another recipe that I came up with during those first few months of the Covid-19 pandemic, when we were stuck at home trying to keep our spirits up amid the tragedy facing the world. I had just made a coquito bread pudding and suddenly thought: What if I turn French toast into a bread pudding? As I mulled over this French toast casserole creation, I decided to take my experiment a little further, layering the bread with a pineapple–cream cheese mixture and drenching it all in a custardy coconut mixture. This infuses it with the flavor of a piña colada—Puerto Rico's signature cocktail, which was declared our national drink in 1978. It cooks up beautifully in the oven and is so easy to put together, it's my go-to French toast recipe when making breakfast for my family and friends.

Makes 8 to 10 servings

One (8-ounce/225g) package cream cheese, softened

½ cup/60g powdered sugar

One (20-ounce/570g) can crushed pineapple, drained

3 tablespoons salted butter

1 loaf Texas toast, cubed

3 large eggs

One (13.5-ounce/380g) can coconut milk

Splash of vanilla extract

½ cup/120ml coconut cream

½ cup/120ml whole milk

Ground cinnamon to taste, *LQTDT*♥

½ cup/100g brown sugar

½ cup/20g coconut flakes

In a medium bowl with an electric or hand mixer, whip the cream cheese and powdered sugar until smooth. Fold in the pineapple and set aside.

Grease a 9 by 13-inch baking dish with ½ tablespoon of the butter. Spread half of the cubed Texas toast evenly in the dish, dollop the cream cheese and pineapple mixture over the bread cubes, top with the remaining cubed bread, and set aside.

In a large bowl, whisk together the eggs, coconut milk, vanilla extract, coconut cream, milk, and cinnamon until well combined.

Pour the coconut-egg mixture evenly over the cubed bread in the baking dish, pressing down slightly to ensure all the bread is soaked. Refrigerate for at least 1 hour to let the bread soak.

Preheat the oven to 350°F/175°C.

In a small bowl, mix together the brown sugar and coconut flakes. Sprinkle the mixture evenly over the casserole.

In a small saucepan over medium-low heat, melt the remaining butter, then drizzle it over the top of the casserole.

Cover the casserole with aluminum foil, place it in the oven, and bake for 30 minutes.

Remove the foil and continue baking for an additional 15 to 20 minutes, until the top is golden brown and the center is set.

Let the casserole cool for a few minutes before serving.

Omi Tip: This is a perfect breakfast to leave in the fridge overnight and cook the next day. If desired, garnish with extra coconut flakes or a drizzle of maple syrup, ¡lo que te diga tu corazón!

2

Almuerzo en el campo
Lunch in the countryside

My grandparents' farm in Río Grande provided sustenance and love, but above all, it helped my abuelo realize his dream of having enough acreage to give his children the opportunity to build their own homes on his land. The first one to break ground and help fulfill his vision was my titi (aunt) Marta. Turning blueprints into an actual house takes hard work and a lot of time, so my grandfather had a temporary wooden home built above their main house for Titi Marta and her three kids, my cousins Glorimil, Angie Enid, and Fernando (aka "el karateca"). This meant that every summer, I was always only a few steps away from a grandparent, aunt, or cousin—a stark contrast to the loneliness I felt in Rhode Island during the school year. The vibrant symphony of voices chattering away interrupted by bursts of roaring laughter always made my soul feel at home.

Once I was done with my morning chores, I'd meet my cousins in the driveway to play and relax until we were called inside for lunch. My prima Glorimil and I were obsessed with making mixtapes, so we usually headed to the marquesina (the garage, although the car was never parked there), turned the radio on, and put a blank tape in the cassette player. Then, one of us would nervously hold a finger over the record button, ready to press it down when one of our favorite tunes began blaring through the speakers. This was back when Daddy Yankee and Nicky Jam were considered underground musicians and Shakira had just released her first album.

While recording, we danced to the contagious beats, imagining what it would be like to see them live, or maybe even to be a rising star like them.

As we twirled and giggled, the daily yet unpredictable tropical rain shower of el campo would drizzle down on us. But we never sought shelter—there was a beautiful sense of freedom when we played or danced in the rain, and Abuela or Titi Marta never told us to come inside. The rain usually stopped after about ten or fifteen minutes, and the clouds would disperse, giving way to the hot sun and warm breeze that would dry us off while we continued our shenanigans.

Meanwhile, on the other side of the house, my abuelo finished up his farm chores while my abuela busied herself preparing lunch inside. I swear, I don't think that woman ever stopped. As she got older, she'd take mini breaks to gather her strength, but even then, she would've put the Energizer bunny to shame. Around ten in the morning, once she was done cooking, my abuelito would put on a clean shirt, and my abuelita would swap her at-home camisa for a showier shirt, which she'd glam up with jewelry, a nice headscarf, a spritz of her favorite perfume, and a flash of red lipstick. Then they'd head outside to their gold four-door Volvo and drive into town to run their daily errands. When they came back, Abuelita always had a sweet treat for us to enjoy outside, which she'd give to us with a kind smile before heading back to her beloved kitchen.

When we were called in to lunch, I'd stroll in, yearning for a few more minutes of playtime, but also hungry from all the morning activities. Sometimes my cousins ate with us; other times it was just my abuelos and me. Without fail, my abuelo would already be in his preferred spot: a rattan rocking chair set diagonally across from the TV. I'd take my usual place on the tile floor in front of the sofa facing the TV. After hours spent outside, there was nothing like the feeling of those cool tiles on my warm skin. On weekdays, *Entrando por la cocina,* my abuelito's all-time favorite lunchtime show, would play on the screen. As we chuckled at the skits, my abuelita would set the day's lunch on an aluminum tray in my abuelito's lap and hand a plate over to me. She'd then shuffle back into the kitchen, come out with her own food, sit down on the corner seat of the couch beneath the living room window, perpendicular to me, and dig in. Abuela wasn't a dainty eater—she'd fill her mouth with food until her cheeks were as round as a full moon, which we all found incredibly endearing.

Though it is traditionally considered the heartiest meal of the day, lunch in Puerto Rico has become somewhat lighter in the busy modern day, now consisting of stews, salads, mashed root vegetables, and brothy soups, such as the Caldo de pescado (page 86), Asopao de pollo (page 81), and Sopa de plátano (page 87). But when I was a kid, lunch was all about my abuelito el consentido, the pampered one. That meal was always catered to him, which meant we usually had his all-time favorite: bacalao (salted cod). He was crazy about his bacalao, it would show up on our plates in soups, stews, salads, or straight-up with a side of root vegetables, as in Bacalao con viandas (page 76). Viandas (starchy root vegetables and fruits) were another lunch staple. They grew right outside, ready to be harvested fresh whenever needed. My abuela would pickle, boil, or mash them, as in Majado de viandas (page 75).

I usually finished my plate first, but I'd stick around and wait until my abuelo was almost done with this food. Then, I'd get up, walk by his rocking chair, and ask him if he was going to eat that last bite—"¿Tú te vas a comer eso?"—to which he'd always reply, "Toma, toma, mija, coge ahí," relinquishing it to me. It was our own unspoken lunch ritual. On the outside, he seemed gruff, but on the inside, he was a softy who treasured his grandkids.

Once the three of us were done eating, my abuelita would clean up while my abuelo shuffled over to the kitchen for his lunchtime cafecito and then outside to sit and smoke his cigar. I always joined him, not to smoke, of course, just to sit by his side in silence and share the moment with him—our moment. Nowadays, anytime I smell a cigar, I miss my abuelo Pedro.

During that window of free time, if my cousins were already back in school (classes begin in early August in Puerto Rico), I often walked out to the glorieta, an area at the side of the house that had a yellow cement table and two half-moon-shaped cement benches under a tin roof, with a hammock hanging in the corner. I've never been able to stay still, and to this day I'm not a napper, but I loved lying in that hammock during that post-lunch lull. It calmed me. I'd come up with random games, like grabbing the sides of the hamaca, folding them over myself to make a cocoon, flipping myself upside down to face the floor, and then peering through the fabric to spy on the ants, salamanders, and tiny lizards weaving across the ground.

Those lunches and early afternoons will always remain with me.

Te conozco, bacalao
Salted cod, my abuelo's all-time favorite

Ask any Puerto Rican what bacalao reminds them of, and they will probably say their parents or grandparents. This is an old-school ingredient that dates back to the days of European colonization and trade. Salted cod came on the scene as the Portuguese dish bacalhau. It then made headway in the Atlantic trade business, as the salt preservation kept it edible for months or even years. By the seventeenth century, it had become a staple in European markets and what would later become the United States.

It didn't take long for bacalhau to reach Puerto Rico, as it was a nonperishable source of protein for the seamen arriving on the island. It eventually became a mainstay for soldiers docked in Puerto Rico, as well as for enslaved workers, because it was a cheap, accessible, nourishing, and durable source of food. Religion also played a part in turning this fish into an essential part of Puerto Rican cuisine. Catholicism, the island's largest denomination, required abstaining from meat on Fridays, but fish was allowed.

Because salted cod was affordable, many of the poorer people on the island only had access to bacalao as a protein, hence its nickname "comida de pobres" (poor people's food). But with time and the ingenuity of the Boricua, this simple ingredient transformed into several dishes that are now part of classic Puerto Rican cuisine, such as bacalao guisado, funche de bacalao, bacalaítos, ensalada de bacalao, and bacalao con viandas.

Salted cod became so popular on the island that Puerto Rican salsa legends Héctor Lavoe and Willie Colón turned the already well-known local saying, "Te conozco, bacalao," into one of their all-time famous hits in the late 1960s. The lyric, "Te conozco, bacalao, aunque vengas disfrazado," basically means "I know you, codfish, even when you're in disguise." In the song, the lyric is about seeing through someone's game, but in a way, it's also a play on the many shapes and forms one ingredient can take on.

The history behind this ingredient is likely why it has always been more popular among older generations. Taking a bite of bacalao in any Puerto Rican dish brings on a wave of nostalgia. In my case, it takes me straight to my days with my abuelo Pedro, who couldn't live without his bacalao. I can only assume he grew up eating salted cod in all forms, given that he came from a family that wasn't well off and likely had easy access to this durable protein. Maybe each bite took him back to his childhood, too.

My favorite ways to eat bacalao nowadays are en escabeche (pickled), en ensalada (salad), or my absolute, all-time go-to: Bacalao con viandas (page 76). I love this dish so much that every time I visited my abuela in Puerto Rico, she'd ask me, "¿Quieres que te haga tu viandita con bacalao?" wondering if I wanted that dish as my welcome meal. And I always replied with a resounding and excited yes: "¡Ay, sí, abuela, por favor!" To this day, anytime I have that magic combo, it's a hug for my soul.

Guanimes en coco

Coconut dumplings

Guanimes are basically cornmeal dumplings that look kind of like slimmer Pasteles (page 226). The name is derived from the Taíno word *guanime,* meaning "corn bread," and some parts of Puerto Rico call these dumplings *guanimes;* others, *guanimos.* Depending on what region you're in, they are either scooped and boiled (western Puerto Rico) or wrapped in banana leaves and then cooked (eastern Puerto Rico). I like cooking them in the banana leaves because they infuse the guanimes with a delicious earthy flavor that brings the island to life in every bite. They're usually served alongside Bacalao guisado (page 74), which creates a perfect sweet and savory balance. I love dipping them in the bacalao guisado's juice. If you're lucky enough to have leftovers, do as my aunts and uncles do and enjoy these sweet bites alone with your cafecito the following morning.

Makes 10 to 12 servings

- 10 to 12 banana leaves
- 2 cups/480ml coconut milk
- 1 cup/200g brown sugar
- ½ cup/110g unsalted butter
- 1 tablespoon plus 1 teaspoon kosher salt
- 2 cups/280g yellow cornmeal, plus more as needed
- Kitchen twine or string, for wrapping

Clean the banana leaves and warm them slightly over a flame or in a pan to make them pliable. Then cut them into 8-inch squares and set aside.

Make the masa (dough): In a medium saucepan over medium heat, add ½ cup/120ml water and the coconut milk and heat until almost boiling. Then, add the brown sugar, butter, and 1 teaspoon of the salt and stir until dissolved. Add the cornmeal and stir until the mixture forms a smooth, cohesive, paste-like dough. Adjust, adding a bit more cornmeal or water as needed. Remove from the heat.

Bring a large pot of water to a boil over medium-high heat. Stir in the remaining 1 tablespoon of salt.

Cook the guanimes: Scoop out a ¼-cup portion of the dough, form it into a 4 by 1½-inch rectangle, and place it in the center of a banana leaf square. Fold the banana leaf around the dough lengthwise to create a cylinder and tie the top and bottom ends with string.

Place the guanimes in the boiling water. Cook for 45 minutes to 1 hour, until they feel firm to the touch throughout.

Remove the guanimes from the pot, unwrap, and enjoy.

Omi Tip: Guanimes are shaped either like an oval or a rectangle, depending on what side of the island you're on. In Loíza (on the east side of the island), they're rectangles, so that's how I make them now, too. If you like the flavor of coconut, you can add 1 teaspoon of coconut extract in step 2 of the recipe while boiling the coconut milk and/or ½ cup/40g of shredded coconut to the dough before shaping the guanimes.

Bacalao guisado

Stewed salted codfish

I have a confession to make: I wasn't a bacalao guisado fan as a kid. My abuelo, on the other hand, could have bacalao guisado on its own, with guanimes, viandas, arroz, con lo que sea . . . even scrambled eggs! Salted cod is, as you'd expect, very salty, and it's important to rinse and soak the fish to remove excess salt before adding it to the stew base. Now that I love bacalao, my go-to pairing for this dish is the Guanimes en coco (page 73), but by all means play around to find your perfect side, ¡lo que te diga tu corazón!

Makes 4 to 6 servings

- 1 pound/450g salted cod
- 2 tablespoons extra-virgin olive oil
- 2 tablespoons Achiote oil (page 39)
- 1¼ cups/150g thinly sliced yellow onion (about ½ large onion)
- 1 green bell pepper, diced
- 3 garlic cloves, minced
- 1½ tablespoons Mi Sofrito Fresquecito (page 37)
- 1 large bay leaf
- ½ teaspoon dried oregano
- ¼ teaspoon freshly ground black pepper

Prepare the codfish: Rinse the salted cod, then place in a large bowl, fill with cold water, and soak at room temperature for at least 8 hours, changing the water every 4 hours. For a quicker method, rinse and soak for 45 minutes, then add the cod to a large pot, cover with fresh water, and simmer over medium heat for 15 minutes to remove excess salt. Drain and let it cool slightly.

Once cool enough to handle, flake the bacalao into bite-size pieces, removing any bones and skin, and set aside.

Prepare the guiso: In a large pot over medium heat, add the olive oil and achiote oil and heat until glistening. Add the onion and bell pepper and sauté until the onion is translucent, about 5 minutes.

Add the garlic and cook for about 1 minute, until fragrant.

Stir in the sofrito, bay leaf, oregano, and pepper and cook for another 1 to 2 minutes, until fragrant.

Add the flaked bacalao to the pot and simmer for 10 minutes, allowing the flavors to meld. Remove and discard the bay leaf. Serve the stew with the side of your choice.

Omi Tip: You can usually find bacalao in the fish section of most supermarkets. In the States, look for salted codfish or salted pollock or haddock (abadejo)—both are dried white fish preserved in salt.

Majado de viandas

Mashed root vegetables

Makes 4 to 6 servings

- Kosher salt to taste, *LQTDT*♥
- ½ pound/225g yautía, peeled and cubed
- ½ pound/225g taro root (malanga de coco), peeled and cubed
- ½ pound/225g Asian sweet potatoes (batatas), peeled and cubed
- ¼ cup/55g salted butter
- ½ cup/120ml milk (adjust as needed)
- Freshly ground black pepper to taste, *LQTDT*♥
- ½ teaspoon garlic powder (optional)
- ½ teaspoon onion powder (optional)

Omi Tip: Nowadays, viandas are readily available with the root vegetables in the produce section of most supermarkets. If you have any leftovers of this majado de viandas, use it to make a chicken or ground beef shepherd's pie.

Anytime my abuelita Gloria put a serving of majado de viandas on my plate, she'd always say, "Esto te va a poner bien fuerte, bien saludable"—this dish will make you strong and healthy. I heard that phrase so much growing up that when I first started making these mashed root vegetables for my boys, back when they were toddlers, I automatically said the same thing to them! Now that they're healthy, strong teenagers, this is my go-to as a great alternative to regular mashed potatoes because of its nutritional and sentimental value—I still taste el campo with every earthy bite.

Fill a large pot with water, add a pinch of salt, and place over medium-high heat. Bring the water to a boil; then add the yautía, taro, and batata and cook until the vegetables are tender, 15 to 20 minutes.

Drain the cooked vegetables and return them to the pot, off the heat (or transfer them to a bowl). Add the butter and use a potato masher or a fork to mash the vegetables until smooth. Set aside.

In a small saucepan over medium-high heat, warm the milk. Once it's simmering, remove from the heat and add to the pot of mashed vegetables, mashing and stirring until you reach your desired consistency.

Season with 1 teaspoon salt, the pepper, and garlic powder and onion powder, if using. Adjust the seasoning to taste, ya tú sabes, ¡lo que te diga tu corazón!

Serve the majado de viandas hot, paired as a side dish with Bacalao guisado (page 74), jueyes (crab), chicken, or your favorite protein.

Serenata de bacalao con viandas

Salted codfish salad with root vegetables

Makes 4 to 6 servings

Bacalao

1 pound/450g salted cod (bacalao)

¼ cup/60ml extra-virgin olive oil or avocado oil

1 medium onion, thinly sliced

1 large tomato, diced

1 bell pepper, thinly sliced (red, yellow, or green)

Viandas

Kosher salt to taste, *LQTDT*♥

1 cubanelle (Cuban pepper)

1 bay leaf

1 pound/450g cassava (yuca), peeled and cut into 2- to 3-inch chunks

1 pound/450g yautía, peeled and cut into 2- to 3-inch chunks

1 pound/450g Asian sweet potatoes (batatas), peeled and cut into 2- to 3-inch chunks

1 pound/450g taro root (malanga de coco), peeled and cut into 2- to 3-inch chunks

Vinaigrette

¼ cup/60ml extra-virgin olive oil or avocado oil

¼ cup/60ml white vinegar

2 garlic cloves, mashed in a pilón

For Serving

Chopped cilantro, for garnish

2 ripe avocados, sliced

4 hard-boiled eggs

continued

This is my welcome-home meal when I arrive in Puerto Rico—my abuela always had it ready for me when I walked through her door. Now my mom has held strong to this tradition and I couldn't be happier. In Puerto Rico, the viandas always included pana (breadfruit), because every other tree is a pana tree. Pana is a fruit that is cooked like a vegetable, looks like a potato and a yuca had a baby, and tastes a little sweeter than yuca but not as sweet as a yam. My family lore is that every tree will give you a different-tasting pana, and they would readily fight you over who had the best pana of them all. I wish breadfruit were more readily available in the United States, but it's still pretty hard to find, which is why I did not add it to this recipe. But if you do happen to come across some, go straight to the recipe Tip and add it in!

Prepare the codfish: Rinse the salted cod, then place in a large bowl, fill with cold water, and soak at room temperature for at least 8 hours, changing the water every 4 hours. For a quicker method, rinse and soak for 45 minutes, then add it to a large pot, cover with fresh water, and simmer over medium heat for 15 minutes to remove excess salt. Drain and let it cool slightly.

Once cool enough to handle, flake the bacalao into bite-size pieces, removing any bones and skin, and set aside.

Make the viandas: In a large pot filled with water over medium-high heat, add a generous amount of salt, the cubanelle pepper, and bay leaf and bring to a boil.

Add the viandas—yuca, yautía, batata, and taro—and cook until tender, 20 to 30 minutes. They should be easily pierced with a fork but not falling apart. Remove from the heat, drain, discard the cubanelle pepper and bay leaf, and set aside.

Make the vinaigrette: In a large bowl, combine the olive oil, vinegar, and garlic and whisk vigorously until well mixed and lightly frothy. Set aside.

Make the bacalao: Set a large skillet over medium-low heat and add ¼ cup of olive oil. Once the oil is shimmering, add the onion, tomato, and bell pepper. Sauté until the onion is translucent and the pepper has softened, about 5 minutes. Add the flaked bacalao to the skillet, stirring gently to combine. Remove from the heat.

Serenata de bacalao con viandas, *continued*

Omi Tip: If you have access to pana (breadfruit), by all means, use it! Peel it, cut it into chunks, and add it to the pot of boiling water with the rest of the viandas. If you have leftover uncooked chunks, place them in ziplock bags and freeze to use at another time.

To serve: In a large bowl, combine the bacalao mixture and the vinaigrette, carefully folding until well combined. Taste and adjust the seasoning as needed.

Serve a portion of the boiled viandas on a plate, topped with a generous helping of bacalao and garnished with cilantro. This dish is traditionally enjoyed with a side of aguacate (avocado) and a boiled egg cut in half. As a kid, I always loved washing it all down with a cup of milk—un vasito de leche para tomar.

Macarrones con carne

Meat macaroni

Makes 6 to 8 servings

- 2 tablespoons kosher salt, plus more to taste, *LQTDT*♥
- 1 pound/450g elbow macaroni
- 2 tablespoons extra-virgin olive oil
- 1 pound/450g (93/7 is preferred) ground beef
- 1 small onion, finely chopped
- 1 green bell pepper, finely chopped
- 1 teaspoon Garlic paste (page 39)
- 1 tablespoon Mi Sofrito Fresquecito (page 37)
- 1 teaspoon Sazón (page 43)
- 1 tablespoon Adobo (page 38)
- One (8-ounce/225g) can tomato sauce
- 1 teaspoon granulated sugar
- Freshly ground black pepper to taste, *LQTDT*♥
- Chopped cilantro, for garnish

When Mami first made me macarrones con carne, I saw the light. This dish is so sumptuous that every time I ate it, I felt like I was dining at a high-end restaurant. When I had my sons, I turned this easy recipe into our Monday special, and my ravenous kids devoured it. Once in a while, I'll use ziti or spaghetti instead of elbow macaroni to change it up, but the flavors remain the same. With four sons (and their endless appetites), leftovers are usually only a dream, especially when the dish is a hit. But if possible, make a big batch of this recipe and save the leftovers. Like stews and soups, it's even better the next day.

Make the pasta: Fill a large pot with water and set over medium-high heat. Add the salt and bring it to a boil. Once boiling, add the elbow macaroni and cook according to the package instructions until al dente. Drain and set aside.

Make the meat sauce: In a large skillet over medium heat, add the oil and heat until shimmering. Add the ground beef and cook, stirring often, until browned, about 15 minutes. Add the onion, bell pepper, and garlic paste. Sauté until the vegetables are tender, about 5 minutes.

Stir in the sofrito, sazón, and adobo and cook for 3 to 5 minutes, until fragrant.

Add the tomato sauce and sugar and stir well to incorporate. Bring the mixture to a simmer and cook for about 10 minutes, allowing the flavors to meld.

Add the cooked macaroni to the skillet with the meat sauce. Stir well to combine. Adjust the salt and pepper to taste. Garnish with cilantro before serving.

Omi Tip: If you want to take the flavor of this dish to a new level, when you add the tomato sauce, also add a squeeze of ketchup. This gives the sauce an additional slightly sweet and tangy flavor profile that hits the spot every time.

Funche de bacalao

Cornmeal and codfish pudding

Makes 4 to 6 servings

1 pound/450g salted cod (bacalao)

1 tablespoon Achiote oil (page 39)

1 onion, diced

¼ green bell pepper, diced

¼ red bell pepper, diced

½ teaspoon dried oregano

Leaves of 8 to 10 cilantro sprigs, finely chopped

1 bay leaf

2 cups/280g yellow cornmeal

Kosher salt and freshly ground black pepper to taste, *LQTDT*♥

Guess who loved this dish in my family? That's right—my abuelo. He could go without breakfast just to have twice as much funche de bacalao for lunch. The cooked cornmeal, which is similar to polenta or grits, combined with the bacalao guisado gives this recipe a pudding-like consistency with the same flavor profile as Guanimes en coco (page 73) with Bacalao guisado (page 74), all in one dish. The touch of achiote oil gives this dish a beautiful golden hue. This is one of our classic old-school dishes that has been passed down from one funche-loving generation to the next, but it's not as popular as it used to be. I only make it when my mom and stepdad visit because my kids and husband are not fans, so it's become a special-occasion-only dish for me—but I want to bring it back to the mainstream. Give it a try, and let's help it make a comeback!

Make the bacalao: Rinse the salted cod, then place it in a large bowl, fill with cold water, and soak at room temperature for at least 8 hours, changing the water every 4 hours. For a quicker method, rinse and soak for 45 minutes, then add the fish to a large pot, cover with fresh water, and simmer over medium heat for 15 minutes to remove excess salt. Drain, reserving 2 cups/480ml of the water, and let the bacalao cool slightly.

Once cool enough to handle, flake the bacalao into bite-size pieces, removing any bones and skin, and set aside.

In a large pot over medium heat, add the achiote oil and heat until shimmering. Add the onion, bell peppers, oregano, and cilantro. Sauté until the vegetables are tender, 4 to 5 minutes.

Add the flaked cod to the pot, mix well, and add the bay leaf. Simmer for 10 to 15 minutes, allowing the flavors to meld together.

Make the funche: Add the 2 cups of reserved bacalao water along with 2 cups of fresh cold water to the same pot with the bacalao mixture. Then gradually and slowly pour in the cornmeal, stirring continuously to prevent lumps. Reduce the heat to low and continue stirring until the mixture thickens and begins pulling away from the sides of the pot, 10 to 15 minutes.

To serve, discard the bay leaf, season with salt and pepper to taste, spoon the funche onto plates, and enjoy.

Asopao de pollo

Chicken and rice soup

Makes 6 servings

- 2 tablespoons Achiote oil (page 39)
- 2 pounds/900g chicken thighs, chopped into bite-size pieces
- 1 tablespoon Adobo (page 38)
- 2 teaspoons Sazón (page 43)
- ¼ cup/60ml Mi Sofrito Fresquecito (page 37)
- 1 tablespoon Garlic paste (page 39)
- 1 red bell pepper, diced
- 1 carrot, diced
- 2 celery stalks, diced
- 8 to 10 pimiento-stuffed green olives, halved
- 3 bay leaves
- 1 tablespoon tomato paste
- 1 teaspoon Better Than Bouillon or 1 chicken bouillon cube
- 6 cups/1.4L chicken stock or water
- 1 cup/200g medium-grain white rice, rinsed
- Kosher salt and freshly ground black pepper to taste, *LQTDT*♥
- Chopped cilantro, for garnish
- 1 lime, halved, for garnish

Omi Tip: As we know, rice grains expand during cooking as they absorb water. This recipe makes a thicker soup with a stew-like consistency. If you like your asopao brothier, simply add less rice to the pot.

This is the Puerto Rican chicken soup for the soul, and my mami's asopao de pollo warms your heart with every spoonful. She always serves it with a slice of pan de agua (water bread), which has a light, crispy crust and is soft and airy on the inside, perfect for dipping in a stew or soup. One day, Mami made her asopao de pollo for my godmother, her sister and kids, and me. After savoring every spoonful and chasing it with a bite of bread, I realized I needed one more slice to dip into the last drop of soup at the bottom of the bowl. I set my bowl on the table and dashed to the kitchen for the bread, but when I came back, my bowl was gone! That's when I saw Mami standing at the sink, drying the bowl that had held that last drop of asopao. "¡Mami, pero yo no había terminado!" I yelled—I wasn't done yet! But it was too late. The soup was gone. The scar runs so deep that thirtysomething years later, I still can't forget the last bite of soup-soaked bread that I never got to have that day. Heed this cautionary tale, and make sure no one takes your asopao de pollo until you've swallowed the last bite. It's that good.

In a large pot over medium heat, add the achiote oil and heat until shimmering. Add the chicken pieces and season both sides with the adobo and sazón. Cook until the chicken is browned all over, about 15 minutes.

Stir in the sofrito, garlic paste, bell pepper, carrot, celery, and olives. Cook for 5 minutes, until the vegetables are tender and the sofrito is fragrant.

Add the bay leaves, tomato paste, bouillon, 1 cup/240ml of water, and the chicken stock. Bring to a boil, then add the rice, reduce the heat to medium-low, cover, and cook for about 20 minutes, or until the rice is cooked through and one-quarter of the liquid has been absorbed.

Uncover the pot, stir, and cook the asopao for an additional 2 to 3 minutes. Taste and adjust the salt and pepper as needed.

Garnish with cilantro and a squeeze of lime juice and serve hot.

Asopao de camarones

Shrimp and rice soup

Weekends in Puerto Rico are when family or friends stop by for a visit. Without fail, someone is offering food—but not your everyday weekday food. It has to have a little something extra to remind us that it's time to rest, relax, and enjoy one another's company. Cue this delicious shrimp and rice soup. This recipe was in constant rotation in my big family. As with any of these soups or stews, serve it with slices of fresh bread so your guests can soak up every last drop, or make some Tostones (page 143) as a crispy side that perfectly balances this smooth, ocean-kissed soup.

Makes 4 to 6 servings

1 cup/200g long-grain rice

Shrimp Broth

¼ cup/60ml extra-virgin olive oil or avocado oil

½ large onion, chopped

¼ red bell pepper, chopped

1 pound/450g shrimp tails

4 garlic cloves, roughly chopped

1 tablespoon kosher salt (or to taste, *LQTDT*♥)

3 to 4 cilantro sprigs

2 thyme sprigs

Asopao

1½ tablespoons Achiote oil (page 39)

½ onion, finely chopped

¾ red bell pepper, chopped

1 tablespoon Garlic paste (page 39)

½ cup/120ml Mi Sofrito Fresquecito (page 37)

Kosher salt and freshly ground black pepper to taste, *LQTDT*♥

1 teaspoon dried oregano

1 teaspoon Sazón (page 43)

½ teaspoon ground cumin

4 ounces/115g canned tomato sauce

1 pound/450g large raw shrimp, tails removed and set aside for broth

¼ cup/10g chopped cilantro, plus more for garnish

Lime wedges, for serving

Soak the rice in water for 20 to 30 minutes while you make the broth. Drain the rice and set aside for the asopao.

Make the shrimp broth: In a large stockpot over medium-high heat, add the olive oil. Once the oil is hot, add the onion and bell pepper and cook for about 3 minutes, until the vegetables soften.

Add the shrimp tails (you'll use the rest of the shrimp in the asopao), along with the garlic, salt, cilantro, and thyme. Sauté for another 3 to 4 minutes, until the herbs are soft and fragrant.

Add 8 cups/1.9L of water and simmer the mixture for 10 to 15 minutes. Turn off the heat and allow the broth to cool slightly.

Strain the broth through a colander or sieve into a large bowl, reserving the liquid and discarding the solids. ¡Eso es oro!

Make the asopao: In the same stockpot over medium-high heat, add the achiote oil. Once the oil is hot, add the onion, bell pepper, garlic paste, and sofrito. Cook for about a minute, stirring frequently, until fragrant.

Season with salt and pepper, then add the oregano, sazón, and cumin. Stir to incorporate, then add the tomato sauce and one-quarter cup of the raw shrimp and cook for about 30 seconds. Carefully pour in the reserved shrimp broth and bring to a boil.

Once the broth is boiling, add the soaked and drained rice, reduce the heat to medium, and simmer until the rice is tender and one-quarter of the liquid has been absorbed, 15 to 20 minutes, stirring occasionally.

Once the rice is cooked, add the remaining raw shrimp and the cilantro. Cook for an additional 5 minutes, or until the shrimp are pink and cooked through.

Taste and adjust the salt and pepper as necessary, *LQTDT*♥.

Serve the asopao hot, with lime wedges and more cilantro. Enjoy with a side of tostones (fried plantains) or bread.

Omi Tip: To take this asopao to the next level, after straining the shrimp broth, save the shrimp tails, put them in a blender with the broth, and blend until smooth. Strain the mixture through a cheesecloth into a bowl and use that liquid gold to make the asopao. You won't regret it!

Asopao de gandules con bolitas de plátano

Pigeon pea soup with plantain balls

The Corozal region is la capital del plátano, the plantain capital of Puerto Rico. The region is so proud of this moniker—and their plantains—that almost every dish from there features plantains. (Their baseball team is called los Plataneros de Corozal!) This recipe is my family's version of a classic soup from Corozal. It's so versatile—on its own, it's a little brothy, but the rice, gandules, and plantains give it some heft. You can serve it my favorite way, as I do here, with little golden plantain balls that add a mildly sweet, nutty flavor. Or you can grate the plantain directly into the broth (see Tip). You can even incorporate the plantain by making a bowl out of Mofongo (page 103) and serving the soup inside it. ¡En tu cocina, te mandas!

The first time I tried this soup was when my mom made it for me when I was pregnant with my first son. Life had gotten so busy and filled with responsibilities that I had stopped visiting Puerto Rico. But when I tried this, even though it was my first time eating it, it tasted like home.

Makes 4 to 6 servings

2 green plantains, peeled and grated

1 pinch kosher salt, plus more to taste, *LQTDT♥*

2 tablespoons Achiote oil (page 39)

1 cup/150g diced smoked pork chop

1 onion, diced

1 green bell pepper, diced

1 tablespoon Garlic paste (page 39)

¼ cup/60ml Mi Sofrito Fresquecito (page 37)

One (15-ounce/425g) can pigeon peas (gandules)

1 teaspoon Sazón (page 43)

1 beef bouillon cube

1 teaspoon dried oregano

1 teaspoon ground cumin

1 tablespoon tomato paste

6 cups/1.4L water or chicken broth

Freshly ground black pepper to taste, *LQTDT♥*

Chopped cilantro, for garnish

Prepare the plantain balls: Season the grated plantains with a pinch of salt and mix to incorporate. Form the grated plantain into 8 to 10 golf-size balls (bolitas). Try not to compact them; leave them a little loose. Set aside.

Make the soup: In a large pot over medium-high heat, add the achiote oil. Once the oil is hot, add the smoked pork chop and cook until it starts to brown, stirring often, 6 to 7 minutes.

Add the onion, bell pepper, garlic paste, and sofrito. Sauté until the vegetables are tender, about 5 minutes.

Add the pigeon peas (with their liquid), sazón, bouillon, oregano, cumin, and tomato paste and stir well to incorporate. Pour in the water or chicken broth and bring the mixture to a boil.

Gently add the plantain balls (las bolitas) to the pot to avoid splashing. Then reduce the heat to medium-low and let the soup simmer for about 30 minutes, stirring occasionally, until the consistency is hearty rather than soupy.

Season with salt and pepper and garnish with cilantro before serving.

Omi Tip: If you don't want to go through the trouble of making the plantain dumplings, you can simply grate the plantain into the soup and cook it for the same amount of time. This will make a thicker, more stew-like asopao.

Caldo de pescado

Puerto Rican fish broth

This was a Doña Gloria specialty, a simple broth that uses the head and tail of the fish to infuse it with the flavors of the sea. I loved my abuela's version so much that during one of my latest trips to Puerto Rico, I made it a point to try the caldo de pescado wherever it was served, in search of one that would replicate my abuela's. I eventually realized she had added ingredients that weren't featured in the other broths, like carrots and another mystery plant from her vegetable patch out back. I never found out what that plant was, but I think I've gotten pretty darn close to her golden broth. I made this caldo de pescado and topped it with a Bacalaíto (page 153) to win my first "top dish" on *Next Level Chef*. ¡Gracias, Abuela!

Makes 4 to 6 servings

1 head and 1 tail of red snapper or grouper, cleaned (see Tip)

Kosher salt and freshly ground black pepper to taste, *LQTDT*♥

2 tablespoons extra-virgin olive oil

1 onion, diced

1 green bell pepper, diced

1 tablespoon Garlic paste (page 39)

1 tablespoon Mi Sofrito Fresquecito (page 37)

1 teaspoon dried oregano

1 bay leaf

2 carrots, cut into ½-inch rounds

Chopped cilantro, for garnish

Lime wedges, for serving

Season the fish head and tail with salt and pepper. Set aside.

In a large pot over medium heat, add the oil. Once the oil is hot, add the onion, bell pepper, and garlic paste. Sauté until the vegetables are tender and the garlic paste is fragrant, about 5 minutes. Stir in the sofrito and oregano and cook for 1 to 2 minutes, until fragrant.

Add the bay leaf, carrots, and 6 cups/1.4L of water and bring to a boil. Then reduce the heat to medium-low and simmer for about 20 minutes, or until the carrots are fork-tender.

Gently add the fish pieces to the pot. Simmer for another 10 to 15 minutes, until the fish is cooked through.

Adjust the seasoning; ¡sal y pimienta se quieren casar! Strain, serve the broth, add pieces of fish to each serving, and discard the vegetables. Garnish with cilantro and serve with lime wedges on the side.

Omi Tip: Ask your market's fishmonger to clean the fish head and tail before you take it home. You can eat this dish with a slice of bread or crackers for lunch, or as a stomach warmer. It soothes your belly—te asienta el estómago.

Sopa de plátano

Plantain soup

Makes 4 to 6 servings

- 2 tablespoons avocado oil
- 1 onion, diced
- 1 green bell pepper, diced
- 1 tablespoon Garlic paste (page 39)
- 1 tablespoon Mi Sofrito Fresquecito (page 37)
- 1 teaspoon Sazón (page 43)
- 1 teaspoon dried oregano
- 1 teaspoon Better Than Bouillon or 1 chicken bouillon cube
- 6 cups/1.4L chicken broth or water
- 1 bay leaf
- 1 carrot, sliced
- 3 or 4 green plantains, peeled and cut into 1-inch rounds
- Kosher salt and freshly ground black pepper to taste, *LQTDT*♥
- Chopped cilantro, for garnish
- Plantain chips, for serving

I didn't grow up eating this traditional soup—I discovered it a few years back during a resurgence on social media, when many people were experimenting with its ingredients. And I'm so glad I came across it, because it's delicious and super filling, but not as thick as Asopao de gandules (page 84). Oftentimes, this puréed soup is topped with meat, which makes each spoonful taste like a pastel (page 226). I like to go all-out with the plantain and serve it alongside plantain chips—the crunchiness of the chip adds the perfect contrast to the smoothness of the velvety sopa.

In a large pot over medium heat, add the oil and heat until shimmering. Add the onion, bell pepper, and garlic paste. Sauté until the vegetables are tender, about 5 minutes. Stir in the sofrito, sazón, oregano, and bouillon. Cook for 3 to 5 minutes, until fragrant.

Add the chicken broth (or water), bay leaf, carrot, and plantains to the pot and bring to a boil. Reduce the heat to medium-low and simmer for about 30 minutes, or until the plantains and vegetables are tender.

Remove and discard the bay leaf. Then, using an immersion blender, blend the soup until smooth. If you don't have an immersion blender, carefully transfer the soup to a regular blender and blend it in batches.

Adjust the salt and pepper and garnish with cilantro. Serve hot, with a side of plantain chips.

Ensalada de mariscos

Seafood salad

Makes 6 to 8 servings

Seafood

Kosher salt and freshly ground black pepper to taste, *LQTDT*♥

Lemon wedges from 2 lemons

4 bay leaves

8 garlic cloves

2 pounds/900g shrimp, shells on

2 pounds/900g octopus

2 pounds/900g frozen lobster tails

Salad

1 small red onion, finely chopped

1 green bell pepper, finely chopped

1 red bell pepper, finely chopped

2 tomatoes, diced

¼ cup/40g green olives, sliced

½ cup/120ml extra-virgin olive oil

½ cup/120ml white vinegar

Juice of 2 limes

Kosher salt and freshly ground black pepper to taste, *LQTDT*♥

¼ cup/10g chopped cilantro, for garnish

Omi Tip: If you're worried about ending up with chewy octopus, you can tenderize it before cooking—do this by marinating it in milk overnight. And if you're pressed for time, cook it in a pressure cooker for 25 to 30 minutes.

If you're really short on time, feel free to buy cooked seafood at your local market to cut the prep to only a few minutes. Use about ½ cup of cooked shrimp, ½ cup cooked octopus, and ½ cup cooked lobster meat and you'll be good to go.

This was a weekend special at home and one of our go-to dishes on family beach days. Abuela took her time with the seafood to make sure the shrimp wasn't overcooked, the octopus was soft, and the lobster wasn't chewy. I think that necessary attention to detail is why Puerto Ricans adore this salad but rarely make it at home. When I first started Cooking con Omi on social media, I made this recipe, and it immediately went viral. It's easier than you think, as long as you take time to cook your seafood to perfection.

Prepare the seafood: Fill a large pot with water, add a pinch of salt and pepper, the lemon wedges, bay leaves, and garlic cloves and bring the water to a rolling boil over medium-high heat.

Add the shrimp to the boiling water and cook for 2 to 3 minutes, until they turn pink and opaque. Remove with a slotted spoon and set aside.

Reduce the heat to medium-low, then add the octopus and simmer gently for 45 to 60 minutes, until tender. Test the octopus for doneness by piercing it with a fork; it should be tender but not mushy. Remove with a slotted spoon and set aside.

Increase the heat to medium-high, bring the water to a boil, add the frozen lobster tails and cook for 8 to 10 minutes. The shell should be bright red and the meat opaque when cooked through. Remove and set aside.

Let the seafood cool completely to room temperature. (You can place it in an ice bath to speed up the process.)

Once cooled, peel and devein the shrimp. Shell the lobster and extract the edible meat. Then chop the shrimp, lobster, and octopus into bite-size pieces.

Assemble the salad: In a large bowl, combine the cooked shrimp, octopus, and lobster. Add the onion, bell peppers, tomatoes, and olives. In a small bowl, make the dressing by whisking together the olive oil, vinegar, lime juice, and a seasoning of salt and pepper.

Pour the dressing over the seafood and vegetables and toss gently to combine, ensuring everything is well coated. Refrigerate the salad for at least 1 hour before serving, preferably overnight, to allow the flavors to meld. Garnish with the cilantro before serving.

Empanadas de yuca, coco y jueyes

Cassava, coconut, and crab empanadas

When I take a bite of this empanada, I'm immediately transported to Loíza. Rather than being fried like many other empanadas, these are baked to perfection and have a slightly sweet taste that dances on your palate like a gentle Caribbean wave. Traditionally, they were cooked on a burén (a clay-based plate that originated with the Taíno) over an open fire. Feel free to use different fillings, like chicken or pork, but don't sleep on this crab filling—it will take you to another stratosphere.

Makes 8 to 10 empanadas

Empanada Dough

2 pounds/900g cassava (yuca), peeled

1 pound/450g Caribbean pumpkin (calabaza), peeled

1 cup/240ml coconut milk

1 teaspoon Sazón (page 43)

Kosher salt to taste, *LQTDT*♥

Filling

2 tablespoons extra-virgin olive oil

1 small onion, finely chopped

1 red bell pepper, finely chopped

3 garlic cloves, minced

1 tablespoon Mi Sofrito Fresquecito (page 37)

1 teaspoon Sazón (page 43)

1 teaspoon Adobo (page 38)

1 pound/450g precooked crabmeat (jueyes)

1 tablespoon tomato paste

8 to 10 pimiento-stuffed green olives, halved

Kosher salt and freshly ground black pepper to taste, *LQTDT*♥

To Assemble Empanadas

8 to 10 banana leaves, cut into 10-inch squares

8 to 10 sheets aluminum foil, cut into 10-inch squares

¼ cup/60ml Achiote oil (page 39)

Chopped cilantro, for garnish

Arroz con habichuelas (page 99), for serving (optional)

Omi Tip: You can buy pre-grated yuca at your local Latin market. Check the frozen aisles; it's usually more widely available during the holidays. Also, if you have any leftover crab filling, store it in a container in the refrigerator for up to 3 days or freeze for 1 month.

Make the dough: Grate the cassava and pumpkin together in a food processor or using the finest part of a grater. Make sure it's well grated with no chunks remaining.

Transfer the grated cassava and pumpkin to a large bowl. Add the coconut milk, sazón, and salt and mix until well combined and the dough is soft, pliable, and slightly tacky. Set aside.

Make the filling: In a large skillet over medium heat, add the extra-virgin olive oil and heat until shimmering. Add the onion, bell pepper, and garlic and sauté until the vegetables are tender, about 5 minutes. Stir in the sofrito, sazón, and adobo and cook for 1 to 2 minutes, until fragrant.

Add the crabmeat, tomato paste, olives, and ¼ cup/60ml of water. Cook for 5 to 7 minutes, until the mixture is well combined and heated through and most of the liquid is absorbed. Season with salt and pepper. Remove from the heat and let the mixture cool slightly.

Assemble the empanadas: Place a banana leaf over a sheet of aluminum foil. Brush a small amount of achiote oil on the banana leaf.

Place a small amount of the dough, about ⅓ cup, in the center of the leaf and flatten it out using the back of a spoon to make a circle. Add 1 tablespoon of the crab filling in the center of the dough.

Fold the empanada in half over the filling (the dough should now form a half-moon shape), using the banana leaf and foil to press down and seal the edges shut. Fold the foil over to secure it.

Preheat the oven to 350°F/175°C.

Place the foil-wrapped empanadas on a baking sheet lined with more aluminum foil or parchment paper. Bake for 45 to 50 minutes, until the dough is cooked through and firm.

Unwrap the empanadas and garnish with cilantro before serving. The empanadas are fine alone, but a good Boricua will always include a side of arroz con habichuelas.

Vinegar

3

¡A comer!
Dinner is ready!

At around three in the afternoon, my abuelita would stroll back into her spotless kitchen—her workspace always had to be pristine before any type of cooking took place—ready to concoct the day's final feast. As soon as I heard her shuffling around, I'd walk to the kitchen, lean over the counter, and watch her do her thing.

First, she'd open the refrigerator and pull out the meat she had bought earlier in town, along with whatever ingredients she needed for the meal. Vegetables, herbs, and seasonings were a mainstay on that counter, together with her ever-present yellow can of Betis Spanish olive oil, which was considered to be the good olive oil. Though Puerto Rican cuisine tends to be heavy on fried food, Abuela's weekday recipes were always pretty clean (my abuelos were very healthy eaters, and Abuela's sazón never had artificial colors). There wasn't a week without stews, soups, rice, and beans on the menu, as in any respectable Boricua household.

Most—if not all—of those dishes started with a fresh batch of sofrito sizzling in a pot or pan. As I inhaled the intense and comforting aroma, she'd grab the house phone with the long cord, dial one of her daughters, and place the receiver in the crook of her neck. Abuela never made dinner without talking to one of her children. Eventually, she upgraded to a wireless telephone, el teléfono inalámbrico, freeing her from the twisting, bouncing cord and the inevitable twirling and untwirling to keep it straight. "Ajá, sí, te oigo, sigue, sigue," she'd say, assuring them she could hear them, that they should go on with their story while she continued making dinner.

I'd listen in on Abuela's conversations with my aunts or mom, and when she noticed my presence, she'd say, "Espérate, que esta está comiendo boca." Even though she called me out for eavesdropping, she never asked me to leave. Instead, she'd eventually put me to work. Dinner prep was the only time she'd let me get involved in the kitchen. She'd give me small tasks, like grabbing ingredients from the fridge, mashing the garlic in the pilón, or deseeding the peppers. Anything that didn't involve a knife—she didn't trust that I wouldn't slice my finger off in the process. Even when I became a full-blown teenager, I was still "la nena" in her eyes.

I would often grab my 1997 blue Superior notebook, with little yellow Tweety birds dotting its cover, and diligently take notes of what my abuela was doing, trying to catch any secret ingredient or method I hadn't noticed before. But she was so quick that my notes were often woefully incomplete, such as the ingredient list for a budín, which I spelled "pudín": 2 libras de pan viejo (2 pounds of old bread)... and that was it. Even though my notes left a lot to be desired, they are a clear reminder that my love for cooking started to bloom in that kitchen with my abuela.

My favorite moment on those afternoons was when she hung up the phone, because that meant I now had her full attention. Then began our precious one-on-one time. I barely needed her to ask me a single question before I would jump in and tell her everything that was happening back home in the States, how I felt at school, how I missed everyone so much. She'd listen, without a hint of judgment, and share her wisdom, advice, or simply say, "Yo también fui una muchacha, yo me acuerdo"—she, too, had once been a young girl and understood what I was going through. Then she'd tell me a story of her own. I relished every time she opened up to me, because not only did it help us bond, but it also shed light on how she grew up and where she came from... and where I come from. I loved her stories so much that I often didn't want dinner to be ready, but my hunger got the best of me once I smelled the aromas of her finished dishes.

We usually ate at around five o'clock, watching the news with my abuelo in the living room. *Primer Impacto* would be on, and we were not allowed to talk during Walter Mercado's horoscope reading. If my aunt and cousins were around, they'd come over and join us for dinner, too. Even though we didn't sit at the table, we always ate together.

Back in Rhode Island, dinner with Mami was also early. As soon as the bus dropped me off and I approached our apartment door, I was hit with the inviting aromas of whatever she was cooking, and my stomach would let out a grumble in response. I honestly survived days at middle school and high school on honey buns and Pepsi because I couldn't stand school lunch. The cold burgers, fake-tasting hot dogs, and gross, rubbery pizza couldn't compare to Mami's cooking, so by the time I got home, I was ravenous. I was blessed to be greeted after school with a home-cooked meal, and I am grateful for that to this day.

As soon as the food was ready, Mami and I would sit in the living room and watch *Primer Impacto* while eating our dinner, much like I did with my abuelos back in Puerto Rico. But we never shared as much as I did with my abuela. Mami was strict and would have a fit whenever I returned from Puerto Rico with new makeup, a different haircut, another piercing. I didn't speak to her about the boys I liked—or anything like that—but once in a while, as she made our dinner, she'd open up and tell me some fun stories. And I'd sit there and listen attentively to anything she was in the mood to share.

When my stepdad got home, we'd head back to the kitchen and sit at the table. Once he started eating, Mami would busy herself cleaning—she couldn't stand a dirty plate if her life depended on it—and I'd do my homework or jump into their conversation. I loved sharing that part of the day with them.

Much like Abuela, Mami didn't let me help a lot with the cooking either. Because of this, I was pretty lost once I became an adult and had to cook for myself. I didn't even know how to cook white rice. After many calls to her and to my abuela, I learned to make some basic dishes, and by the time I was married with my first son on the way, I had begun to feel more comfortable with my cooking techniques.

I have four sons, so the actual dinner-making when they were little is somewhat of a blur to me. I focused on making the easiest meal that all of them liked so I could stay sane. Once I perfected my Arroz blanco (page 98) and Habichuelas guisadas (page 100), I began to simplify my cooking methods and experiment with different recipes and Omify them—make them my own—because of course, ¡en mi cocina, yo mando! That's how dishes like Rollo de pollo (page 131) and Yuca rellena de queso envuelta en tocineta (page 159) were born.

When both my husband and I were working nonstop, it was hard for me to cook every night, so we often relied on takeout. But once I started working from home and no longer had to do twenty-five thousand things a day, I was able to make home-cooked dinners for my family more often. They and I were grateful for this shift in our lives. (Friday is still pizza night—Mama needs a break sometimes.) Now my Pollo en fricasé (page 112) and Carne guisada (page 108) make weekly appearances on our table, while the Sancocho (page 107) is a monthly event—I love to make it on Saturdays, because it takes time but lasts a few days. And while I'm cooking, much like I did with my abuela and Mami, my kids hover around the kitchen to check when the food will be ready—or to hunt for a snack to quell their bottomless appetites.

Dinner is by far the most important meal for my family (my husband and kids).

It's our time to sit together, share food, and talk about our day or joke around—when our busy schedules align. But on Sundays, we always make time to eat together, in honor of my late mother-in-law's Sunday dinner tradition. Sunday is my day to have fun in the kitchen with no time constraints—to experiment and to enjoy the process without weekday responsibilities clouding my cooking joy. Some of the dishes I like to cook on weekends are Chillo frito (page 128) with a side of tostones, a rack of ribs with French fries, or my Meat loaf a lo boricua (page 133). Regardless of what I'm making, dinner is an opportunity to celebrate being alive and together with my beloved family.

Habichuelas
Hooked on beans

Habichuelas, a word that derives from the Spanish word *haba* (bean or broad bean) combined with the diminutive *chuela* (used to describe something small), can be traced back to the Taínos, the Indigenous people of the Caribbean. They grew many crops, including staples such as yuca, as well as squash, peppers, pineapples, and beans, which were an essential part of their diet.

Beans are widely used in most Latin American and Caribbean countries, a mainstay in our cuisine. We all identify them with different words. For example, red beans, which are used to make Puerto Rico's classic habichuelas guisadas are called habichuelas coloradas (or colorá—IYKYK), while in the Dominican Republic they're habichuelas rojas. In Mexico, Cuba, Central America, and Colombia, they're called frijoles rojos; in Venezuela, they're caraotas rojas; in Peru and Ecuador, they're frejoles rojos; in Brazil, they're feijão vermelho; in Haiti, they're pois rouges; in Bolivia, Paraguay, Argentina, Uruguay, and Chile, they're porotos rojos. In the United States, they'll often be sold as kidney beans. Whatever you call them, they're a delicious staple ingredient in Latin American cuisine to this day.

When the European colonists arrived on our lands, they introduced rice to the island and incorporated habichuelas into their diet. Both crops thrived thanks to the Indigenous people and the enslaved Africans working the fields. Not long after the appearance of rice, the now-renowned combo of rice and beans became a staple in every household, regardless of the family's status or income.

Habichuelas are an excellent source of nutrition. They're filling, incredibly versatile, and everyone grew up eating them in Puerto Rico . . . except for me. As a kid, I hated habichuelas. There, I said it. I was crazy about white rice and corn; I could eat that all day. I even loved the bean juice from the habichuelas guisadas, but put a bean on my plate, and I'd scrunch up my face, purse my lips, and deny entry into my mouth. When I was six or seven, Titi Loida, my father's first cousin who used to babysit me in Puerto Rico, made it her mission to get me to eat habichuelas. "You have to at least try them," she insisted. I don't remember how she did it, but her negotiation tactics worked, and I gave them another shot. To my surprise, they weren't as gross as I had remembered, and soon after that first bite, I was hooked on them, too.

Once I started cooking as an adult, I started making different types of beans and experimenting with interesting combinations, which allowed me to explore beyond the world of habichuelas colorás and rosadas (pink beans). At first, I used canned beans, but when I learned how to soak dried beans, I never looked back. My favorite go-to is mixing red and pink beans for my Habichuelas guisadas (page 100). Red beans are earthier and have more bite, while pink beans are slightly sweeter and smoother. The differences are subtle, but when combined, the two beans become a power couple. And I can eat them with anything. Well, almost anything—I don't do pigs' feet in my habichuelas. I know my fellow Boricuas love their patitas, and believe me, I've tried, but I just can't stomach them. ¡No me mires con ese tono de voz! We all have our limits.

Arroz blanco

White rice

Makes 4 servings

¼ cup/60ml avocado oil

½ teaspoon kosher salt

1 cup/200g medium-grain white rice, rinsed until the water runs clear

White rice in Puerto Rican cuisine is almost on the level of sofrito—you need it for practically every main dish. Growing up, I watched my abuela and Mami in action in the kitchen all the time, but neither of them allowed me to cook with them, so by the time I left the nest at eighteen, I knew how to take care of myself but had never really cooked. It wasn't a big deal when I was single, but once I met my future husband, a sense of pride hit me, and I wanted to show him that I had sazón. I decided to start with the basics: arroz blanco con habichuelas guisadas. On my first try, my rice was so soggy that it resembled arroz con dulce, without the flavor. (Whatever you do, once your rice is cooking in the pot with water, for the life of you, DO NOT stir the rice! I learned that the hard way.) The next time, I burned my rice. I needed to get it right, so I frantically called Mami: "I don't know what I did, but it's not coming out right—help me, please!" And she replied, "Tienes que practicar si te quieres casar," telling me I had to practice cooking if I wanted to get married. After a few more attempts with Mami's over-the-phone guidance, I finally mastered this essential side dish and eventually became the person who brought the rice to family or church functions in Rhode Island. And I married my guy, so maybe Mami was right!

In a large pot or caldero over high heat, add the oil, salt, and 1⅓ cups/315ml of water and bring to a boil.

Once the water is boiling, add the rinsed rice to the pot and stir well, just one time.

Let the rice cook, uncovered, until it has absorbed most of the water, 10 to 12 minutes.

Reduce the heat to low, cover the pot, and continue to cook for about 25 minutes more. To get the pegao (the crispy browned layer on the bottom), let the rice sit on low heat for a few extra minutes without stirring to allow the layer to form.

Uncover the rice and fluff it with a large spoon. Then remove the rice from the pot and scrape the pegao off the bottom. Serve as a side or top with beans. A forkful of pegao dipped in habichuelas broth ¡no tiene precio!

Omi Tip: If you choose to make short-grain rice (instead of medium-grain), use 1¼ to 1½ cups/300ml to 360ml of water for 1 cup of rice. And if you prefer long-grain rice, then go with 2 cups/480ml of water. If you double the rice, double the water and you'll be good to go. Just resist the urge to overstir!

Arroz con habichuelas

Rice and beans

Not to be confused with white rice and stewed beans, which are two separate dishes, here, our two staple ingredients are cooked *together* in one pot, marrying their flavors into a yellow rice *and* beans dish that can be eaten on its own or as a side. The key to perfectly cooked arroz con habichuelas is the mirepoix, or guiso. That's where the flavor lives, so really focus on the first few steps of this recipe to get it just right. We have arroz con habichuelas every week at home. Serve it as a side dish with Bistec encebollado (page 120) and thank me later!

Makes 4 to 6 servings

- ¼ cup/60ml Achiote oil (page 39)
- ¼ cup/60ml Mi Sofrito Fresquecito (page 37)
- 1 tablespoon Garlic paste (page 39)
- 1 tablespoon tomato paste
- 1 teaspoon dried oregano
- 7 or 8 green olives, halved
- 1 tablespoon bouillon (chicken, beef, or vegetable)
- Kosher salt and freshly ground black pepper to taste, *LQTDT*♥
- One (15-ounce/425g) can pink beans, drained and rinsed
- 2 cups/400g medium-grain white rice, rinsed
- ¼ cup/10g chopped cilantro

In a large pot over medium heat, add the achiote oil and heat until it shimmers. Add the sofrito and garlic paste and sauté until fragrant, about 5 minutes.

Stir in the tomato paste, oregano, olives, and bouillon and cook for another 2 minutes—this creates the guiso, which should look like a paste and smell very fragrant. Add salt and pepper and adjust seasoning to taste.

Add the beans to the pot and stir gently to incorporate. Then add the rinsed rice and stir to coat it with the guiso.

Add 3 cups/315ml of water, increase the heat to medium-high, and bring to a boil. Continue cooking until the rice absorbs the liquid completely, 8 to 10 minutes. Stir the rice from the bottom to the top just once; then cover, reduce the heat to low, and cook for another 20 minutes.

Remove the pot from the heat and let it sit, covered, for 5 minutes. Then uncover, fluff the rice with a fork, stir in the chopped cilantro, and serve hot.

Omi Tip: Before sautéing your sofrito, stir-fry some cubed cooked ham or smoked pork chops in the achiote oil until golden brown, 5 to 7 minutes—then add the sofrito. This will give an amazing depth of flavor to your rice.

Habichuelas guisadas

Stewed beans

You can't call yourself Boricua if you don't have habichuelas guisadas on the regular. These stewed beans are almost as essential to Puerto Rican cuisine as sofrito and white rice. It's such a staple that even if you've made the juiciest meat or stew, serving it with a side of rice on its own is never enough. It's like having a peanut butter and jelly sandwich without the jelly—you need those habichuelas to complete the plate. I make this recipe at least four times a week; my boys can't get enough of it. If it were up to them, they'd have Arroz blanco (page 98), these habichuelas guisadas, and Chicharrón de pollo (page 116) every single day of the week. That's the Puerto Rican in them coming out strong, and I'm here for it!

Makes 4 to 6 servings

- 1 cup/160g dried pink beans
- 1 cup/160g dried red beans
- 1 medium onion, quartered
- ¼ green bell pepper
- 3 garlic cloves
- 1 bay leaf
- 2 tablespoons Achiote oil (page 39)
- ½ cup diced smoked ham steak
- ¼ cup/60ml Mi Sofrito Fresquecito (page 37)
- 1 teaspoon Better Than Bouillon or 1 chicken bouillon cube
- 1½ tablespoons tomato paste
- 1 large russet potato, peeled and diced
- ½ cup/60g peeled and diced Caribbean pumpkin (calabaza) or acorn squash
- 8 to 10 pimiento-stuffed green olives, halved
- 1 teaspoon Sazón (page 43)
- 1 tablespoon Adobo (page 38)
- 1 teaspoon dried oregano
- Kosher salt and freshly ground black pepper to taste, *LQTDT*♥
- Chopped cilantro, for garnish (optional)

Rinse the pink and red beans and soak them in 4 cups/950ml of water overnight. Drain and rinse before cooking.

In a large pot over medium-high heat, add the soaked beans and 4 cups/950ml of fresh water. Add the onion, bell pepper, garlic, and bay leaf. Bring to a boil, then reduce the heat to low and simmer for about 1 hour, or until the beans are tender and can be pierced easily with a fork. Remove from the heat and set aside. (Don't drain—you'll use the cooking liquid later.)

In a separate large pot over medium heat, add the achiote oil and heat until it shimmers. Stir in the diced smoked ham, sofrito, bouillon, and tomato paste and cook for 2 to 3 minutes, until fragrant and darkened in color.

Add the potato, calabaza, olives, and cooked beans with their liquid. Stir in the sazón, adobo, and oregano and mix well to combine. Pour in 1 cup/240ml of water, if needed, to submerge the beans and all the vegetables. Reduce the heat to medium-low and cook for 20 minutes, or until the vegetables are tender.

Taste and adjust the seasoning with salt and pepper as needed. Garnish with cilantro, if desired. Serve hot with white rice and enjoy!

Omi Tip: If time is of the essence, you can skip soaking the beans and simply use two 15-ounce cans of beans. I don't drain or rinse them, but you can—it's a matter of preference.

Mofongo

Mashed plantain with garlic and pork crackling

Makes 4 to 6 servings

- 1½ cups/120ml chicken broth, plus more for serving
- 1 cup/240ml vegetable oil, for frying
- 4 green plantains, peeled and cut into 2-inch rounds
- 6 garlic cloves, minced
- 2 tablespoons salted butter
- ½ cup/35g pork cracklings (chicharrones) or cooked bacon, cut into small pieces
- Kosher salt or Adobo (page 38) to taste, *LQTDT*♥

Omi Tip: Mofongo is versatile—it can adapt to any dish you make, depending on how you shape it. You could press it into a cup or bowl and fill the middle with meat, then turn it out onto a plate. You could leave it pressed into a bowl and ladle your favorite soup inside. En tu cocina tú mandas—play around with it and make it yours.

On days when I'm not in the mood for rice and beans, I make mofongo because, like white rice, it really goes with everything. Mofongo is basically fried and mashed green plantains that are shaped into a large ball (see Tip). And unlike tostones, which require double-frying, mofongo is fried just once, which makes it easier to prepare. Peel, fry, mash, and you're done. Just make sure to not let the plantains sit for too long after frying, as they can get tough. Your best bet is to fry and mash immediately. If you still find the plantain is too tough to mash, add a little water or warm chicken broth to help soften it. If you want to turn this into an even heartier meal, top it with the meat of your choice and enjoy its rich, savory flavor with just the right hint of garlic.

In a small saucepan over medium heat, add the chicken broth and bring to a simmer. Once simmering, remove from the heat and set aside.

In a large skillet over medium-high heat, add the oil and heat until it shimmers. Add the plantain rounds and fry for 5 to 8 minutes, until golden brown and tender on both sides. Use a slotted spoon to remove the plantains from the oil and set on paper towels to drain excess oil.

Transfer the fried plantains to a large mortar and pestle (or a mixing bowl with a potato masher). Add the garlic, butter, and pork cracklings and mash until well combined. Add the chicken broth, a little at a time, to soften the plantains and achieve a cohesive, chunky mashed potato–like texture.

Season with salt or adobo and mix well. Shape the mofongo into 4 to 6 individual portions/balls and serve hot, with extra chicken broth on the side for dipping or drizzling.

Pastelón

Sweet plantain and meat casserole

Some people like to call pastelón "Caribbean lasagna" because the dish is layered with meat and cheese, sort of like an Italian lasagna. But instead of pasta sheets, we use sliced ripe plantains, which gives the dish a hint of sweetness that to me is pure magic. In my house, pastelón is a treat, because I like to take my time getting the right cheeses and meat and searching for the right size of plantains. I like to use a thicker plantain that I can slice lengthwise to create perfect layers. I layer each component of my pastelón like a lasagna (first plantain, then meat and vegetables, then cheese, repeat), but others prefer to boil and mash the ripe plantains and add them on top of the meat filling, like a shepherd's pie. The taste is practically the same in both versions, so it's up to you what path you take.

Makes 6 to 8 servings

¾ cup/180ml vegetable oil, for frying, plus more for greasing

6 ripe sweet plantains, peeled and sliced 1⁄16 inch thick lengthwise

¼ cup/60ml Mi Sofrito Fresquecito (page 37)

2 pounds/900g (93/7) ground beef, or ground turkey

1 cup/140g frozen mixed vegetables (e.g., bell peppers, carrots, peas, corn, *LQTDT*♥)

One (8-ounce/225g) can tomato sauce

1 tablespoon Adobo (page 38)

1 teaspoon Sazón (page 43)

1 teaspoon beef bouillon

Kosher salt and freshly ground black pepper to taste, *LQTDT*♥

2 cups/200g shredded mozzarella

1 cup/200g shredded sharp cheddar cheese

2 large eggs, beaten and seasoned with 1 teaspoon Adobo

In a large skillet over medium heat, add the oil and heat it until it shimmers. Add the plantain slices and fry for 5 to 7 minutes, until golden brown on both sides. If needed, fry in batches to avoid overcrowding the skillet—you need enough room to flip them comfortably. Use a slotted spoon to remove the plantains from the skillet and set on paper towels to drain excess oil.

In a separate large skillet over medium heat, add the sofrito and sauté until fragrant, about 5 minutes. Add the ground meat and cook until browned, about 15 minutes. Stir in the mixed vegetables, tomato sauce, adobo, sazón, and bouillon. Cook until the vegetables are tender and the mixture is well combined, about 10 minutes. Season with salt and pepper and remove from the heat.

Preheat the oven to 350°F/175°C.

Grease an 8 by 8-inch baking dish with oil and arrange half of the fried plantain slices in an even layer across the bottom. Spread half of the meat and vegetable mixture over the plantains, then sprinkle with half of each of the cheeses. Repeat to make a second layer, finishing with the remaining cheeses.

Pour the beaten eggs evenly over the top layer of cheeses. This will help bind the pastelón together.

Bake for 20 to 25 minutes, until the cheese is melted and bubbly and the eggs are set.

Remove from the oven and let the pastelón cool for a few minutes before slicing. Serve hot, with a generous helping of Arroz con habichuelas (page 99) on the side.

Omi Tip: If you like creamy lasagna, try adding thin slices of cream cheese in between the meat and plantains. Thank me later.

Sancocho

Hearty meat and vegetable stew

Sancocho es obligado en casa—it's a year-round must at home. Most Latin American and Caribbean countries have their own version of this stew, which usually turns cheap cuts of meat and vegetable scraps into a rustic and filling meal. I love the Puerto Rican version, so I kept it classic, but I did add one ingredient that usually isn't included in our sancocho: batata. In the States, I use Asian sweet potato (with white flesh and purple skin) instead of the regular orange-fleshed one because it has a fluffier texture that I love.

Makes 8 to 10 servings

- 1½ pounds/680g beef stew meat, cut into 2-inch chunks
- 1½ pounds/680g boneless, skinless chicken thighs, cut into chunks
- 3 tablespoons Adobo (page 38)
- 2 tablespoons extra-virgin olive oil
- ½ pound/225g ham or smoked pork chops, cut into chunks
- 1 large onion, diced
- 1 green bell pepper, diced
- 1 tablespoon Garlic paste (page 39)
- ½ cup/120ml Mi Sofrito Fresquecito (page 37)
- ¼ cup/60ml Mojo de Omi (page 37)
- 1 tablespoon Sazón (page 43)
- 1 teaspoon ground cumin
- 2 tablespoons tomato paste
- 1 teaspoon chicken bouillon
- 2 bay leaves
- 8 to 10 cups/2 to 2.5L beef or chicken broth or water, plus more as needed
- 2 green plantains, peeled and cut into 1-inch pieces
- 2 yautía, peeled and cut into 2-inch chunks
- 1 large cassava (yuca), peeled and cut into 2-inch chunks
- 1 Asian sweet potato (batata), peeled and cut into 2-inch chunks
- ½ small Caribbean pumpkin (calabaza), peeled and cut into 2-inch chunks
- 2 carrots, peeled and cut into ½-inch rounds
- 2 ears of corn, cut into 2-inch segments
- 2 to 3 green cooking bananas (guineos verdes), peeled, for bolitas
- Kosher salt and freshly ground black pepper to taste, *LQTDT*♥
- Chopped cilantro, for garnish
- Lime wedges, for serving

Season the beef and chicken chunks with 1 tablespoon of the adobo.

In a large pot over medium-high heat, add the olive oil and heat until it shimmers. Add the seasoned beef and chicken and cook for 20 minutes, until the meat is browned on all sides and has released its liquids.

Add the ham or smoked pork chops and continue to cook for another 20 minutes, until the pork is tender and most of the liquid has been absorbed.

In the same pot, add the onion, bell pepper, and garlic paste and cook for about 5 minutes, until the vegetables begin to soften. Stir in the sofrito, mojo, sazón, the remaining 2 tablespoons of adobo, the cumin, tomato paste, bouillon, and bay leaves and cook for another 2 to 3 minutes.

Pour in the broth or water, bring to a boil over medium-high heat, and simmer for about 10 minutes. Add broth or water as needed along the way to replace what evaporates.

Add the plantains, yautía, yuca, batata, calabaza, and carrots to the pot. Continue to simmer for another 30 minutes, or until the vegetables are tender. Add the corn during the last 15 minutes of cooking.

Make the bolitas: Using the finest part of a grater (or a food processor), grate the green bananas and season with salt. Using a spoon, form the grated banana into roughly 1-tablespoon-size dumplings and add to the center of the pot one at a time. Cook for 10 minutes, until the bolitas turn light golden and slightly increase in size.

Taste the sancocho and adjust the seasoning with salt and pepper. Remove and discard the bay leaves before serving. Garnish each bowl with cilantro and serve with lime wedges on the side.

Carne guisada

Beef stew

Makes 4 to 6 servings

- 2 tablespoons Achiote oil (page 39)
- 2 pounds/900g beef stew meat, cut into 1½-inch chunks
- 1 large onion, diced
- 1 green bell pepper, diced
- 1 tablespoon Garlic paste (page 39)
- ¼ cup/60ml Mi Sofrito Fresquecito (page 37)
- 1 teaspoon Sazón (page 43)
- 1 tablespoon Adobo (page 38)
- 8 green olives, pitted
- 1 teaspoon dried oregano
- ½ cup/120ml red wine or one (12-ounce/360ml) beer of choice
- 1 tablespoon tomato paste
- 4 cups/950ml beef broth
- 2 large russet potatoes, peeled and cut into 1-inch chunks
- 2 carrots, peeled and cut into 1-inch chunks
- 2 bay leaves
- Kosher salt and freshly ground black pepper to taste, *LQTDT*♥
- Chopped cilantro, for garnish
- Arroz blanco (page 98), for serving (optional)

Omi Tip: If your beef is still not tender at the 40-minute mark, continue to add ½ cup/120ml of water in 15-minute intervals, checking after each interval until the beef reaches your desired level of tenderness.

My hubby will have seconds of this carne guisada every time I make it, and my boys lap it up, too, so I usually don't have the luxury of leftovers—it's that good! The key to this stew is to achieve the right texture. To do that, the secret is to leave it alone: Once you've added all the ingredients, reduce the heat and let it do its thing. Don't rush it—it's a set-it-and-forget-it type of dish. You'll know you hit the sweet spot when the meat pulls apart easily with a fork. I know many people like to make this recipe in a pressure cooker, but I feel it lacks some of its signature depth of flavor with the sped-up process. En mi cocina, the slow cook on the stovetop is the way to go.

In a large pot over medium-high heat, add the achiote oil and heat until it shimmers. Add the beef chunks and brown on all sides, 8 to 10 minutes. Remove the beef from the pot and set aside.

In the same pot, add the onion, bell pepper, and garlic paste and sauté until the onion is translucent, about 5 minutes. Stir in the sofrito, sazón, adobo, olives, and oregano and cook for another 2 minutes, until fragrant.

Pour in the red wine or beer to deglaze the pot and use a wooden spoon to scrape any browned bits from the bottom. Simmer for about 2 minutes, then add the tomato paste and stir to incorporate.

Pour in the beef broth. Bring to a boil, then reduce the heat to low and simmer for about 5 minutes.

Return the browned beef to the pot. Add the potatoes, carrots, and bay leaves. Simmer for 30 to 40 minutes, until the beef is tender and the vegetables are cooked through.

Season with salt and pepper. Simmer for an additional 5 minutes.

Remove and discard the bay leaves before serving. Garnish with cilantro and serve hot, typically over white rice.

Arroz con pollo

Chicken with rice

Arroz con pollo is a weekly staple from my past and present. It's packed with flavor to create a perfect meal that feels like home no matter where you are. If you have leftovers, pair it with Mofongo (page 103) or add some broth and turn it into a warm, comforting soup.

Makes 4 to 6 servings

1 pound/450g chicken thighs, bone-in and skinless

1 pound/450g chicken breasts, bone-in and skinless

2 tablespoons Adobo (page 38)

3 tablespoons Achiote oil (page 39)

1 large onion, diced

1 red bell pepper, diced

1 tablespoon Garlic paste (page 39)

¼ cup/60ml Mi Sofrito Fresquecito (page 37)

One (8-ounce/225g) can tomato sauce

¼ cup/60ml Mojo de Omi (page 37)

1 teaspoon Sazón (page 43)

1 teaspoon Better Than Bouillon or 1 chicken bouillon cube

4 cups/950ml chicken broth or water

8 green olives, pitted

2 bay leaves

2 cups/400g long-grain rice, rinsed

Kosher salt and freshly ground black pepper to taste, *LQTDT♥*

Chopped cilantro, for garnish

Season the chicken thighs and breasts with 1 tablespoon of the adobo.

In a large pot over medium-high heat, add the achiote oil and heat until it shimmers. Add the seasoned chicken thighs and breasts and cook for 4 to 5 minutes on each side, until browned. Remove the chicken from the pot and set aside.

In the same pot, add the onion, bell pepper, and garlic paste. Sauté until the onion is translucent, about 5 minutes.

Stir in the sofrito, tomato sauce, mojo, sazón, the remaining tablespoon of adobo, and the bouillon and cook for another 2 minutes.

Add the broth or water and bring to a boil—at this point, the mixture will look like a delicious soup.

Add the chicken back to the pot, then add the olives, bay leaves, and rice and stir to incorporate. Cook for 7 to 8 minutes, allowing the rice to absorb the flavors. Season with salt and pepper to taste, cover, reduce the heat to low, and simmer for about 20 minutes, until the rice is finished cooking.

Remove and discard the bay leaves before serving. Garnish with cilantro and serve hot.

Pollo en fricasé

Chicken fricassée

Whether you grew up with pollo en fricasé or you are trying it for the first time, I guarantee this hearty dish will wrap you in a comforting embrace with every bite. You may be familiar with French chicken fricassée, which is braised in white wine and stock and served with a buttery sauce. Puerto Rican pollo en fricasé is tomato-based and usually braised in red wine or beer. I like to use beer, but I also included a grape juice alternative in this recipe if you want to avoid the alcohol altogether. I love the way the smooth sauce coats the rice when serving. It's a homey yet also elegant dish that will leave your family and guests begging for more.

Makes 6 servings

6 chicken drumsticks, skinless

6 chicken thighs, bone-in, skinless

2 tablespoons Adobo (page 38)

1 teaspoon dried oregano

1 pinch kosher salt, plus more to taste, *LQTDT♥*

Freshly ground black pepper to taste, *LQTDT♥*

¼ cup/60ml Achiote oil (page 39)

3 tablespoons Mi Sofrito Fresquecito (page 37)

1 tablespoon Garlic paste (page 39)

¼ cup/35g chopped onion

2 celery stalks, cut into 1-inch pieces

2 large carrots, peeled and cut into 1-inch pieces

2 large russet potatoes, peeled and cut into 1-inch cubes

½ cup/75g diced assorted bell peppers

2 tablespoons diced jarred roasted red peppers

8 to 10 green olives, halved (optional)

½ cup/120ml tomato sauce

3 or 4 bay leaves

2 or 3 culantro leaves, or 6 to 8 cilantro leaves, roughly chopped

12 ounces/360ml light beer, or ½ cup/120ml Concord grape juice

2 teaspoons Sazón (page 43)

1 teaspoon Better Than Bouillon or 1 chicken bouillon cube

¼ cup/10g chopped cilantro, for garnish

Arroz blanco (page 98), for serving

Habichuelas guisadas (page 100), for serving

Tostones (page 143), for serving

Clean the chicken, pat dry, and trim some of the excess fat around the thighs, leaving some for flavor. Make shallow slits on each piece of chicken so the seasoning can penetrate the meat.

In a large bowl or container, season the chicken with 1 tablespoon of the adobo, the oregano, and salt and pepper. Mix well to incorporate and place in the refrigerator to marinate for 30 minutes to 1 hour.

In a large pot over medium heat, add the achiote oil and heat until it shimmers. Add the sofrito and cook until fragrant, 1 to 2 minutes.

Add the chicken drumsticks and thighs and brown them on all sides, 12 to 15 minutes total.

Add the garlic paste, onion, celery, carrots, potatoes, bell peppers, roasted red peppers, olives (if using), tomato sauce, bay leaves, and culantro. Pour in your choice of liquid (beer or grape juice) and bring the mixture to a boil.

Add 1½ cups/360ml of water to cover the chicken and vegetables. Stir in the remaining tablespoon of adobo, the sazón, and bouillon. Reduce the heat to low, cover the pot, and simmer for 45 minutes, or until the chicken is cooked through and the vegetables are tender. Stir occasionally and adjust the seasoning to taste.

Remove and discard the bay leaves before serving. Garnish with cilantro and serve hot with arroz blanco, habichuelas guisadas, and tostones.

Tostones, page 143

Habichuelas guisadas, page 100

Arroz con coco, page 117

Omi's mayoketchup, page 38

Chicharron de pollo,
page 116

Chicharrón de pollo

Fried chicken bites

I make this chicharrón de pollo at home a few times a month, and I have to say it's a crowd-pleaser! I love the perfectly crunchy outside and tender, flavorful inside that you get from tossing the chicken in flour before frying. It's also an easy meal—kind of like chicken nuggets. I usually make these with scraps of chicken I have left over from other dishes, which makes it inexpensive, too.

Makes 4 to 6 servings

- 2 pounds/900g bone-in, skin-on chicken thighs, cut into bite-size pieces
- ¼ cup/60ml Achiote oil (page 39)
- ¼ cup/60ml white vinegar
- 2 tablespoons Adobo (page 38)
- 2 teaspoons dried oregano
- 6 garlic cloves, minced
- Kosher salt and freshly ground black pepper to taste, *LQTDT*♥
- 1½ cups/210g all-purpose flour
- 1 teaspoon Sazón (page 43)
- 1 teaspoon garlic powder
- Vegetable oil, for frying
- Lime wedges, for serving
- Omi's mayoketchup (page 38), for serving

In a large bowl, combine the chicken pieces, achiote oil, vinegar, 1 tablespoon of the adobo, the oregano, garlic, salt, and pepper. Mix well and place in the refrigerator to marinate for at least 2 hours, or preferably overnight.

In another large bowl, combine the flour with the remaining tablespoon of adobo, the sazón, and garlic powder.

Dredge the marinated chicken pieces in the flour mixture, ensuring they are thoroughly coated. Shake off any excess flour and set the chicken pieces aside.

In a large skillet over medium-high heat, add enough canola oil to cover the bottom of the pan and heat until it shimmers. Working in batches to avoid overcrowding the pan, add the chicken pieces and fry until they are golden brown and crispy, 13 to 15 minutes per batch. The internal temperature of the chicken should be 165°F/75°C. Use a slotted spoon to remove the chicken from the pan and set on paper towels to drain excess oil.

Serve hot with lime wedges on the side and mayoketchup for dipping. This is typically eaten alone as an appetizer, or enjoyed as a main with Arroz blanco (page 98) con Habichuelas guisadas (page 100).

Omi Tip: Make sure to leave the skin on the chicken—it makes the flavor and crunchy texture ten times better.

Arroz con coco

Coconut rice

Arroz con coco is a beloved side dish in Puerto Rico's coastal towns, especially in Loíza, which is known for having the most amazing coconut rice. Often paired with fresh seafood, for me, this slightly sweet rice cooked in coconut milk evokes memories of lazy Sundays by the sea. East and West Africans use coconut milk to enrich their stews, grains, and fish—a technique that was later adapted to local staples and turned into traditional Afro-Caribbean dishes. This coconut rice is just one example of a dish that carries echoes of our ancestors in every bite.

Makes 6 servings

One (13.5-ounce/400ml) can full-fat coconut milk

½ teaspoon kosher salt, or to taste, *LQTDT*♥

1 tablespoon coconut oil or vegetable oil

2 cups/400g medium-grain white rice, rinsed

In a caldero or other heavy pot over medium-high heat, pour in the coconut milk and cook until it begins to thicken and the oil separates out.

Add 1 cup/240ml of water, the salt, and oil. Stir well, then taste the liquid—it should be just a little salty with a hint of sweetness. Adjust the salt to taste as needed.

Add the rinsed rice, stir well, and bring to a boil. Decrease the heat to medium-low and simmer, uncovered, until the liquid is mostly absorbed and small air holes form on top of the rice, 10 to 12 minutes.

Stir the rice once, then cover tightly, decrease the heat to low, and let it steam for 20 minutes without lifting the lid. Fluff the rice with a fork and serve hot!

Camarones al ajillo

Garlic shrimp

When I first made the recipe for this classic Puerto Rican antojito (snack) and posted it on social media, it went viral overnight. Like many of our iconic dishes, we don't realize how easy it is to make them at home until we try. The trick to getting the taste just right is to keep an eye on the shrimp and cook it just long enough to get that slightly firm, juicy bite, avoiding the rubbery, chewy texture that develops when it's in the pan for too long. I like to make this dish at home rather than order it at a restaurant because I like it extra buttery and with a zing of lemon in each bite. Make this as an appetizer or snack, or pair it with Arroz blanco (page 98) and Habichuelas guisadas (page 100) or Mofongo (page 103) to turn it into a stunning main dish.

Makes 4 to 6 servings

1 pound/450g large shrimp, peeled and deveined, tails on

1 teaspoon Adobo (page 38)

1 teaspoon Sazón (page 43)

2 tablespoons extra-virgin olive oil

¼ cup/55g Mantequilla criolla (page 42)

1 large onion, sliced

½ green bell pepper, sliced (optional)

3 or 4 garlic cloves, minced

½ cup/120ml white wine or cooking wine

2 tablespoons chopped cilantro

Kosher salt and freshly ground black pepper to taste, *LQTDT*♥

Juice of ½ lemon

Season the shrimp with the adobo and sazón and set aside.

In a large skillet over medium heat, warm the olive oil and melt the mantequilla criolla. Once the butter is melted, add the onion and bell pepper (if using) and cook until the onion is translucent, about 5 minutes.

Stir in the garlic and cook until fragrant, about 1 minute.

Add the shrimp to the skillet and cook until they turn pink and opaque, 2 to 3 minutes on each side. Remove the shrimp from the skillet and set aside.

In the same skillet, pour in the white wine and let it simmer for a couple of minutes to reduce slightly, then stir in the cilantro and adjust the salt and pepper.

Add the shrimp back into the skillet and pour the lemon juice over them. Give the mixture a final stir and serve immediately.

Omi Tip: Don't sleep on the white wine sauce in this dish. You can make it alone and drizzle it on any other fish to put an instant smile on your face.

Bistec encebollado

Steak and onions

Makes 4 to 6 servings

- 2 pounds/900g cube steak
- ⅓ cup/80ml extra-virgin olive oil
- ¼ cup/60ml rice vinegar (or white vinegar)
- 5 garlic cloves, mashed in a pilón
- 1 tablespoon dried oregano
- 1 tablespoon Adobo (page 38)
- Kosher salt and freshly ground black pepper to taste, *LQTDT*♥
- 2 large onions, thinly sliced
- ¼ cup/60ml Mi Sofrito Fresquecito (page 37)
- Arroz blanco (page 98) or Arroz con habichuelas (page 99), for serving

Omi Tip: To maximize the tenderness of your bistec, avoid adding too much water at the beginning of your cooking process. Only add the water once the steak has less than ¼ cup/60ml of marinating liquid remaining in the pan.

Like Bacalao con viandas (page 76), this is another dish I request as a welcome-home or goodbye meal. The ingredients are simple, the recipe is easy, and it tastes like home. Cube steak, one of the cheapest cuts available at a butcher shop, originally made this a struggle meal. But the addition of sweet, caramelized onions helps tenderize the meat and adds another layer of flavor that turns these two simple ingredients into the stars of this dish. The more onions, the merrier! Some people like to add sazón with color to brighten up the bistec encebollado, but trust me—don't do it, ¡me lo están dañando! I love color on my plate, but the moment you add sazón to this dish, it turns into a bistec guisado.

In a large bowl, combine the cube steak, half of the olive oil, the vinegar, garlic, oregano, adobo, salt, and pepper. Add half of the sliced onions and mix well. Place in the refrigerator to marinate for at least 20 minutes, or overnight for best results.

In a large skillet over medium heat, add the remaining olive oil and the sofrito and stir to combine. Add the marinated steak, cover, and let it cook for about 20 minutes—the steak and onions will sweat out any liquid. Once the liquid is gone, add ¼ cup/60ml of water, reduce the heat to medium-low, and simmer for another 15 to 20 minutes, until the steak is tender. Add the remaining half of the sliced onions and continue cooking until translucent, 12 to 15 minutes. Serve alongside arroz blanco.

Carne frita encebollada

Fried pork and onions

This may sound similar to the bistec encebollado, but in this case, we use pork shoulder cut into chunks, which is fried and then combined with sautéed onions. The first time I tried to make this dish on my own, my husband and I were in the early years of our marriage and had just moved into a brand-new apartment. I followed my abuela's and mom's instructions to a tee, including leaving some of the marinade on the pork so the flavors would really come through. I heated up the oil in the pan to fry the meat, but when I added the pork, still covered in marinade, it exploded like an oil well. The room filled with smoke, and there was oil everywhere: on the pristine wooden floor, the impeccable cabinets, and when I looked up, bendito—it was all over the brand-new popcorn ceiling. Miraculously, I was physically spared, but my emotions were a wreck. With tears streaming down my face, I walked outside to take a breather before cleaning up the disaster in the kitchen. I learned my lesson and eventually dared to try again, this time taking the necessary precaution of patting the marinated pork chunks dry before frying them—to get an extra crispy, caramelized crust . . . and to avoid an oil splatter catastrophe.

Makes 4 to 6 servings

- 2 pounds/900g pork shoulder or pork butt, cut into 1-inch chunks
- ¼ cup/60ml Achiote oil (page 39)
- ¼ cup/60ml white vinegar or Mojo de Omi (page 37)
- 2 teaspoons Adobo (page 38)
- 2 teaspoons dried oregano
- 6 garlic cloves, minced
- Kosher salt and freshly ground black pepper to taste, *LQTDT*♥
- Vegetable oil, for frying
- 2 large onions, thinly sliced
- Lime wedges, for serving
- Omi's mayoketchup (page 38), for serving
- Arroz blanco (page 98), for serving
- Habichuelas guisadas (page 100), for serving

In a large bowl, combine the pork, achiote oil, vinegar, adobo, oregano, garlic, salt, and pepper. Mix well and place in the refrigerator to marinate for at least 1 hour, or preferably overnight.

In a large skillet over medium heat, add 2 tablespoons of canola oil and heat until it shimmers. Add the onions and cook until they are soft and translucent, 5 to 7 minutes. Remove the onions from the skillet and set aside.

In the same skillet over medium-high heat, add enough canola oil to cover the bottom and heat until it shimmers. Pat the marinated pork chunks with a paper towel to remove excess liquid and add them to the skillet in batches, being careful not to overcrowd the pan. Fry the pork until golden brown and crispy on all sides, 15 to 18 minutes total per batch. Use a slotted spoon to remove the pork from the skillet and set on paper towels to drain excess oil.

Once all the pork has been fried, return it to the skillet, along with the cooked onions. Toss everything together and cook for another 2 to 3 minutes to allow the flavors to combine.

Serve hot, with lime wedges and mayoketchup and arroz blanco and habichuelas guisadas on the side. And if you want to make your plate even better, add a few maduros (see Omi Tip, page 127) or Tostones (page 143) and slices of avocado.

¡A comer!

Omi Tip: If you want to save time, while you cook the onions on the stove, cook the pork in an air fryer. Then add the air-fried pork to the skillet with the sautéed onions. You can also use the marinade in this recipe for chuletas (pork chops).

Salmón con piña

Salmon with pineapple

When I made it to the top ten on *Next Level Chef*, we were challenged to make a knockout appetizer and cocktail. The platform with the ingredients appeared, and after fighting over some scallops with a fellow contestant, I relinquished them and grabbed salmon instead. Eager to infuse the fish with my signature tropical flavors, when the mid-round platform dropped with cocktail ingredients, I immediately grabbed the piña colada box, which included a whole pineapple, the perfect ingredient to round out my appetizer. What no one knew was that I make a version of this dish as a main course at home—my husband loves it so much he says he'd choose it as his last meal. The pineapple salsa gives it boricua flair with a pop of color, flavor, and refreshing texture that I live for—plus, it looks beautiful on the plate. With my husband in mind, I whipped up my appetizer, and I won top dish! This recipe serves four as a main course, but you can cut the salmon into smaller pieces if you want to serve it as an app for a larger crowd.

Makes 4 servings

Marinade

2 tablespoons extra-virgin olive oil or avocado oil

2 tablespoons lime juice

2 garlic cloves, minced

1 teaspoon dried oregano

1 tablespoon brown sugar

Kosher salt and freshly ground black pepper to taste, *LQTDT*♥

4 salmon fillets (4 to 6 ounces each)

Pineapple Salsa

1 cup/150g diced fresh pineapple

½ red bell pepper, diced

½ yellow bell pepper, diced

½ green bell pepper, diced

¼ red onion, finely chopped

¼ cup/10g chopped cilantro

½ teaspoon lemon zest

Kosher salt and freshly ground black pepper to taste, *LQTDT*♥

Salmon

2 tablespoons extra-virgin olive oil or avocado oil

½ cup/120ml pineapple juice

¼ cup/60ml chicken or vegetable broth

1 tablespoon soy sauce

1 tablespoon honey

1 tablespoon brown sugar

1 teaspoon cornstarch mixed with 1 tablespoon water (optional, for thickening)

Marinate the salmon: In a small bowl, add the olive oil, lime juice, garlic, oregano, and brown sugar, salt, and pepper, and mix to thoroughly combine.

Place the salmon fillets in a large shallow dish and pour the marinade over them. Place in the refrigerator to marinate for at least 30 minutes.

Make the pineapple salsa: While the salmon marinates, in a medium bowl, add the pineapple, bell peppers, red onion, cilantro, lemon zest, salt, and pepper. Mix well and set aside to let the flavors meld.

Cook the salmon: In a large skillet over medium-high heat, add the oil and heat until it shimmers. Remove the salmon from the marinade and place it in the skillet, skin side down. Cook for 4 to 5 minutes on each side, until the salmon is cooked through and flakes easily with a fork. Remove the salmon from the skillet and set aside.

In the same skillet, add the pineapple juice, broth, soy sauce, honey, and brown sugar. Stir to combine and bring to a simmer. If you prefer a thicker sauce, add the cornstarch mixture and stir until the sauce thickens, 3 to 4 minutes.

Return the salmon to the skillet and spoon the sauce over the fillets. Cook for an additional 2 minutes to let the flavors combine.

Serve the salmon fillets with any extra sauce drizzled over them, topped with the pineapple salsa. Serve with your favorite side dishes, such as Arroz con coco (page 117) or a fresh salad.

Omi Tip: If you cut the salmon into cubes, it makes a great base for a poké bowl.

ANTOJITOS
DEL
CALLEJÓN
Coca-Cola

Espagueti a lo boricua

Puerto Rican spaghetti

Makes 6 to 8 servings

2 teaspoons kosher salt

1 pound/450g spaghetti

1 pound/450g (93/7) ground beef (or lean ground pork, chicken, or turkey)

1½ teaspoons Adobo (page 38)

1 teaspoon Sazón (page 43)

½ teaspoon dried oregano

1 small yellow onion, diced

1 tablespoon Garlic paste (page 39)

One (24-ounce/680g) can tomato sauce

¼ cup/60ml Mi Sofrito Fresquecito (page 37)

4 cilantro sprigs, plus more for garnish

1 tablespoon granulated sugar

Grated Parmesan cheese, for garnish

To this day, anytime my mom makes this dish for me, I'm in food heaven. Espagueti a lo boricua was my favorite dish to eat after school, so when I eat it now, I'm filled with nostalgia. You really can't go wrong with a spaghetti-and-meat combo, especially one with all the classic Puerto Rican flavors I bet you've come to love by now. If you want to make it extra Boricua, serve it with a side of maduros (fried sweet plantains, page 127) and a little bit of ketchup on top. This is our way of serving it—no me mires con ese tono de voz, ¿capisce?

Fill a large pot with water and bring to a boil over medium-high heat. Add 1 teaspoon of the salt and the spaghetti. Cook the spaghetti according to the package instructions but drain it 1 minute before it's fully cooked. Set aside.

In a large skillet over medium-high heat, add the ground beef. (Add a bit of oil before adding the meat if using ground chicken or turkey.) Sprinkle the remaining teaspoon of salt, the adobo, sazón, and oregano over the meat. Use a spatula to break up the beef and cook until evenly browned, about 15 minutes.

When the beef is almost fully browned, push it to the edges of the pan, then add the onion and garlic paste to the center of the pan. Add the tomato sauce, sofrito, and cilantro stems and stir well to combine with the meat. Cook, stirring occasionally, until fragrant, about 5 minutes.

Add the sugar (this balances out the acidity of the tomato sauce), stir well, and reduce the heat to medium-low. Cover partially with a lid, leaving a crack for steam to escape, and cook for 15 to 20 minutes.

Taste the sauce and adjust the salt, if needed, and remove the cilantro stems. Add the cooked spaghetti to the sauce, in batches to prevent clumping, and toss to coat the pasta.

Garnish with cilantro and Parmesan cheese and serve hot.

Con bif

Corned beef stew

Many may frown upon the idea of canned corned beef, but I dare you to find out how you feel about it after you try this dish. "Con bif," which is how we pronounce corned beef, is made like a stew, but once it's cooked, it's more like a super-moist picadillo. Instead of, or in addition to, adding homemade French fries to the stew, try adding some sliced maduros (see Tip) and/or canned corn. I encourage you to play around and make this one your own!

Makes 4 to 6 servings

French Fries/Fried Potatoes

Vegetable oil, for frying

4 large potatoes (russet or Yukon Gold work well), peeled and cut into ¼-inch-thick strips

Con Bif (Corned Beef)

2 tablespoons Achiote oil (page 39)

2 tablespoons Mi Sofrito Fresquecito (page 37)

1 small onion, diced

1 small green bell pepper, diced

2 garlic cloves, minced

Two (12-ounce/340g) cans corned beef

One (8-ounce/225g) can tomato sauce

1 teaspoon Adobo (page 38)

1 teaspoon Sazón (page 43)

1 teaspoon dried oregano

8 to 10 green olives, halved (optional)

1 cup/130g corn kernels (optional)

¼ cup/65g ketchup

Arroz blanco (page 98), for serving

Habichuelas guisadas (page 100), for serving

Make the French fries: In a deep fryer or a large pot, add a few inches of vegetable oil. Heat the oil to 350°F/175°C (use an instant-read thermometer to monitor the temperature of the oil).

Add the sliced potatoes to the deep fryer or pot and fry in batches to avoid overcrowding, 3 to 4 minutes per batch, until the fries are pale and soft but not browned. Remove the fries from the oil with a slotted spoon and set aside on paper towels to drain excess oil.

Make the con bif: In a large skillet over medium heat, add the achiote oil and heat until it shimmers. Add the sofrito, onion, bell pepper, and garlic and sauté for 2 to 3 minutes, until fragrant and the vegetables are softened.

Add the corned beef to the skillet and break it up with a spoon. Add the tomato sauce, adobo, sazón, and oregano, stir well to combine, and cook for 15 minutes, until it has thickened slightly into a stew.

In the skillet with the corned beef, add the French fries, olives (if using), and corn (if using). Bring the mixture to a simmer, reduce the heat to low, cover, and simmer for 15 to 20 minutes, until it resembles a thick chili. Add the ketchup—this helps round out all the flavors—and mix well.

Taste and adjust the seasoning as needed. Serve con bif over a bed of arroz blanco and habichuelas guisadas.

Omi Tip: Many people add maduros, sweet plantains, to their corned beef recipe. Just slice them, fry them once, so they're golden but still soft, and add to the skillet with the corned beef in place of the fried potatoes.

Chillo frito

Fried snapper

My dad used to love going deep-sea fishing off the coast of Puerto Rico on weekends, and he would come back with buckets filled with fish that my mom would fry up for us to eat. The fish he caught was predominantly red snapper, which is native to Puerto Rico's coastal waters, and a staple of our island's cuisine. Over the years, this chillo frito has become one of my go-to weekend dishes at home—I like to make it on Saturdays along with tostones, French fries, or mofongo. A mouthwatering coconut sauce brings this dish together, infusing the fried snapper (and its side dish) with a tropical flavor that takes me back to those weekends with my grandparents on the island.

Makes 2 to 4 servings

Coconut Sauce

1 tablespoon extra-virgin olive oil

1 small onion, finely chopped

2 garlic cloves, minced

1 small bell pepper, finely chopped

1 tablespoon Adobo (page 38)

One (13.5-ounce/400ml) can coconut milk

Kosher salt and freshly ground black pepper to taste, *LQTDT*♥

Juice of 1 lime

Fish

2 whole red snappers (about 13 inches and 1 pound/450g each), cleaned, scaled, and butterflied

1 teaspoon Adobo (page 38)

1 teaspoon garlic powder

1 teaspoon paprika

Kosher salt and freshly ground black pepper to taste, *LQTDT*♥

1 cup/140g all-purpose flour

Vegetable oil, for frying

Chopped cilantro, for garnish

Make the coconut sauce: In a medium saucepan over medium heat, add the olive oil and heat until it shimmers. Add the onion, garlic, and bell pepper and sauté until the vegetables are soft and the onion is translucent, about 5 minutes. Stir in the adobo and cook for another 1 to 2 minutes, until fragrant.

Pour in the coconut milk, stir well to incorporate with the sautéed vegetables and spices, and bring the mixture to a gentle simmer. Season with salt and pepper, stir gently, and simmer for 10 to 15 minutes, stirring occasionally, until it thickens slightly.

Stir in the lime juice for a fresh, tangy flavor, remove the pan from the heat, and set aside.

Make the fish: Rinse the red snappers under cold water and pat dry with paper towels. Season the fish inside and out with the adobo, garlic powder, paprika, salt, and pepper.

Add the flour to a large, shallow bowl. Dredge the seasoned fish in the flour, shaking off any excess.

Add about an inch of canola oil to a large skillet over medium-high heat. Once the oil shimmers, carefully add the fish and fry until golden brown and crispy, 5 to 7 minutes per side. Use a slotted spoon to remove the fish from the skillet and set on paper towels to drain excess oil.

Serve the chillo frito hot, pour the coconut sauce over it, and garnish with cilantro.

Omi Tip: This is a versatile coconut sauce—feel free to pair it with shrimp or any other fish. Place it on top of Majado de viandas (page 75) or serve with Arroz blanco (page 98) con Habichuelas guisadas (page 100) y Tostones (page 143).

EL KIOSKO
DE MERY

Rollo de pollo

Chicken roll

I had chicken cordon bleu on my mind when I came up with this recipe. But I decided to Omify it by incorporating sweet plantains into the filling and wrapping the whole thing with bacon instead of breading it. This combo creates a sweet-and-savory balance that delights the senses, and the cream sauce turns each bite into perfection.

Makes 4 servings

Chicken Rolls

Kosher salt and freshly ground black pepper to taste, *LQTDT*♥

2 ripe plantains (amarillos), peeled and cut into chunks

4 large chicken breasts (8 to 10 ounces/225g to 280g each), pounded thin

1 tablespoon Adobo (page 38)

1 teaspoon garlic powder

1 teaspoon dried oregano

4 thin slices deli ham

1 cup/100g shredded mozzarella cheese

8 to 10 strips bacon

2 tablespoons extra-virgin olive oil

Cream Sauce

2 tablespoons unsalted butter

2 garlic cloves, minced

1 cup/240ml heavy cream

½ cup/120ml chicken broth

¼ cup/8g grated Parmesan cheese

Kosher salt and freshly ground black pepper to taste, *LQTDT*♥

Chopped parsley (optional)

Make the chicken rolls: Fill a medium saucepan with water and add salt to taste. Bring to a boil over medium heat, then add the plantains and cook until tender, 10 to 15 minutes.

Drain and mash the plantains (using a potato masher) until smooth. Season with salt and pepper and set aside.

Preheat the oven to 375°F/190°C.

Lay the chicken flat on a cutting board. Season both sides with the adobo, garlic powder, oregano, salt, and pepper.

Spread a layer of mashed plantains, about one-quarter of the mixture, on one side of each chicken breast. Then place a slice of ham on top of the plantain mash, followed by a sprinkle of shredded mozzarella cheese.

Carefully roll up each chicken breast, starting at one end and rolling tightly around the filling. Wrap each chicken roll with 2 to 3 bacon slices, securing the ends with toothpicks if necessary.

In a large oven-safe skillet over medium-high heat, add the olive oil and heat until it shimmers. Add the chicken rolls to the skillet and sear on all sides until the bacon is crispy and browned, 2 to 3 minutes per side.

Transfer the skillet to the oven and bake for 20 to 25 minutes, until the chicken is cooked through and the internal temperature reaches 165°F/75°C.

Make the cream sauce: While the chicken is baking, prepare the cream sauce. In a small saucepan over medium heat, melt the butter. Add the garlic and sauté until fragrant, about 1 minute.

Stir in the heavy cream and chicken broth and bring to a simmer. Cook until slightly thickened, 5 to 7 minutes.

Stir in the grated Parmesan cheese and season with salt and pepper. If desired, add parsley for extra flavor. Remove from the heat and set aside.

Remove the chicken rolls from the oven and let them rest for a few minutes. Drizzle the cream sauce over the top of the chicken rolls, slice, and serve with your favorite sides.

Omi Tip: This recipe is a little more involved, so I usually make it as a weekend or special-occasion dish.

Meat loaf a lo boricua

Puerto Rican meat loaf

I came up with this dish a few years ago while playing around with a meat loaf recipe. No one at home really liked meat loaf made the traditional American way, but I was asked to make it as part of a brand collaboration, so I decided to give it an Omified twist that would bring in some of the flavors my family loves. That's how I came up with this version, featuring a mofongo filling, a crispy bacon top, and a sweet-and-savory guava glaze. Now that this meat loaf has been accepted at home, I make it on special occasions—when it comes out of the oven, it's a showstopper, and it continues to impress once sliced and served.

Makes 6 to 8 servings

Mofongo Filling

½ cup/120ml chicken broth

1 cup/240ml vegetable oil, for frying

4 green plantains, peeled and cut into 1-inch rounds

6 garlic cloves, minced

2 tablespoons salted butter

½ cup/35g pork cracklings (chicharrones) or cooked bacon, cut into small pieces

Kosher salt or Adobo (page 38) to taste, *LQTDT*♥

Meat Loaf

1 pound/450g (85/15) ground beef

1 pound/450g ground pork

1 small onion, finely chopped

2 garlic cloves, minced

½ cup/60g breadcrumbs

1 large egg

¼ cup/60ml whole milk

1 tablespoon Worcestershire sauce

1 teaspoon Adobo (page 38)

1 tablespoon Mi Sofrito Fresquecito (page 37)

1 teaspoon dried oregano

Kosher salt and freshly ground black pepper to taste, *LQTDT*♥

8 to 10 strips bacon

Guava Glaze

½ cup/155g guava paste

1 tablespoon apple cider vinegar

1 tablespoon brown sugar

1 teaspoon soy sauce

Make the mofongo filling: In a small saucepan over medium heat, add the chicken broth and bring to a simmer. Once simmering, remove from the heat and set aside.

In a large skillet over medium-high heat, add the oil and heat until it shimmers. Carefully add the plantains to the oil and fry for 5 to 8 minutes, until golden brown and tender. Use a slotted spoon to remove the plantains from the skillet and set on paper towels to drain excess oil. Cook in batches to avoid overcrowding the pan.

In a large mortar and pestle (or a mixing bowl with a potato masher), add the fried plantains, garlic, butter, and chicharrones and mash until well combined. Add the chicken broth, a little at a time, to help soften the plantains—the mixture should reach a cohesive but still chunky mashed potato–like texture. Season with salt and pepper. Set aside to cool.

Make the meat loaf: Preheat the oven to 350°F/175°C. Line an 8½ by 4½-inch loaf pan with parchment paper, or lightly grease it with cooking spray.

In a large bowl, combine the ground beef, ground pork, onion, garlic, breadcrumbs, egg, milk, Worcestershire sauce, adobo, sofrito, oregano, and a pinch of salt and pepper. Mix just until all the ingredients are well combined—be careful not to overmix (overmixing can make the meat loaf heavy and dense).

Spread half of the meat mixture on the bottom of the prepared loaf pan.

Mold the mofongo into a cylinder roughly 1 inch thick and 6 inches long and place it in the center of the meat mixture in the loaf pan. This should leave about 1 inch of the meat mixture exposed on either end.

continued

Omi Tip: Feel free to brush the guava glaze onto the meat loaf in increments, at the 15-, 30-, and 45-minute marks. The more glaze you give it, the prettier it will look and tastier it will be.

Add the remaining meat mixture on top of the mofongo and press down on it to seal the mofongo in on all sides.

Place one layer of the bacon strips across the top of the meat loaf lengthwise, tucking the ends in along the sides of the loaf.

Bake the meat loaf in the oven for 45 minutes.

Make the guava glaze: While the meat loaf is baking, in a small saucepan over medium heat, combine the guava paste, ¼ cup/60ml of water, the apple cider vinegar, brown sugar, and soy sauce. Cook, stirring frequently, until the guava paste melts and the mixture is smooth and slightly thickened, 7 to 8 minutes. Set aside.

After the meat loaf has been baking for 45 minutes, remove it from the oven and brush the top with the guava glaze. Then, return the meat loaf to the oven and bake for 45 more minutes, or until the internal temperature reaches 165°F/75°C.

Remove from the oven and let the meat loaf rest for about 10 minutes before slicing. Serve with your favorite sides and enjoy!

Amarillos en almíbar

Sweet plantains in syrup

When you think of sweet plantains in syrup, you likely associate it with dessert. But this old-timer is a versatile side as well. As a kid in Puerto Rico, I often had amarillos en almíbar alongside a main course. Its spiced syrup is as delicious with a savory dish as it is with a scoop of ice cream (a tropical version of bananas Foster) or on its own.

Makes 4 to 6 servings

½ cup/110g salted butter

4 ripe plantains (amarillos), peeled and sliced into 1-inch pieces

½ cup/100g brown sugar

2 cinnamon sticks

1 teaspoon vanilla extract

¼ teaspoon ground cloves

¼ teaspoon ground nutmeg

⅛ teaspoon lime zest

In a large skillet over medium-high heat, melt the butter, add the plantain slices, and fry until golden brown on both sides, 3 to 4 minutes. Remove and set aside. Cook in batches to avoid overcrowding the pan.

In the same skillet, again over medium-high heat, add the brown sugar, 2 cups/480ml of water, the cinnamon sticks, vanilla extract, cloves, and nutmeg. Stir to combine and bring the mixture to a boil. Reduce the heat to medium-low and simmer until the mixture thickens into a syrup, 10 to 15 minutes.

Return the fried plantains to the skillet, gently stirring to coat them in the syrup, and continue cooking for another 5 to 10 minutes, until the plantains absorb the flavors of the syrup.

Remove and discard the cinnamon sticks, sprinkle in the lime zest, and serve.

Omi Tip: The ripe plantains in this recipe have to be, as we say, "a punto de mime," in other words, so ripe they're turning black. That's what makes them extra sweet. Add a splash of spiced rum to the syrup for a deeper, more elevated flavor.

4

De chinchorreo
Street food frituras loved by all

The first time I ever heard the word *chinchorrear*, I was already an adult living in Rhode Island. Chinchorrear, or irse de chinchorreo, is a new twenty-first-century term that describes a group of people getting together during the weekend and hopping from one chinchorro (food stand) to another across different areas of Puerto Rico. It's similar in concept to a pub crawl, but instead of drinking beer in bars, you're outdoors, getting a taste of Puerto Rico's famous fried foods, juices, and cocktails.

One of the terrible effects of the many hurricanes that hit our beautiful island in the early 2000s was school closures, which left a number of school buses out of service, wasting away in some car lot or the local junkyard. Once chinchorreando started to become popular, residents decided to repurpose the old buses into chinchorreo buses that would take locals and tourists to chinchorros all over the island.

The old buses were made vibrant and celebratory, painted in bright colors with messages and murals and equipped with stereos—and they're still popular in Puerto Rico today. The chinchorreo tours include music, singing, dancing, and guides to accompany you on the cheerful ride across the island. For locals who want to enjoy cocktails along the way, it's a safe means of transportation that takes the responsibility of driving off their hands, so they can kick back, relax, and enjoy the ride, the food, the drinks (which we'll get into in chapter 5, page 161), and the whole vibe. With many different routes that cruise along the coastlines or venture inland, the chinchorreo experience has provided a boost for the economy in regions of Puerto Rico that tourists and locals alike may not be able to visit otherwise.

El chinchorreo didn't exist when I was growing up. What we know today as a chinchorro was called a parada back then. And instead of full-blown food stands, we had el hombre del carrito (the man with the food cart), la señora de la tiendita que hace las mejores alcapurrias (the lady from the bodega who makes the best alcapurrias), or la señora de la casa amarilla (the lady in the yellow house). These spots were usually unmarked, places that you discovered through word of mouth. You had to know someone who would take you there—there was no address or Google Maps to guide you.

And the act of chinchorrear, well, that was exactly what my family did when I was a kid almost every Sunday, minus the party bus. When Mami and I lived in Puerto Rico, my grandparents would pick us up in the morning and take us on a day trip somewhere new. I'd excitedly climb into the back seat of their gold Volvo next to Mami and wonder where we'd visit next. As we settled in for the ride, I'd smell a whiff of my abuela's perfume and catch a glimpse of her kind eyes in the rearview mirror, then look over at the nape of my abuelo's neck peeking out of his signature Panama hat and crisp guayabera, his weathered hand resting on the wheel, guiding us down the highway to a new adventure.

Sometimes we'd go to the town where my abuelo got his cigars; other times, we'd explore new areas until someone in the car would say, "Let's stop here, aquí venden rico," there's good food here. I clearly remember one ride in Guayama, driving down a long dirt road to Pozuelo Beach in search of a spot someone recommended, where we had the best empanadillas de jueyes ever. We returned often to that parada just for them. Unknowingly, we were the OGs of chinchorreo!

Whenever we tried a new food that made us do a happy dance, my abuela would say, "Ah, pero eso yo lo hago fácil," talking about how she could easily make that. It was almost like a challenge to her. We'd return home, and in the subsequent days, she'd work on re-creating the dish. She'd come to life in her kitchen, with my aunt by her side, the two of them mixing, blending, and frying ingredients like chemists, searching for the perfect balance of seasoning and texture. They were patient, determined to replicate the flavors that had made our eyes roll back in bliss. And they always got it. It was an art—it was magic.

Once my abuelos moved to Río Grande, our weekend adventures turned to the sea, and our domingos en familia became Sundays at the beach. We would wake up with the sun to pack the car with coolers filled with Sandwichitos de mezcla (page 231) for the kids, as well as fresh ingredients my abuela and aunt had prepared earlier that morning or the night before, specifically for this outing. Abuela packed her favorite pot, my aunts brought seasoned, ready-to-cook food in disposable aluminum pans, and my abuelo loaded bags of charcoal in the trunk. By eight in the morning, we were on our way to Playa Seven Seas, our favorite beach.

As a kid, I always thought the ride to Playa Seven Seas was so long, but in reality it was only about a thirty-minute drive from our home in Río Grande. We always left early to make sure we'd be able to get a good parking spot on the street (there were no parking lots back then) and, most importantly, claim the perfect stretch on the beach. We needed room for more than just a few towels and beach chairs—we set up a full production. I already mentioned the pot, baking tins, and charcoal, but there was also the grill, the table, the chairs, and even

the tendedero—that's right, we brought our own clothesline to hang our towels. We took our Sundays at the beach so seriously that one of my uncles eventually bought a porta potty, so we could relax and enjoy our all-day family event without hectic bathroom runs.

Once we made ourselves at home on the beach, the cooking began. I'm talking arroz con pollo, con bacalao, or anything that could be turned into a hearty one-pot meal that was plentiful enough to feed our entire family. My aunt was in charge of the ensalada de mariscos, which we would stuff into freshly fried arepas.

Aside from the food, what I loved most was lounging on a towel or a chair near my aunts, uncles, and grandparents and hearing them joke around and talk, hablando de todo y de nada, while they cooked or played dominoes. That dominoes table was where the real conversations went down, and I often preferred to eavesdrop instead of playing in the water with my cousins. My curiosity always got the best of me.

On the days we craved frituras, my abuelo was the one who knew where to find la señora de las alcapurrias or el señor de los jueyes, so we'd head over to these secret spots with him to buy Alcapurrias (page 144) exploding with flavor, along with fresh empanadillas (see page 150) or Bacalaítos (page 153). And if we craved something sweet, we'd beg the adults for a few bucks and run to the nearest carrito on the beach, pushed by a señor selling mantecados (ice creams), limber (a popular Puerto Rican ice pop–like treat, served frozen in a cup without a stick), or piraguas (shaved ice with fruit syrup).

When I was in my late teens and my cousin got her driver's license, we had the chance to head down to the shore on our own, and we couldn't get enough of our newfound freedom. Puerto Rico, teenagers, summertime, the soft sand, the hot sun, the warm breeze, the frituras and fresh juices—what more could we ask for? We never wanted it to end.

Plátanos
The ever-present ingredient

Plantains are the most versatile fruit in the Puerto Rican arsenal of ingredients. They are so important that it would be nearly impossible to eat one of our feasts without a beloved plátano on your plate. Their main-character energy shows up in Pastelón (page 104) and Mofongo (page 103), and they play a supporting side-dish role in Tostones (page 143) and maduros (page 127), or they can impart a more subdued flavor in soups and masas (doughs).

We eat plantains at every stage of ripeness: green (unripe), yellow (ripe), and a punto de mime (so ripe that the skin turns black). Their flavor will change depending on their ripeness, as well as the cooking method and seasoning, which can turn them into anything from a salty snack like tostones to a caramelized side like maduros.

Native to Southeast Asia, plantains reached Puerto Rican shores around the sixteenth century with the arrival of Spanish colonizers and the transatlantic slave trade. Enslaved Africans planted plantain trees, which thrived in the tropical climate, the fruit becoming their main source of food. Given how affordable, adaptable, and filling plantains are, they became a critical crop in Puerto Rico, grown commercially and in backyards alike. Over time, plantains went from a survival food to a culinary staple symbolizing heritage, resilience, and comfort in our everyday dishes and holiday spreads.

My family members in Puerto Rico have so many plantain trees growing in their backyards that someone is always bringing over un racimo de plátanos cut directly from their tree—a cluster of plantains with rows of the fruit still attached to the stem. A single one has enough plantains to feed several families. Some people also sell these racimos at food stands to make some extra cash—I recently asked a vendor at an outdoor market how much a racimo would cost, and he said seventy dollars!

My abuela always had un racimo de plátanos tucked away in a corner of her terrace. Anytime she needed plantains (which was almost daily), she'd head out to the terraza and pick a green, yellow, or black one to use in her asopaos, main and side dishes, or frituras. I don't remember a day in my life without some type of plantains.

I love plátanos in all their culinary forms, such as Bolitas de plátano rellenas de jueyes (page 156), Piononos (page 154), and Arañitas (page 155), but my all-time favorite are maduros. So, when plantains showed up as our surprise mid-round drop on episode six of *Next Level Chef*, I thought I was dreaming. I lunged forward and grabbed three green plantains, and a yellow one. And although on-screen, you only see me making tostones al ajillo for my dish, I also sliced and fried up that perfectly ripe yellow plátano and turned it into a serving of maduros just for my homesick heart. After we were done, I took my plate of leftover tostones and maduros and munched on them on the elevator ride down to meet the judges. No one could take the smile off my face after I tasted that rich, sweet, caramelized slice of home.

Picadillo

Puerto Rican picadillo

Picadillo is basically seasoned ground beef stewed in a tomato sauce. This dish is eaten across Latin America, but this version is quintessentially Puerto Rican, thanks to the inclusion of sofrito, achiote oil, adobo, and more flavors that we love. It's mainly used as a filling or stuffing in several of our traditional recipes, such as Alcapurrias (page 144), Rellenos de papa (page 151), and Piononos (page 154), to name a few. So make sure you flag this recipe as you will be coming back to it often!

Makes 6 to 8 servings

2 tablespoons Achiote oil (page 39)

1½ tablespoons Mi Sofrito Fresquecito (page 37)

1 small onion, finely chopped

1 small green bell pepper, finely chopped

2 garlic cloves, minced

1 pound/450g (90/10) ground beef

½ cup/120ml tomato sauce

8 pimiento-stuffed green olives, halved

1 tablespoon Adobo (page 38)

1 teaspoon Sazón (page 43)

1 teaspoon dried oregano

½ teaspoon freshly ground black pepper

Kosher salt to taste, *LQTDT*♥

¼ cup/10g chopped cilantro

In a large skillet over medium heat, add the achiote oil and heat until it shimmers. Add the sofrito, onion, bell pepper, and garlic and sauté until the vegetables are soft and fragrant, about 5 minutes.

Add the ground beef to the skillet and cook, breaking it up with a spoon, until it is browned and cooked through, about 10 minutes.

Stir in the tomato sauce, olives, adobo, sazón, oregano, pepper, and salt to taste. Mix well to combine, reduce the heat to low, and let the mixture simmer for 15 to 20 minutes, allowing the flavors to meld.

Stir in the cilantro just before serving the picadillo (or using it in another recipe).

Omi Tip: Though it's most often used as a stuffing, picadillo can also be eaten as a main dish, served with classic Arroz blanco (page 98) and Habichuelas guisadas (page 100), with a side of maduros (page 127) for good measure.

Tostones al ajillo y limón

Fried green plantains with garlic and lime

Crispy, golden tostones (smashed twice-fried plantains) are a beloved staple in Puerto Rico. They're made with green plantains, which have a more neutral flavor and a firmer texture than sweet, ripe ones, giving them a starchier bite. Pair them with seafood, Mofongo (page 103), and Carne frita encebollada (page 123), or enjoy them on their own, drizzled in their signature garlic sauce or dipped in Omi's mayoketchup (page 38). When making tostones, my trick is to dip them in garlic water after their first fry to infuse them with that irresistible flavor before frying a second time.

Makes 6 to 8 servings

- 1 cup/240ml vegetable oil, for frying
- 3 green plantains, peeled and cut into 2-inch-thick slices
- 4 garlic cloves, mashed in a pilón
- ¼ cup/60ml extra-virgin olive oil
- ¼ cup/60ml lime juice (about 2 limes)
- Kosher salt and freshly ground black pepper to taste, *LQTDT*♥

In a large skillet over medium-high heat, add the vegetable oil and heat until it shimmers. Add the plantain slices to the skillet and fry for 2 to 3 minutes on each side, until they are golden but not fully cooked. Use a slotted spoon to remove the fried plantains from the oil and set on paper towels to drain excess oil, reserving the oil in the skillet. Turn off the heat for the time being.

In a bowl, mix half of the mashed garlic with 1 cup/240ml of water. Add the fried plantain slices to the garlic water and soak for 1 to 2 minutes to infuse them with a delicious garlic flavor.

Remove the plantains from the garlic water and pat them dry with paper towels.

Using a tostonera (plantain press) or the flat bottom of a glass, gently flatten each plantain slice to about a ½-inch thickness.

Reheat the oil in the skillet until it shimmers. Add the flattened plantains back to the skillet and fry a second time for 2 to 3 minutes on each side, until they are crispy and golden brown. Remove the tostones from the skillet and set on fresh paper towels to drain excess oil.

In a small saucepan over medium heat, add the olive oil and heat until it shimmers. Add the remaining mashed garlic and sauté until fragrant, 1 to 2 minutes. Remove from the heat and stir in the lime juice.

Drizzle the garlic sauce over the tostones, sprinkle with salt and pepper, and serve immediately while still hot and crispy.

Alcapurrias

Fried plantain and meat fritters

Makes 20 servings

Masa (Dough)

10 to 12 green cooking bananas (guineos verdes)

1 white yautia (yautías blanca)

1 green plantain

2 teaspoons kosher salt

1 teaspoon Sazón (page 43)

1 tablespoon Achiote oil (page 39)

Alcapurrias

Vegetable oil, for frying, plus more for greasing

1 recipe Picadillo (page 142)

Omi's mayoketchup (page 38), Pique (page 43), or hot sauce, for serving

I am an alcapurrias snob—I admit it wholeheartedly, with no shame. If I see an alcapurria that doesn't look or taste a certain way, I'll turn my nose up at it. My perfect alcapurria is around 6 to 7 inches long with a masa made from blended green bananas, yautía blanca, and plantains, and evenly filled with beef picadillo. The masa *and* the filling must be packed with flavor and fried to perfection so that each bite delivers a tasty crunch and reveals the juicy picadillo with visible speckles of olives and peppers. While beef picadillo is the classic filling, fillings vary, from shredded chicken to bacalao to cheese to jueyes (crab), which is my second-favorite. But please, por el amor de Dios, don't add calabaza to the masa of your alcapurrias. Pumpkin has a high water content, which will leave you with a sad, soggy fritter that will take the joy out of the experience. Hazme caso, por favor.

Make the masa (dough): Peel the green bananas, yautía, and plantain and cut them into small pieces. As you cut, place the pieces in a large bowl filled with cold water to prevent browning.

Drain the water and add the pieces to a food processor. Blend until a smooth, thick dough forms. Work in batches as needed to avoid overfilling the food processor.

Transfer the masa to a large bowl and add the salt, sazón, and achiote oil and mix well until evenly combined.

Make the alcapurrias: Lightly grease a 10 by 10-inch sheet of parchment paper with vegetable oil.

Place about ¼ cup of the masa onto the parchment paper and spread it out into a 6-by-3-inch rectangle. Add a tablespoon of picadillo in the center of the masa and spread it lengthwise along the size of the masa rectangle, then use the parchment paper to carefully fold the masa over the filling widthwise, shaping it into a log. If the filling isn't completely enclosed, add a little more masa to help seal it completely and smooth it out with the back of a greased spoon. Transfer the alcapurria to a separate plate lined with parchment paper and repeat this step, using the same sheet of parchment paper to continue shaping 3 more alcapurrias.

continued

Alcapurrias, *continued*

Omi Tip: If you make more alcapurrias than you want to fry, freeze them for up to 3 months and fry them at a later date. If freezing, use squares of parchment paper to separate each one and freeze flat on a tray covered in plastic wrap to prevent frostbite. You can fry them directly from frozen—do not thaw.

Use a new sheet for every 3 to 4 alcapurrias shaped. You should have about 20 alcapurrias total once done.

In a deep frying pan or large pot over medium-high heat, add 2 to 3 inches of the canola oil and heat to 350°F/175°C (use an instant-read thermometer to monitor the temperature of the oil). Gently slide the alcapurrias off the parchment paper into the hot oil one at a time. You can fry multiple alcaupurrias at a time but avoid overcrowding the pan. Fry until golden brown and crispy, 7 to 8 minutes per side.

Remove the alcapurrias from the pan and set on paper towels to drain excess oil. Serve hot, with a side of mayoketchup, pique, or your favorite hot sauce.

Sorullitos

Sweet cornmeal sticks

Sorullitos con café are the ultimate pairing, ¡es lo más rico que existe! You can have these cornmeal fritters stuffed with cheese for breakfast, or with a cup of hot chocolate later in the evening. My abuela used to make this sweet-and-savory treat every morning and serve it as a side next to eggs and bacon or, in my case, with my go-to cremitas and fruit. Nowadays, you can find them at some chinchorros served with a side of mayoketchup (page 38).

Makes 15 or 16 servings

Cornmeal Dough

1 teaspoon kosher salt

1 tablespoon granulated sugar

1 tablespoon unsalted butter

1½ cups/210g fine yellow cornmeal

½ cup/15g grated Parmesan cheese

½ cup/50g shredded mozzarella cheese

Sorullitos

1 tablespoon granulated sugar, for sugar water

1 cup/100g shredded mozzarella cheese (or queso de papa)

Vegetable oil, for frying

Make the dough: In a medium saucepan over medium-high heat, bring 2 cups/480ml of water, the salt, sugar, and butter to a boil. Once the water is boiling, gradually add the cornmeal, stirring continuously to prevent lumps.

Once the cornmeal is incorporated, reduce the heat to low and stir continuously until the mixture thickens and pulls away from the sides of the pan, 5 to 7 minutes. Remove from the the heat and stir in the Parmesan and mozzarella cheese. Let the dough cool slightly, until it is safe to handle.

Make the sorullitos: In a small bowl, combine the sugar with 1 cup/240ml of water to make a sugar water. Wet your hands in the sugar water, then grab a golf ball–size amount of the cornmeal dough and flatten it into a disc in your hand.

Place a heaping teaspoon of mozzarella cheese in the center of the disc. Fold the dough over the cheese and shape it into a small log. Pinch the seam and ends to seal, ensuring the cheese is fully enclosed.

Repeat to make 15 or 16 sorullitos with the rest of the dough and cheese, making sure to wet your hands in the bowl of sugar water to keep the dough from sticking to your fingers before each one.

In a deep skillet or deep fryer over medium-high heat, add 2 inches of oil and heat to 350°F/175°C (use an instant-read thermometer to monitor the temperature of the oil).

Fry the sorullitos in batches until golden brown and crispy, 3 to 4 minutes per batch.

Use a slotted spoon to remove the sorullitos from the skillet and set on paper towels to drain excess oil.

Serve the sorullitos hot with your favorite dipping sauce on the side, such as garlic aioli, mayoketchup, or a spicy mayo.

Omi Tip: The art to making a perfect sorullito is in learning how to shape it into a cylinder without the dough sticking to your hands and fingers. My trick is to keep a small bowl of sugar water nearby to wet my hands as I form the dough.

GENUINE
1876

Los tacos de Doña Connie

Doña Connie's tacos

Makes 20 servings

Masa (Dough)

3 cups/420g all-purpose flour, plus more for kneading

2 teaspoons kosher salt

½ cup/120ml vegetable oil, plus more for frying

Filling

Kosher salt to taste, *LQTDT*♥

3 to 4 medium russet potatoes, peeled and diced

1 recipe Picadillo (page 142)

Omi Tip: You can freeze the unfried tacos for up to 3 months, then thaw and fry at a later date.

Growing up in Puerto Rico, I had these pastelito-like tacos at school and at events all the time. But it wasn't until I was twelve or thirteen that I realized I had the taco-making queen living in my house. Mami's tacos—which sort of resemble Mexican taquitos—are so good that people in Rhode Island started buying boxes of them. She makes the dough from scratch, with love, and folds potatoes into the picadillo filling, making the tacos extra hearty. We are such fans of Mami's tacos that whenever she stays at our house, she always makes us a batch before leaving—gifting us a little piece of her that makes missing her just a tiny bit easier.

Make the masa: In a large bowl, combine the flour and salt. Gradually add 1 cup/240ml of water and the oil and mix until a dough forms.

Remove the dough from the bowl, place it on a floured surface, and knead until it becomes smooth and elastic and it no longer sticks to your hands, about 10 minutes.

Cover the dough with a damp cloth and let it rest for 20 minutes.

Make the filling: Fill a large pot with water, add a pinch of salt, and bring to a boil over medium-high heat. Add the potatoes, return to a boil, and cook until fork-tender, 10 to 15 minutes, then drain.

Add the picadillo to the pot with the potatoes and gently fold it until well combined.

Make the tacos: Divide the dough into small balls, each about the size of a golf ball. On a flat surface lightly dusted with flour, using a rolling pin, roll out each ball into a flat oval, about 6 inches in diameter.

Place a spoonful of the picadillo and potato filling in the center of each oval and spread lengthwise. Fold the dough over the filling and shape it into a log, pinching and sealing the seam and ends shut to prevent the filling from leaking out.

In a deep frying pan or large pot, add 2 to 3 inches of the oil and heat to 350°F/175°C (use an instant-read thermometer to monitor the temperature). Carefully place the tacos in the hot oil, a few at a time, crowding the pan. Fry until golden brown and crispy, 5 to 7 minutes.

Remove the fried tacos from the pan and set on paper towels to drain excess oil. Serve warm and eat to your heart's content!

Empanadilla de pizza

Pizza turnover

I went to school in Puerto Rico through sixth grade, and there was nothing like heading to the school's tiendita to buy a warm empanadilla de pizza and a Coca-Cola Icee. I'm talking about the ones with the trenza, the braid-like fold, not the ones with the fork-crimped edges, which technically makes it a pastelillo in my eyes. Semantics aside, one bite instantly wraps me up in the warm memories of my Puerto Rican schooldays.

Makes 15 or 16 servings

Empanadillas

2 cups/280g all-purpose flour

½ teaspoon kosher salt

½ teaspoon baking powder

¼ cup/55g cold unsalted butter, cubed

Vegetable oil, for frying

Filling

1 cup/240ml marinara sauce

2 cups/200g shredded mozzarella cheese

1 teaspoon garlic powder

½ teaspoon dried oregano

½ teaspoon dried basil

¼ cup/8g grated Parmesan cheese

¼ cup/30g finely chopped pepperoni or pan-fried salami (optional)

Make the dough: In a large bowl, combine the flour, salt, and baking powder and use a pastry cutter or your fingers to cut in the cold butter until the mixture resembles coarse crumbs. Gradually add ½ cup/120ml of cold water, mixing until a dough forms.

Remove the dough from the bowl, place on a lightly floured surface, and knead until smooth, about 8 minutes. Wrap the dough in plastic wrap and refrigerate for at least 30 minutes.

Make the filling: In a bowl, mix together the marinara sauce, mozzarella, garlic powder, oregano, basil, and Parmesan cheese. Add the pepperoni or salami, if using, and mix well.

Make the empanadillas: On a lightly floured surface, roll out the dough until it's about ⅛ inch thick. Using a round cutter or a small bowl (4 to 5 inches in diameter), cut out 15 or 16 discs.

Place 1½ tablespoons of the filling in the center of each dough circle and fold the dough over the filling to form a half-moon shape. Pinch to seal and then create the famous "trenza" (braid-like fold) with the dough: Starting at one end of the sealed edge, pinch the bottom into a tiny triangle and fold it back over itself toward the empanadilla, pressing it down gently. Continue this process all the way up the sealed edge of the empanadilla, by gently pulling on the triangle and folding it back onto itself, to create a braided pattern.

Fry the empanadillas: In a deep skillet or deep fryer over medium-high heat, add 2 to 3 inches of the oil and heat to 350°F/175°C (use an instant-read thermometer to monitor the temperature of the oil).

Carefully add the empanadillas to the pan in batches, to avoid overcrowding. Fry until golden brown and crispy, 2 to 3 minutes per side. Use a slotted spoon to remove the empanadillas from the skillet and set on paper towels to drain excess oil. Serve warm.

Omi Tip: Feel free to use any deli meat other than pepperoni. En tu cocina ú mandas.

Rellenos de papa

Stuffed potato balls

I feel like the DNA of this recipe is part of a local and international language, because many countries have their own version of a stuffed potato ball. The sazón used in our version is what really makes this Puerto Rican. Rellenos de papa were another treat I couldn't get enough of when I went to school in Puerto Rico. My favorite are the traditional picadillo-stuffed kind, as in this recipe. But feel free to play around with the fillings to make it your own. You can use eggs, other kinds of ground meat, shredded chicken, chopped steak, lo que te diga tu corazón.

Makes 10 or 11 servings

- 5 or 6 large russet potatoes, peeled and cut into chunks
- 1 teaspoon kosher salt
- ½ teaspoon garlic powder
- ½ teaspoon onion powder
- ¼ teaspoon freshly ground black pepper
- ¼ cup/35g cornstarch, plus 1 cup/140g for coating
- ½ recipe Picadillo (page 142), for filling
- 1 cup/140g all-purpose flour
- Vegetable oil, for frying

In a large pot over medium-high heat, add the potatoes and enough water to cover them. Add the salt and bring to a boil, then cook until the potatoes are tender, 15 to 20 minutes. Drain the potatoes, return them to the pot, and mash until smooth. Add the garlic powder, onion powder, pepper, and ¼ cup of the cornstarch and mix well.

Let the potato mixture cool to room temperature, then take ⅓ cup of the potatoes and shape it into a ball the size of a baseball. Repeat with the remaining potato mixture until you have 10 or 11 potato balls.

Using your thumb, make a well in the middle of a potato ball and add a teaspoon of the picadillo in the well. Pinch the potato ball closed to seal the picadillo inside and smooth it out so there are no cracks. Repeat to stuff the remaining potato balls.

Add the flour to a shallow bowl. Add the remaining cup of cornstarch to a separate shallow bowl and whisk in about ½ cup/120ml of water (adjust as needed) to form a thick slurry. Roll each potato ball in the flour, then dip it in the cornstarch slurry, making sure each ball is evenly coated.

In a deep skillet or deep fryer over medium-high heat, add enough vegetable oil to fully cover the potato balls. Heat the oil to 350°F/175°C (use an instant-read thermometer to monitor the temperature).

Carefully add the potato balls to the hot oil, working in batches to avoid overcrowding the pan. Fry until golden brown and crispy, 3 to 4 minutes per batch. Use a slotted spoon to remove the fried potato balls from the skillet and set on paper towels to drain excess oil.

Serve the rellenos de papa hot, with your favorite dipping sauce on the side—that's Omi's mayoketchup (page 38) for me.

Omi Tip. To prevent the rellenos from splitting open, make sure to thoroughly drain the potatoes before mashing to remove excess moisture. If the potato balls are still splitting, you can add a bit more cornstarch to seal them completely. Also, avoid overcrowding the skillet so you have plenty of space to turn them on all sides.

Bacalaítos

Codfish fritters

Makes 10 to 12 servings

- 1 pound/450g salted cod (bacalao)
- 2 cups/280g all-purpose flour
- 1 teaspoon baking powder
- 1 tablespoon Adobo (page 38)
- 1 teaspoon Sazón (page 43)
- ¼ cup/10g finely chopped cilantro
- ¼ cup/60ml Mi Sofrito Fresquecito (page 37)
- ¼ cup/60ml extra-virgin olive oil
- Vegetable oil, for frying
- Lime wedges, for serving

Omi Tip: If you're feeling super creative, that's great—¡en tu cocina tú mandas! You can use this same batter for other things, including for dipping your Piononos (page 154) before frying. It's a game-changer!

Bacalaítos are the current star attraction when it comes to chinchorreo. The average bacalaíto nowadays has grown to about the size of a plate, and an unspoken competition has emerged to see who can make the largest bacalaíto on the island. That's all fun and good, but size doesn't mean anything if your fritter doesn't have the right consistency. A true bacalaíto needs to stand sturdy in your hand, even if it's the size of your head. And it should be crunchy throughout, with pockets in the fried dough hiding bites of soft, flaked bacalao. If you're trying to defend your bacalaíto to me and it flops over so you have to carry it around like a taco, you might as well argue with a wall, because I'm not hearing it. I like my bacalaítos the size of a regular pancake, crisp and firm, with grease running down the side of my hand as I eat it.

Prepare the bacalao: Rinse the salted cod under cold water to remove excess salt. Then set a large pot over medium-high heat, add the cod, cover with water, and bring to a boil. Once the water is boiling, reduce the heat to medium-low and simmer for 15 to 20 minutes.

Drain the cod and let it cool. Once cool enough to handle, flake the fish into small pieces with your fingers, removing any bones and skin.

Make the batter: In a large bowl, combine the flour, baking powder, adobo, and sazón. Add the flaked cod, cilantro, and sofrito and stir to incorporate. Gradually add the olive oil and 1½ cups/360ml of water, stirring until a smooth batter forms. Add water a little bit at a time as needed—the batter should be thick but pourable.

Fry the bacalaítos: In a deep skillet or fryer over medium-high heat, add 1 inch of vegetable oil and heat to 350°F/175°C (use an instant-read thermometer to monitor the temperature of the oil).

Using a ladle, carefully add spoonfuls of the batter to the hot oil, using the back of the ladle to flatten them slightly so they look like pancakes. Work in batches, taking care to avoid overcrowding the pan.

Fry the bacalaítos until golden brown and crispy, 3 to 4 minutes per side. Use a slotted spoon to remove the bacalaítos from the skillet and set on paper towels to drain excess oil.

Serve the bacalaítos hot, with a squeeze of fresh lime juice or your favorite dipping sauce.

Pionónos

Sweet plantain and meat rolls

The sweet-and-savory flavor profile of this dish speaks to my heart. Pionónos consist of a ring-shaped maduro, filled with picadillo and cheese, dipped in perfectly seasoned batter, and flawlessly fried not once, but twice. These are a treat and well worth the work. You can easily find pionónos at chinchorros on the island, but for those of us living far away from home, it's wonderful to have a recipe up our sleeve when the craving hits. Serve with some rice and beans to turn this tropical bite into a full-blown meal.

Makes 8 to 10 servings

Fried Plantains

4 ripe plantains (yellow with black spots)

Vegetable oil, for frying

Batter

1 cup/140g all-purpose flour

1 teaspoon baking powder

½ teaspoon Adobo (page 38)

4 large eggs, beaten

Pionónos

1 recipe Picadillo (page 142), for filling

Toothpicks, for making rings

1 cup/100g shredded mozzarella cheese (or your favorite melting cheese)

Vegetable oil, for frying

Fry the plantains: Peel the plantains and cut them each lengthwise into 4 long, thin strips.

In a large skillet over medium heat, add about 2 inches of oil and heat until it shimmers. Fry the plantain slices until golden brown on both sides, 2 to 3 minutes per side. Use a slotted spoon to remove the fried plantains from the skillet and set aside on paper towels to drain excess oil.

Make the batter: In a bowl, combine the flour, baking powder, and adobo. Gradually add 1 cup/240ml of water, whisking until smooth. Add water a little bit at a time as needed—the batter should be thick but pourable. Add the eggs and whisk to incorporate.

Make the pionónos: Form a fried plantain slice into a ring, securing the ends together with a toothpick. Repeat with the rest of the slices and place the plantain rings on a large plate. Fill each plantain ring with picadillo, then top with mozzarella cheese.

In a deep skillet over medium heat, add 2 to 3 inches of oil and heat until it shimmers.

Dip each filled plantain ring in the batter, ensuring it is fully coated, and carefully place the battered plantain rings into the hot oil, working in small batches to avoid overcrowding. Fry the rings until the batter is golden brown and crispy, 3 to 4 minutes per side. Use a slotted spoon to remove the plantain rings from the skillet and set on paper towels to drain excess oil. After the first frying, let the pionónos cool slightly (turn off the heat in the meantime).

Reheat the oil until it shimmers, return the pionónos to the skillet, and fry them again for 2 to 3 more minutes—this will give you that extra crispiness. Use a slotted spoon to remove the pinonos from the skillet again and set on paper towels to drain excess oil once more.

Serve the pionónos hot—the fresher, the better!

Omi Tip: If you don't want to fry them, baking your pionónos in a muffin pan is totally acceptable. Simply form the pionóno in the muffin cup, skip the batter bath, and instead beat 1 egg and top each pionóno with about 1 teaspoon of the beaten egg. Bake at 350°F/175°C for about 15 minutes, until they are set and the tops are lightly browned.

Arañitas de camarones
Shrimp fritters

Seafood items are featured on most chinchorreo menus (unsurprisingly for an island), and these garlicky arañitas are some of the tastiest among them. They have the perfect plantain-to-shrimp ratio, and when you bite into one, it's like a cloud on the inside, with a delicious outer crunch. I urge you to swap out your regular side of Tostones (page 143) for these arañitas for a delicious twist on your everyday meals (see Tip).

Makes 6 to 8 servings

- 4 green plantains, peeled
- 1 pound/450g shrimp, peeled, deveined, and finely chopped
- 1 teaspoon Sazón (page 43)
- 1 tablespoon Adobo (page 38)
- 2 garlic cloves, mashed in a pilón
- ¼ cup/10g finely chopped cilantro
- Kosher salt and freshly ground black pepper to taste, *LQTDT*♥
- Vegetable oil, for frying

Grate the plantains using the finest side of a grater or a food processor. In a large bowl, combine the grated plantains, the shrimp, sazón, adobo, garlic, and cilantro and mix until well combined. Season with salt and pepper.

Take small handfuls of the mixture and shape them into flat patties or nests about the size of your palm. Press them together, but DO NOT compact them too much—just enough to ensure they hold together during frying. It's okay to see some plantain flakes around the edges; that's what gives it a spider (aka arañita) effect.

In a deep skillet or deep fryer over medium-high heat, add 3 inches of oil and heat to 350°F/175°C (use an instant-read thermometer to monitor the temperature of the oil).

Carefully place the arañitas in the hot oil, working in batches to avoid overcrowding the pan. Fry until golden brown and crispy, 3 to 4 minutes per side. Use a slotted spoon to remove the arañitas from the skillet and set on paper towels to drain excess oil.

Serve the arañitas hot with your favorite dipping sauce on the side, such as a garlic aioli, ketchup, or spicy mayo.

Omi Tip: You can also make arañitas without the shrimp—the end result will make you feel like you're snacking on a bag of platanutres con ajo (packaged plantain chips with garlic). Simply omit the shrimp when making the mixture. Remember not to compact the arañita mixture too much—being gentle will create a more cloudlike interior with maximum crunch on the outside.

Bolitas de plátano rellenas de jueyes

Crab-filled plantain balls

Imagine a Relleno de papa (page 151)—but made with amarillos (ripe plantains) and filled with jueyes (crab)—and you've got this Omified chinchorreo-inspired dish. I like to use canned crabmeat, mostly because I don't have time to crack all those legs, pero en tu cocina tú mandas. Make sure to shape the bolitas in your hand and seal them well before frying. Whether you serve this alone or as an appetizer, or add your favorite sides and turn them into a main dish, you're sure to wow your guests, because you won't find these frituras anywhere else but in my house (and now, yours)!

Makes 6 to 8 servings

Bolitas de plátano (Plantain Balls)

- 4 ripe plantains (amarillos), peeled and cut into chunks
- 2 teaspoons kosher salt
- 1 teaspoon Adobo (page 38)
- 1 teaspoon garlic powder
- 1 teaspoon dried oregano
- ½ cup/70g cornstarch, for coating (optional)
- Vegetable oil, for frying

Picadillo de jueyes (Crab Filling)

- 2 tablespoons extra-virgin olive oil
- 1 small onion, finely chopped
- 1 small green bell pepper, finely chopped
- 2 garlic cloves, minced
- ¼ cup/60ml Mi Sofrito Fresquecito (page 37)
- 1 pound/450g crabmeat (fresh or canned)
- ¼ cup/60ml tomato sauce
- 1 teaspoon Adobo (page 38)
- 1 teaspoon dried oregano
- ¼ cup/40g green olives, sliced
- Kosher salt and freshly ground black pepper to taste, *LQTDT*♥

Prepare the plantains: In a large pot over medium-high heat, add the plantain chunks, cover with water, and add 1 teaspoon of the salt. Bring to a boil and cook until tender, 20 to 25 minutes.

Drain the plantains, add them to a medium bowl, and mash them with a fork or potato masher until smooth. Season with the remaining teaspoon of salt, the adobo, garlic powder, and oregano and set aside to cool.

Make the picadillo de jueyes: In a large skillet over medium heat, add the olive oil and heat until it shimmers. Add the onion, bell pepper, and garlic and sauté until the vegetables are softened, 3 to 4 minutes. Stir in the sofrito and cook for another 2 minutes, until fragrant.

Add the crabmeat, tomato sauce, adobo, oregano, and olives and stir to combine. Cook for 10 to 15 minutes, allowing the flavors to meld. Season with salt and pepper.

Make the plantain balls: Take about 1½ tablespoons of the mashed plantain mixture and flatten it in your palm.

Place about 1 teaspoon of the crab filling in the center and carefully pinch the plantain mixture around it to form a ball. Repeat with the remaining plantain mash and crab filling. There should be 17 to 20 balls, depending on their size. If desired, roll the plantain balls in the cornstarch until fully coated for an extra-crispy finish.

In a deep fryer or deep skillet over medium-high heat, add 2 inches of vegetable oil and heat until it shimmers.

Fry the bolitas in batches to avoid overcrowding the skillet, until golden brown and crispy, 3 to 4 minutes per side. Use a slotted spoon to remove them from the oil and set on paper towels to drain excess oil.

Serve the bolitas de plátano warm with a side of Pique (page 43) for an extra kick.

Omi Tip: If you have any leftover crab filling, store it in a container in the refrigerator for up to 3 days or freeze for 1 month. Also, if you're not a fan of the sweet-and-salty flavor profile of this recipe, use Mofongo (page 103) instead and fill it with picadillo de jueyes . . . ¡delicioso!

Queso frito con salsa de guayaba

Fried cheese with guava sauce

A somewhat newer player on the scene, this fried cheese with guava dipping sauce is quickly becoming a staple in Puerto Rico. And I'm not surprised—these two flavors are a common pairing on the island, so they speak straight to my Boricua heart. When I make this at home, my boys like to eat the fried cheese with fried salami instead of the guava sauce, but I personally need this salsita to complete the dish. Have it as a snack, an appetizer, or a dessert, lo que te diga tu corazón.

Makes 18 to 20 fried cheese slices

Queso frito (Fried Cheese)

1 cup/140g all-purpose flour

1 teaspoon paprika

½ teaspoon garlic powder

½ teaspoon onion powder

½ teaspoon freshly ground black pepper

1 pound/450g queso blanco or queso de freír (frying cheese), cut into thick slices

Vegetable oil, for frying

Salsa de guayaba (Guava Sauce)

1 cup/315g guava paste

1 tablespoon lime juice

1 tablespoon honey

Make the queso frito: In a shallow bowl, combine the flour, paprika, garlic powder, onion powder, and pepper. Dredge each slice of cheese in the flour mixture, ensuring it is well coated.

In a large skillet over medium heat, add 1 inch of oil and heat until it shimmers. Add the cheese slices to the skillet and fry until golden brown and crispy, 2 to 3 minutes per side. Use a slotted spoon to remove the cheese slices from the skillet and set on paper towels to drain excess oil.

Make the salsa de guayaba: In a small saucepan over medium heat, add the guava paste and ½ cup/120ml of water and cook, stirring frequently, until the guava paste has melted and the mixture is smooth, 5 to 7 minutes. Remove from the heat, add the lime juice and honey, and stir to incorporate. Let cool slightly.

Serve the queso frito hot, with the salsa de guayaba on the side for dipping.

Omi Tip: This guayaba sauce isn't overly sweet and plays well with other flavors, so go ahead and drizzle it on other savory dishes for a sweet-and-salty bite.

Yuca rellena de queso envuelta en tocineta

Cheese-stuffed yuca wrapped in bacon

I was clearly obsessed with rolls a few years back, because this is another Omified dish that I came up with around the same time I created my Rollo de pollo (page 131). In this case, I had vegetables on the mind, and yuca was the winner. These mini rolls are assembled in layers and then rolled up—you start with a layer of bacon, followed by mashed yuca, sweet fried plantains, and cheese. Then, guava glaze is drizzled over them just before serving, a perfect finishing touch. I originally made this recipe as one giant roll, but I decided to experiment with a mini version meant to be served as an appetizer. If you ask me, these mini rolls are something you could potentially find being sold at a chinchorro one day!

Makes 4 servings

1½ pounds/680g cassava (yuca), peeled and cut into chunks

1 teaspoon kosher salt, plus more to taste, *LQTDT*♥

1 teaspoon Adobo (page 38)

1 teaspoon garlic powder

1 teaspoon dried oregano

16 strips bacon

4 mozzarella string cheese sticks

1 recipe Guava glaze (page 133), for serving

Prepare the yuca: Fill a large pot with water, add salt to taste, and bring to a boil over medium-high heat. Add the yuca and boil until fork-tender, 20 to 25 minutes.

Drain the yuca, place it in a large bowl, and mash with a fork or potato masher until smooth. Season with the salt, adobo, garlic powder, and oregano. Set aside.

Make the rolls: Preheat the air fryer or oven to 375°F/190°C.

On a sheet of parchment paper, lay down 4 of the bacon slices, slightly overlapping each other to form a rectangle. Spread a layer of mashed yuca to cover the bacon. Then place a cheese stick in the center of the mashed yuca, lengthwise. Carefully roll the bacon and yuca mixture around the mozzarella stick to form a log. Secure the ends of the bacon with toothpicks if necessary. Repeat with the remaining bacon, yuca mixture, and mozzarella sticks to create a total of 4 mini rolls.

Place the yuca rolls seam sides down in the air fryer basket and air fry for 20 to 25 minutes, turning halfway through, until the bacon is crispy and the cheese is melted. Or, to cook in the oven, place on a baking sheet lined with parchment paper and bake for 25 to 30 minutes, turning halfway through, until the bacon is crispy and the cheese is melted.

Remove the rolls from the air fryer or oven and let them rest for a few minutes. Drizzle with the guava glaze before serving and enjoy hot.

Omi Tip: The firmer you wrap the rellenas, the more compact they'll stay. Feel free to use toothpicks to hold it all together if you're having trouble. Also, feel free to double the recipe if you have a big family or are hosting a gathering.

5

Un brindis boricua
Drinks with a Puerto Rican soul

Whether you're at home, at a restaurant, or de chinchorreo (see page 137), refreshing jugos (juices), rich batidas (shakes), and delicious, fresh cocteles (cocktails) are a key part of daily life on the island. Jugo de china, freshly squeezed orange juice, was ever-present on our breakfast table. My abuela also made sure to have fresh tamarind, passion fruit, or grapefruit juice in the fridge. Those were our go-to drinks with any meal at home.

Batidas were a treat my abuela made later in the evening, after dinner. I relished those sweet, creamy, flavor-packed smoothies and shakes because she didn't make them every night. When I was a toddler, I was such a picky eater that I basically survived on the batida-like concoctions Mami made me, such as grape juice blended with an egg yolk or warm milk with molasses. Mami would get so distressed when I wouldn't eat, but my abuelo would always say to her, "No te preocupes, que ella no se va a morir. Cuando ella tenga hambre, ella va a comer." Don't worry, she's not going to die. When she's hungry, she'll eat. Mami would perk up a little and head back into the kitchen, praying that day would come soon.

I can't say I remember those nutritious drinks very fondly, but there's one smoothie that I still love to this day: the batida de champola. I could have lived my entire childhood on that sweet blend of guava nectar and milk. Thankfully, my abuelo was right: Eventually, I stopped being a fussy eater. Nowadays, Mami likes to say, "She eats everything—and she's taught me how to eat things I didn't even know existed." She's right. What a role reversal!

Cocteles are a different story. Mami has never had an alcoholic beverage or smoked a cigarette in her life, and at my abuelos' home, there were no beers in the fridge, no bar with bottles of hard liquor—my abuelo's only real indulgence was his cigars. But during some of our weekend trips, they'd set out in search of a traditional artisanal drink called maví. It's made from the bark of the mauby tree, which is native to the Caribbean and south Florida. First, the bark is boiled in water with ginger, orange peel, and cinnamon sticks, to make a spiced tea known as "pie de maví." The pie de maví is then strained and added to water mixed with several cups of sugar, then stirred until a foam appears on the surface. That liquid is funneled into bottles and left to ferment for one to three days.

This rare, cherished home-brewed Puerto Rican beverage wasn't easy to find—they usually had to know someone who made it and then hope they had a batch for sale. Luckily, Abuelo knew that someone. Since the fermentation process does produce some alcohol, I was only allowed a few sips from their glass of maví. It is incredibly sweet with a slightly tangy aftertaste and is considered good for digestion.

Funnily enough, even though my abuelo didn't really drink, he did make home-brewed pitorro. A type of moonshine rum also known as ron cañita or ron aguardiente, pitorro is a fermented spiced sugarcane juice that is bottled and buried in the ground early in the year, then dug up right before the holidays, once it's become a distilled liquor. Abuelo liked to add his signature mix of fruits and spices—including raisins and figs according to Mami—and right before the holidays, he'd dig up his bottle so that Abuela could use it to make Coquito (page 169), a coconut nog, for our family members who were visiting from the States. That was the old-school way of making coquito, before we started using rum. But be warned, pitorro is a "'tate quieto," in other words, if you drink one too many, it will creep up on you, so be extra careful when sipping.

The other renowned pitorro maker in our family is my titi Marta. She likes to make them with different flavors, such as guava, tamarind, and coconut, to name a few, and then stash the bottles under her sink. Anytime we're at her place, she'll walk the adults to that under-the-sink cabinet, open the door, and say, "¿Cuál quieres probar?," asking us which one we'd like to try. It tastes like a warm, spiced rum with sweet notes of whatever fruit was added. I've only dared a few sips here and there; the smell alone could knock me out, but many of my aunts and uncles love it.

The production of rum in Puerto Rico is directly linked to the expansion of sugarcane cultivation on the island back in the 1700s, which made rum more commercially viable. In the 1800s, with the industrialization of the distillation process came the foundation of Destilería Serrallés, the oldest distillery in Puerto Rico. Located in Ponce, Destilería Serralés is still operating today and produces the renowned Don Q rum. In the 1930s, Bacardí, which was founded in Cuba, moved most of its operation to Puerto Rico, where it now operates the world's largest premium rum distillery, near Cataño. So, it's no surprise this ingredient shows up in so many of our cocktails.

When I finally turned twenty-one, I traded my jugos and refrescos for mojitos and piña coladas on nights out. I'm not a huge drinker, but during the holidays, I love having a glass of creamy Coquito (page 169) or Sangría roja (page 174). But if you find me in San Juan, you'll likely see me with a Mojito de coco (page 171) in hand, or a traditional Piña colada (page 166) topped with a cherry. ¡Salud!

Piña colada
Puerto Rico's national drink

There is a hot debate over who was the true inventor of the now-classic piña colada. The stories feature three bartenders and two hotels. The first one begins with the Caribe Hilton, an iconic hotel located at the mouth of the Condado Lagoon in San Juan. The Caribe Hilton opened in 1949 next to the remnants of the eighteenth-century Spanish Fortín San Gerónimo del Boquerón. Considered one of the first modern luxury hotels on the island, the Caribe Hilton attracted big-name stars such as Rita Moreno, Sophia Loren, and Elizabeth Taylor.

It is said that in 1954, only a few years after the Caribe Hilton's grand opening, one of its bartenders, Ramón "Monchito" Marrero, was asked by the hotel to create a signature cocktail that represented the essence of Puerto Rico. As the story goes, Marrero spent the following three months experimenting with different flavors and combinations until he invented what is now considered the all-time classic piña colada.

But origin stories are not always so simple. During that same year, Ricardo García, another bartender at the same hotel, claimed that *he* was the original inventor of this cocktail. He claimed to have invented it due to a shortage of fresh coconuts on the island, which led him to turn to canned cream of coconut instead.

But the debate doesn't end there! Nine years later, in 1963, a *third* bartender, Ramón Portas Mingot, who was working at the then-new restaurant Barrachina in Old San Juan, laid claim to the title of piña colada inventor. And let's not forget the legend of el Pirata Cofresí, aka Roberto Cofresí, considered the Caribbean Robin Hood, who allegedly mixed white rum, pineapple juice, and coconut milk in the 1800s and served it on his ship to avoid a rebellion among his crew. It's said that he took the recipe to his grave, so it will forever remain a mystery.

For what it's worth, in 1978, Caribe Hilton reached three million sales of the frozen cocktail, and Puerto Rico declared the piña colada its national drink. We will never know its true inventor, but my personal favorite is Marrero's version, made with white rum, Coco López cream of coconut, heavy cream, fresh pineapple juice, and ice and crowned with a maraschino cherry. That's all I need to put a big smile on my face.

Piña colada

Makes 1 serving

- 2 ounces white rum
- 1 ounce Coco López cream of coconut
- 1 ounce heavy cream
- 6 ounces/180ml fresh pineapple juice
- ½ ounce lime juice
- ½ ounce passion fruit purée (optional)
- ½ cup/65g crushed ice
- 1 fresh pineapple wedge, for garnish
- 1 maraschino cherry, for garnish

I can't write a cookbook that's a love letter to Puerto Rican cuisine without including Puerto Rico's official national cocktail. In recent years, I've seen all kinds of decked-out piña coladas—served inside a pineapple, topped with whipped cream, bedazzled with gummy bears—but I still like the old-school version best, simply garnished with a slice of pineapple and a maraschino cherry. The classic Ramón "Monchito" Marrero recipe doesn't include lime, but I added it here to give this signature cocktail a little flair of my own. If you want to Omify it a step further, add a bit of passion fruit purée. My kids, and many Boricuas, are also fans of the virgin piña colada. If that's your jam, simply omit the rum—just remember the Coco López cream of coconut is nonnegotiable.

In a blender, combine the rum, cream of coconut, heavy cream, pineapple juice, lime juice, passion fruit purée (if using), and crushed ice. Blend the mixture until it's smooth and creamy.

Pour the mixture into a chilled glass, garnish with a pineapple wedge and a maraschino cherry, and enjoy—you'll be immediately transported to my isla del encanto.

Omi Tip: Before blending your ingredients, add a tablespoon of the maraschino cherry juice to the blender. It won't change the color, but it adds depth of flavor that will elevate your piña colada to new heights. You can also use dark rum instead of white rum. I even tried making a piña colada with whiskey, and it was pretty good! The art is in finding the perfect cream of coconut–to–pineapple juice ratio.

Coquito

Coquito is the Puerto Rican holiday season in a bottle. I remember my grandparents making this spiced coconut-flavored nog of sorts in the kitchen of their Río Grande home. My abuelo would crack the brown coconuts open and remove the meat, which my abuela would then blend in her faithful Osterizer and then strain through a cheesecloth to extract the coconut milk, one of the key ingredients for this classic drink. Nowadays, we cut corners and use canned coconut milk, although it does give the coquito a hint of a processed aftertaste. So, if you ever have the opportunity to taste coquito made with fresh coconuts, don't miss out—you'll be blown away by the fresh burst of flavor.

Makes 1 liter

Spiced Tea

4 cinnamon sticks

10 whole cloves

2 whole star anise

8 whole allspice berries

½ teaspoon freshly grated nutmeg

Coquito

One (13.5-ounce/400ml) can coconut milk

One (14-ounce/415ml) can sweetened condensed milk

One (12-ounce/350ml) can evaporated milk

One (15-ounce/440ml) can Coco López cream of coconut

1 cup/240ml white rum (preferably Don Q, but Bacardí will work)

2 teaspoons vanilla extract

1 teaspoon ground cinnamon, plus more for garnish

Make the spiced tea: In a medium saucepan over medium-high heat, bring 2 cups/480ml of water to a boil. Add the cinnamon sticks, cloves, star anise, allspice, and nutmeg. Reduce the heat to medium, cover, and let simmer for about 15 minutes.

Remove the pot from the heat and let it cool slightly. Strain the tea through a fine-mesh strainer or cheesecloth, then discard the spices. Allow the tea to cool completely before using it in the coquito.

Make the coquito: In a blender, combine the coconut milk, sweetened condensed milk, evaporated milk, and cream of coconut. Blend until smooth.

Add the rum, vanilla extract, ground cinnamon, and ¼ cup /60ml of the cooled spiced tea. Blend again until well mixed. Taste and adjust the rum and/or spices to your liking, ¡lo que te diga tu corazón!

Pour the coquito into a glass bottle or jar and refrigerate for at least 2 hours before serving. This step is necessary, as the flavors will develop while it chills.

Serve the coquito cold, shaking well before you pour it into glasses. Sprinkle with cinnamon, if desired.

Omi Tip: Coquito can last for up to a month in the fridge. The longer it stays in the fridge, the more "curao," or fermented, it will become. That means that over time, it's much more dangerous—it goes down smoother and it's easier to drink one glass too many. If you want to make a kid-friendly/alcohol-free version of coquito, follow the same steps above, but omit the rum. Store any leftover spiced tea in the fridge for up to a week so you have it handy in case you want to make the Pumpkin spice coquito (page 170).

Pumpkin spice coquito

Comparing coquito recipes and deciding who made the best batch of the season is practically a holiday tradition in Puerto Rico. Given this unspoken competition, people have gotten creative, adding different flavors to help their coquito stand out from the crowd—Nutella, for instance, is a popular addition. In the fall of 2020, in the midst of the annual autumn pumpkin spice craze, I wondered why there wasn't a pumpkin spice coquito floating around the Internet yet. So I came up with this recipe, which immediately blew up when I posted it on social media. This isn't just a wonderful marriage of flavors—it also gives you the perfect excuse to start enjoying coquito even earlier than usual. If you ask me, that's a win-win!

Makes 1 liter

- One (13.5-ounce/400ml) can coconut milk
- One (14-ounce/415ml) can sweetened condensed milk
- One (12-ounce/350ml) can evaporated milk
- One (15-ounce/440ml) can Coco López cream of coconut
- 1 cup/225g pumpkin purée (not pumpkin pie filling)
- 1 cup/240ml white rum (adjust to taste, *LQTDT*♥)
- 1 teaspoon vanilla extract
- 1 teaspoon ground cinnamon, plus more for garnish
- 1 teaspoon pumpkin pie spice
- ¼ cup Spiced tea (page 169), cooled completely

In a blender, combine the coconut milk, sweetened condensed milk, evaporated milk, cream of coconut, and pumpkin purée. Blend until smooth.

Add the rum, vanilla extract, cinnamon, pumpkin pie spice, and the cooled spiced tea. Blend again until well combined. Taste and adjust the rum and/or spices to your liking, ¡lo que te diga tu corazón!

Pour the coquito into a glass bottle or jar and refrigerate for at least 2 hours before serving. This step is necessary, as the flavors will develop as the coquito chills.

Serve the pumpkin spice coquito cold, shaking it well just before pouring into glasses. Sprinkle the top with cinnamon, if desired.

Omi Tip: To make an extra-rich pumpkin spice coquito, switch out the white rum for the same amount of dark rum or whiskey. If you omit the alcohol, this recipe also makes an amazing coffee creamer!

Mojito de coco

Coconut mojito

Originally from Cuba, Puerto Rico's not-so-distant neighbor, the mojito quickly made its way into Puerto Rican hearts and has become a staple cocktail on the island. The original mojito recipe, of course, uses lime, mint, and sugar, but mojitos now come in a variety of flavors, including passion fruit, mango, guava, pineapple, and many more. My all-time favorite is the mojito de coco. A sip of this creamy yet refreshing beverage hits me with a tropical wave of joy every time.

Makes 1 serving

10 to 12 fresh mint leaves, plus 1 mint sprig for garnish

1 ounce store-bought or homemade simple syrup (adjust to taste, *LQTDT*♥)

2 ounces/60ml white rum (preferably Don Q or Bacardí)

1 ounce Coco López cream of coconut

1 ounce fresh lime juice (from about 1 lime)

Ice cubes for shaking, plus more for serving

1½ ounces club soda or sparkling water

1 lime wedge, for garnish

Shredded coconut, for garnish (optional)

In a sturdy glass or cocktail shaker, add the mint leaves and simple syrup. Using a cocktail muddler or the back of a spoon, gently muddle (apply pressure to) the mint leaves to release their oils. Be careful not to tear the leaves too much.

Add the rum, coconut cream, and lime juice to the glass or shaker. Fill the glass or shaker with ice cubes. Shake well until all ingredients are combined and chilled.

Strain the mixture into a tall glass filled with fresh ice cubes. Top off with the club soda or sparkling water and stir gently to combine. Garnish with the sprig of mint, the lime wedge, and a sprinkle of shredded coconut on top, if desired. Serve immediately.

Omi Tip: If you want to keep this mojito authentically Puerto Rican, make sure to use Don Q or Bacardí rum. Anuncio no pagado.

Ponche

Punch

Makes 1 liter

- One (12-ounce/350ml) can evaporated milk
- One (14-ounce/415ml) can sweetened condensed milk
- One (15-ounce/440ml) can Coco López cream of coconut
- 1 teaspoon vanilla extract
- ½ teaspoon ground cinnamon
- ¼ teaspoon ground nutmeg
- 1 cup/240ml white rum, or *LQTDT*♥
- 4 egg yolks, beaten
- Cinnamon sticks, for garnish (optional)

Omi Tip: Since there are raw egg yolks in the recipe, ponche doesn't last long in the fridge—make sure to drink it within a day!

I often hear people say that coquito is our version of an eggnog, but personally, when I think of a Puerto Rican eggnog, I think of ponche. Ponche is basically a coquito made with egg yolks, which deliver a thicker consistency and richer flavor. Feel free to use dark rum instead of white rum here, as it plays well with the rest of the ingredients. And remember, el coquito no lleva huevo, mi gente. If it has eggs, it's ponche—end of discussion!

In a blender, combine the evaporated milk, sweetened condensed milk, and cream of coconut. Blend until smooth.

Add the vanilla extract, ground cinnamon, and nutmeg to the blender. Blend again until well mixed.

Gradually add the rum to the mixture, blending continuously. Adjust the amount of rum to your liking, ¡lo que te diga tu corazón!

With the blender running on low speed, slowly add the beaten egg yolks. Blend until fully incorporated.

Pour the mixture into a large pitcher or bottle and refrigerate for at least 2 hours—this step is necessary so the flavors can meld.

Serve the ponche in small glasses, each garnished with a cinnamon stick.

Sangría roja

Spiced red sangria

Makes 1 large punch bowl, about 2 liters

- 1 bottle/750ml red wine (a fruity red like Merlot or Rioja works well)
- 1 cup/240ml white Puerto Rican rum, such as Don Q
- 1 cup/240ml orange juice (preferably freshly squeezed)
- 1 cup/240ml fresh pineapple juice
- ½ cup/120ml lemon juice (preferably freshly squeezed)
- ¼ cup/60ml store-bought simple syrup (adjust to taste, *LQTDT*♥)
- 1 orange, sliced into ½-inch rounds
- 1 lemon, sliced into ½-inch rounds
- 1 lime, sliced into ½-inch rounds
- ½ cup/75g diced pineapple
- ½ cup/85g diced mango (optional)
- ½ teaspoon ground allspice
- ½ teaspoon ground cloves
- ½ teaspoon ground ginger
- Ice cubes, for serving
- ½ cup/120ml club soda or lemon-lime soda (optional)
- Fresh mint leaves, for garnish (optional)

This sangría was a staple at our family celebrations, and as a young girl, I loved to sneak a little bit of it into my cup. The fruit infuses the drink with sweet notes that mask the wine and rum, so be careful, because it may taste refreshing, but it is not a kid-friendly punch. Sangría roja is usually made during the holiday season, but if you want to make a non-spiced summertime drink, use white wine instead of red, and forgo the allspice, cloves, and ginger. Serve this in a big punch bowl to show off its beautiful color and carefully sliced-and-diced fruit.

In a large pitcher or punch bowl, combine the red wine, rum, orange juice, pineapple juice, lemon juice, and simple syrup. Stir well to mix.

Add the sliced orange, lemon, lime, pineapple, and mango (if using). Then add the allspice, cloves, and ginger and stir gently to combine.

Refrigerate the sangría for at least 1 hour but preferably for 4 hours or overnight for best results, so the flavors can meld.

Add the ice cubes to the sangría just before serving. If you prefer a fizzy sangría, add the club soda or lemon-lime soda at this point and give it a gentle stir. Serve the sangria in glasses garnished with fresh mint leaves, if using.

Omi Tip: Don't add the ice cubes ahead of time—they'll melt and water down the sangría while it chills in the fridge.

Limonada de coco
Coconut limeade

Makes 6 to 8 servings, about 1½ liters

- 1 cup/240ml fresh lime juice (from 8 to 10 limes), strained to remove pulp and seeds, if any (about 8 to 10 limes)
- One (13.5-ounce/400ml) can coconut milk
- One (14-ounce/415ml) can sweetened condensed milk
- 1 cup/170g ice cubes, plus more for serving
- ¼ cup/50g granulated sugar (adjust to taste, *LQTDT*♥)
- Lime wedges, for garnish (optional)
- Fresh mint leaves, for garnish (optional)

When I first heard of Brazilian limeade, limonada Suíça, its flavors spoke to my heart. It's a creamy concoction made with limes blended together with condensed milk—ingredients so tempting that I just had to play around with the recipe and make my own version. That's how this limonada de coco was born. It was a hit on my social media, and it also became a smash at home—my boys can't get enough of it. I like to make this recipe in the spring and summer, as it's super refreshing on a hot day. If you're throwing a summer bash, be sure to add this to your drink menu as a great virgin cocktail option.

In a blender, combine the lime juice, coconut milk, sweetened condensed milk, 2 cups/480ml of cold water, the ice cubes, and sugar. Blend until smooth.

Taste the limeade and adjust to taste, adding more sugar if needed. Blend again briefly to mix.

Pour the coconut limeade into glasses filled with ice. Garnish with lime wedges and mint leaves, if desired. Serve immediately and enjoy!

Omi Tip: If you have access to fresh brown coconuts, use 1 coconut instead of the canned coconut milk. Remove the coconut water from the coconut and set aside. Break open the coconut and remove the flesh with a butter knife. Combine the flesh, the reserved coconut water, and 1 cup/240ml of water in a blender and blend until smooth. Strain the coconut mixture through a cheesecloth and squeeze out any remaining liquid. Use 1¾ cups/415ml of your homemade coconut milk instead of the canned version. Or, to turn this drink into a decadent yet refreshing shake, add a scoop of vanilla ice cream to the blender and enjoy.

Jugo de tamarindo
Tamarind juice

Whenever we'd open the fridge in my abuela's kitchen, there would always be a large plastic pitcher inside with a cheerful flower design and a green lid—and it was always filled with jugo de tamarindo. This tangy and refreshing tamarind juice can be enjoyed any time of day, any day of the week. If you can't find dried tamarind pods at your local market, check online, or look for them at a Latin or Indian grocery store.

Makes 1 large pitcher, about 1 liter

½ pound/225g dried tamarind pods, shells removed

1 cup/200g granulated sugar (adjust to taste, *LQTDT♥*)

¼ cup/60ml fresh lime juice

½ teaspoon ground ginger (optional)

Ice cubes, for serving

In a large bowl, add the tamarind pods and cover with 4 cups/950ml of water. Let the tamarind soak for about 1 hour to soften.

After an hour, use your hands to mash the tamarind pods, releasing the pulp into the water. Remove and discard any pods or shells.

Pour the tamarind-water mixture through a fine-mesh strainer into a large pitcher, pressing down as you strain to extract as much liquid as possible.

Add the sugar to the pitcher and stir until dissolved. Add the lime juice and mix well. If you like a bit of spice, add the ginger and stir to incorporate.

Refrigerate the jugo de tamarindo for at least 1 hour, the colder the better . . . ¡mientras más frío mejor! Once chilled, serve over ice.

Omi Tip: You can use any leftover tamarind juice to make limber, the Puerto Rican ice pop in a cup. It's as easy as filling a disposable plastic cup with the tamarind juice, putting it in the freezer, and freezing overnight. Voilà, you've got your very own homemade limber! To enjoy, squeeze the cup so the limber pops up and eat directly out of the cup.

Jugo de toronja

Grapefruit juice

This was another Abuela Gloria staple that could be found in her fridge most days of the week. Hers used freshly squeezed grapefruits on their own, but I've Omified it here by adding coconut water, lime juice, and sugar, which takes the slight bitterness away while keeping it simple and refreshing. Feel free to start with this recipe and play around with the flavors until you find the combination you love most. ¡En tu cocina tú mandas!

Makes 1 large pitcher, about 2 liters

4 large grapefruits (preferably pink or red, which are sweeter)

½ cup/120ml coconut water

½ cup/100g granulated sugar (adjust to taste, *LQTDT*♥)

¼ cup/60ml fresh lime juice

Ice cubes, for serving

Fresh mint leaves, for garnish

Wash the grapefruits thoroughly. Cut them in half and use a citrus juicer to extract the juice. You should end up with about 4 cups/950ml of grapefruit juice.

In a large pitcher, add the grapefruit juice, 2 cups/480ml of cold water, and the coconut water. Stir well to combine.

Add the sugar to the pitcher and stir until completely dissolved, then taste and adjust the sugar to your preferred sweetness. Stir in the lime juice, then refrigerate the jugo de toronja for at least 1 hour, or until well chilled.

Serve the juice over ice, in glasses garnished with fresh mint leaves.

Omi Tip: Make it fancy and add slices of fresh tropical fruits (such as kiwi, papaya, or starfruit) for garnish, *LQTDT*♥.

Batida de champola

Champola smoothie

As a kid, I loved when my abuela or my mom would make me a traditional batida de champola with guava and milk—it was such a treat. I decided to mix it up here and add my own spin on the original—that's where the smooth coconut milk and refreshing lime juice come in. I think these flavors pair beautifully with the sweet guava flavor—my all-time favorite batida to this day.

Makes 1 pitcher

1 quart/1L guava nectar

One (12-ounce/350ml) can coconut milk

¼ cup/60ml fresh lime juice

¼ cup/50g granulated sugar (adjust to taste, *LQTDT*♥)

Ice cubes

Fresh mint leaves, for garnish

In a large pitcher, combine the guava nectar, coconut milk, lime juice, and sugar. Stir well, until the sugar is completely dissolved. Taste and adjust the sugar as needed.

Refrigerate the mixture for at least 1 hour, or until well chilled. Serve the chilled champola over ice in glasses garnished with fresh mint leaves.

Omi Tip: In my opinion, guava is the tastiest flavor of batida, but batida de champola can be made with a variety of fruits, so pick your favorite flavor and run with it.

Batida de lechosa

Papaya smoothie

Makes 3 or 4 servings

2 cups/340g frozen or fresh ripe papaya, peeled, deseeded, and cut into chunks

1 cup/170g frozen or fresh mango, cut into chunks

4 to 6 dates, pitted, to taste, *LQTDT*♥

1 teaspoon vanilla extract

1 tablespoon fresh lime juice

1 cup/240ml almond milk

Ice cubes (optional)

Fresh mint leaves, for garnish (optional)

The classic batida de lechosa consists of papaya blended with sugar, milk or water, and ice. I've always loved this batida, but it's too much sugar to have on a regular basis, so I decided to create a healthier version. I replaced the sugar with dates for a touch of sweetness and mango chunks, which provide more essential vitamins and minerals. When I drink this smoothie, I still enjoy a burst of flavors from home, and I feel great knowing it's good for me.

In a blender, combine the papaya, mango, dates, vanilla extract, lime juice, and almond milk. Blend until smooth and creamy.

Taste the shake and add more dates if needed for additional sweetness. Blend again to incorporate. If you prefer a colder, slushier drink, add a handful of ice cubes to the blender and blend until smooth.

Pour the batida into glasses and garnish with fresh mint leaves, if desired. Serve immediately.

Omi Tip: You can substitute the mango with banana, pineapple, or any tropical fruit . . . the possibilities are endless!

RICO

6

To' lo melao
All things sweet

When I think of Puerto Rican desserts, the first two that come to mind are quesitos (cream cheese–filled pastries) and flans. Those are my all-time favorites, the ones I can't get enough of when I'm home. But the list doesn't stop there. We also have tembleques, tres leches, flancochos, budines, arroz con dulce—to name a few. And you can usually find any of these traditional sweet treats at most local bakeries.

Las panaderías in Puerto Rico aren't your run-of-the-mill bakeries. When you step into one of these glorious-smelling shops, you will find everything from the baked goods you expect to see to bread, cake, candy, and even milk and juice. While you're there, feel free to order a sandwich with the bakery's freshly baked pan de agua, pan sobao (white bread made with lard), or pan de medianoche (a yeasted bread used to make the popular Cuban medianoche sandwich). Whenever I walked into a panadería as a little girl, I was pulled like a magnet to the display cabinet filled with every dessert you could imagine—and I yearned to have them all. If I close my eyes, I can picture the rows of cakes, flans, loaves, and pastries. The possibilities were endless, but our wallets weren't, so we only bought a slice of cake or a candy as a treat on special occasions. Thankfully, I was lucky enough to have amazing bakers in my family, so whatever we didn't get at the panadería would oftentimes be made at home.

When my grandmother and her daughters got together in that kitchen, it turned into a cooking contest à la *Next Level Chef*. Each of them would focus on their own specialty, yet they also *worked* in perfect harmony—it was always best to step away and let them do their thing.

They'd fill the kitchen with warm laughter while they baked, and when they were done, they loved to step back and admire their creations.

Abuela Gloria made delicious desserts across the board, but her favorites were any that had to be baked or cooked, such as Puerto Rican dulce de coco, a bite-size caramel-like treat made with shredded coconut. When she made dulce de coco, she'd grab the ingredients, head to her outdoor kitchen, and set them next to her charcoal grill, atop the wood and tile counter that reached the top of her belly. That may sound tall, but she was only four foot nine, so it was custom-built to fit her petite stature. I loved watching her cook out there, over the grill, stirring a simmering pot filled with shredded coconut (or papaya, if she was making dulce de lechosa). Abuela was also the reigning queen of arroz con dulce. Eso sabía a gloria, como su nombre—that tasted glorious, just like her name.

Abuela didn't make desserts every day, but she always had something sweet to offer us after our meals. Sometimes it was one of these more elaborate treats; other times, it was a simple fruit salad with queso de papa on top. I loved our lunches and dinners, but dessert was my favorite. And like with our savory meals, my abuelo always saved his last bite for me, which made my heart (and my taste buds) happy.

Mami's sweet specialty is undoubtedly her budines. Her rich, custard-like bread puddings are so good that when she lived in Rhode Island, people would offer to pay her to make some for them. Both Mami and Abuela Gloria were too territorial in their kitchens to let any of us kids help out with cooking, and that was especially true when it came to desserts. So, I was honored when Mami offered to show me how to make one of her renowned budines. By then, of course, I was also a grown woman—and I was still floored.

As much as I love all things sweet, at heart, I'm not a baker. If I have to use exact measurements and bake at a specific temperature for a specific amount of time, I usually set aside my entire afternoon, because it's going to require all my attention. The way my brain works isn't really compatible with baking, which is more like an exact science. I'm all about lo que me diga mi corazón, so following the rules doesn't come easily to me.

But I also never shy away from a challenge—and that's why I think this is the most Omified chapter in this book. I just couldn't help tinkering with many of these dishes to infuse the classic recipes with my own personal twists.

As I embraced dessert-making, I quickly discovered my own specialty: flan, a creamy custard topped with a caramel sauce. I can make flan with my eyes closed. And it gives me room to experiment with different flavor profiles and try new combos, which fills me with joy. When I make flan, I enjoy turning into a dessert chemist in search of the perfect ratio of ingredients to bring my vision to life. And my social media followers love it, too—almost all my flans have gone viral. ¡Gracias, mi gente!

Don't let the idea of baking intimidate you. Believe me, if I can do it, so can you. Plus, I've added a few shortcuts here to make your life easier, so you've got no excuse not to try! Remember, even if you're using a box mix, a cake still has to be made at home, so it's homemade in my eyes! I encourage you to jump headfirst into this sweets-filled chapter and let me know which recipes become your favorites.

El coco
A taste of home

The coconut is a key player in Puerto Rican cuisine. It appears in our main dishes, sauces, side dishes, frituras, drinks, and most certainly in our desserts. Luckily, cocos are plentiful on the island. Puerto Rico also exports coconuts and coconut-based products to the United States, Latin America, and other islands in the Caribbean, with possible future expansion to Europe and Asia.

With this fruit so entrenched in our food and our culture, you might assume the coconut is native to Puerto Rico—but in fact, it's not indigenous to the Caribbean at all. Coconut palm trees originated in Southeast Asia and were first introduced to our island by Spanish colonizers in the fifteenth century.

Coconut trees thrived in Puerto Rico's tropical climate and were quickly adopted into everyday life. The trees didn't just provide fruit, but also oil and materials for shelter and even clothing. With time, cocos became a part of our agriculture, food, and cultural evolution, and they are now an inherent part of the Puerto Rican spirit. What would our food and drinks be without coconut water, shredded coconut, coconut milk, and of course, cream of coconut? There would be no coquito, tembleque, dulce de coco. Thankfully the coco is here to stay. My abuela loved anything made with coconuts, and so do Mami and I. A little sprinkle of toasted shredded coconut on top of almost any dish adds a tropical note that makes everything taste better.

As for the coconuts themselves, you may have noticed that they're sometimes green and sometimes brown. They all come from the same coconut palm; the color simply represents the fruit's maturity, which translates to how much water and flesh they have inside their shells. The green coconut is the baby of the family. It's usually harvested from the tree about six months after it has gone from flower to fruit. At this stage, they are considered young and unripe. They have a smooth green shell, a thin layer of soft, gelatinous flesh, and a lot more coconut water inside. Green coconuts are used to make the packaged coconut water you buy at the store—but nothing tops the fresh coconut water you can order from a chinchorro in Puerto Rico. The vendor will grab a green coco, hack off the top with a machete, stick a straw in the opening, and hand you that delightful coco frío with its signature mild, sweet taste, ideal for quenching your thirst on a hot summer's day.

As coconuts mature, their skin turns brown and husky, and the water is mostly absorbed as the layer of meat thickens within. By the time the brown coco is harvested—ten to twelve months after flowering—its flesh is harder and denser, ideal for producing coconut milk and coconut oil.

If a coconut is harvested at the twelve-month mark or later, the meat inside is dried up, making it perfect for shredding or turning into coconut flour for baking. I'm continually amazed by how versatile the coconut can be, but to keep it simple, just remember: Green is for drinking, brown is for cooking.

Tres leches de coquito

Coquito tres leches cake

Makes 6 to 8 servings

Cake

Cooking spray, for greasing

1 box of white or yellow cake mix, plus the ingredients listed on the cake mix box (usually a few eggs, vegetable oil, and water)

1 recipe Coquito (page 169)

Whipped Cream

1 cup/240ml heavy cream

2 tablespoons powdered sugar

½ teaspoon vanilla extract

1 teaspoon coconut extract

Ground cinnamon, for garnish

Toasted shredded coconut, for garnish

Omi Tip: Try this recipe with your favorite chocolate box cake mix instead—thank me later!

A classic Mexican tres leches, as its name will tell you, is made with three milks: evaporated milk, condensed milk, and heavy cream. Puerto Rican coquito (page 169) happens to use all three of these milks, so coming up with this recipe was a no-brainer to me. I love it because it's a great way to use any leftover bottles of coquito you might have lying around after the holidays—and if that's not the case, well, it's a perfect excuse to make a fresh batch of coquito earlier in the year. Who said we needed to wait until the holidays, anyway?

Make the cake: Preheat the oven according to the cake mix instructions (usually 350°F/175°C) and grease a 9 by 13-inch baking pan with cooking spray.

Prepare the cake mix as directed on the box, pour the batter into the greased baking pan, and bake according to the package instructions.

Once done, let the cake cool completely in the pan. Then, use a fork or skewer to poke holes all over the surface of the cake.

Slowly pour the coquito over the entire cake, making sure it seeps into the holes and no dry patches are left. Cover the cake and refrigerate for at least 4 hours or overnight to allow the cake to absorb the milk mixture.

Make the whipped cream: In a large bowl, using an electric or hand mixer, beat the heavy cream, powdered sugar, vanilla extract, and coconut extract until stiff peaks form.

To serve: Spread the whipped cream evenly over the soaked cake right before serving. Sprinkle cinnamon and toasted shredded coconut on top of the whipped cream. Cut into squares and serve chilled.

Flan de guayaba y queso

Guava and cheese flan

If you know me, you know that I can't get enough of guayaba y queso. I love this flavor partnership in all shapes and forms. When I first tried to develop this recipe, I imagined visible swirls of guava running through the flan. But after several failed attempts, I decided to blend it all together and let the guayaba infuse the entire flan with its sweet and tangy flavor. This flan is me in dessert form all day, all the way.

Makes 12 servings

- 1½ cups/300g granulated sugar
- One (14-ounce/415ml) can sweetened condensed milk
- One (12-ounce/350ml) can evaporated milk
- 5 large eggs
- 6 ounces/170g cream cheese, softened
- 7 ounces/200g guava paste, at room temperature
- 1 teaspoon vanilla extract

In a small saucepan over medium heat, combine the sugar and ¼ cup/60ml of water. Cook, stirring occasionally, until the sugar is dissolved.

Increase the heat to medium-high and continue to cook, this time without stirring, until the sugar completely dissolves and turns a golden color, 7 to 10 minutes. Then, begin gently swirling the dissolved sugar in the saucepan until the color turns amber, about 2 minutes.

Remove the saucepan from the heat and carefully add 2 tablespoons/30ml of warm water, swirling until fully combined—you should have a deep amber-brown caramel.

Quickly pour the caramel into a flan mold (a special pan used to make flan) or 12 individual ramekins, swirling so the caramel coats the bottom of the dish evenly. Set aside to cool and allow the caramel to harden.

Preheat the oven to 350°F/175°C.

In a blender, combine the sweetened condensed milk, evaporated milk, eggs, cream cheese, guava paste, and vanilla extract. Blend until fully combined and smooth.

Pour the flan mixture over the hardened caramel in the mold or ramekins.

Place the mold or ramekins in a larger baking dish. Fill the larger dish with hot water until it reaches halfway up the sides of the flan mold or ramekins, creating a water bath, or bain-marie.

Bake for about 1 hour, or until the flan is set and a knife inserted in the center comes out clean.

Remove the flan mold or ramekins from the water bath and let cool to room temperature. Then transfer to the refrigerator to chill for at least 4 hours, or overnight, to fully set.

To serve, run a knife around the edges of the baking dish to loosen the flan. Invert the flan onto a serving plate, so the caramel is on top, and enjoy.

Omi Tip: When blending the flan mixture, make sure the cream cheese and guava are at room temperature. This will ensure everything can blend smoothly and will prevent lumps in your flan.

Flan de yuca y coco

Cassava and coconut flan

Makes 12 servings

2 cups peeled and chunked yuca, about 1 pound/400g

2 cinnamon sticks

Pinch of ground allspice

1 cup/200g granulated sugar

One (13.5-ounce/400ml) can coconut milk

One (12-ounce/350ml) can evaporated milk

½ cup/120ml Coco López cream of coconut

½ cup/120ml sweetened condensed milk

4 large eggs

1 teaspoon vanilla extract

Yuca plays very well with other ingredients—much like avocados, it absorbs and takes on the star ingredient's flavor, which in this case is the beloved coconut. In this recipe, the starchiness of the yuca makes the flan a little denser, but when you take a bite, it still melts in your mouth. I'm sure this kind of flan already exists somewhere out there in the world, but I had never seen or tasted it, so I put my experimenting cap on and gave it a shot. I hope you love this smooth, creamy, tropical flan just as much as I do.

Fill a saucepan with water, add the yuca, cinnamon sticks, and allspice, and bring to a boil over medium-high heat. Boil the yuca until tender, about 20 minutes. Drain, discard the cinnamon sticks, and set aside.

In a separate saucepan over medium heat, combine the sugar and ¼ cup/60ml of water. Cook, stirring occasionally, until the sugar dissolves and turns a light golden color, 5 to 6 minutes.

Quickly pour the caramel into the bottom of a flan mold or 12 individual ramekins, tilting the dish to coat the bottom evenly. Set aside to cool and allow the caramel to harden.

Preheat the oven to 350°F/175°C.

In a blender, combine the boiled yuca, the coconut milk, evaporated milk, cream of coconut, sweetened condensed milk, eggs, and vanilla extract. Blend until smooth and well combined.

Pour the flan mixture over the hardened caramel in the mold or ramekins.

Place the flan mold or ramekins in a larger baking dish. Fill the larger dish with hot water reaching halfway up the sides of the mold or ramekins to create a water bath, or bain-marie.

Bake for 35 to 40 minutes, until the flan is set and a knife inserted into the center comes out clean.

Remove the mold or ramekins from the water bath and let cool to room temperature. Then transfer to the refrigerator for at least 4 hours, or overnight, to fully set.

To serve, run a knife around the edges of the flan to loosen it from the mold, then invert onto a serving plate so the caramel is on top.

Flancocho de chocolate y dulce de leche

Chocolate and dulce de leche flancocho

My boys love this dessert, especially my youngest, who is a chocolate fiend. Also known as chocoflan, this cake is a marriage between a chocolate cake and a classic flan. (The name "flancocho" comes from combining "flan" and "bizcocho," the Puerto Rican word for cake.) It's sometimes called an "impossible cake" because the layers invert while baking, giving you a final dessert that's half of each. I decided to kick it up a notch by adding in some thick, rich dulce de leche, which gives the flan an incredible depth of flavor.

Makes 6 to 8 servings

Cooking spray or butter, for greasing

1½ cups/300g granulated sugar

1 box chocolate cake mix, plus the ingredients listed on the box (usually a few eggs, vegetable oil, and water)

One (14-ounce/415ml) can sweetened condensed milk

One (12-ounce/350ml) can evaporated milk

One (13.4-ounce/395ml) can dulce de leche

One (8-ounce/225g) package cream cheese, at room temperature

4 large eggs

1 teaspoon vanilla extract

Grease a Bundt pan with cooking spray or butter. Preheat the oven to 350°F/175°C.

In a small saucepan over medium heat, combine the sugar and ¼ cup/60ml water and cook, stirring occasionally, until the sugar is dissolved.

Increase the heat to medium-high and continue to cook, this time without stirring, until the sugar completely dissolves and turns a golden color, 7 to 10 minutes. Begin gently swirling the dissolved sugar in the saucepan until the color turns amber, about 2 minutes.

Remove the saucepan from the heat and carefully add 2 tablespoons/30ml of warm water, swirling until fully combined—you should have a deep amber-brown caramel.

Quickly pour the caramel into the greased Bundt pan, swirling to coat the bottom evenly. Set aside to cool so the caramel can harden.

Prepare the chocolate cake mix batter according to the instructions on the box. Carefully pour the cake batter evenly on top of the cooled caramel in the Bundt pan.

In a blender, combine the sweetened condensed milk, evaporated milk, dulce de leche, cream cheese, eggs, and vanilla extract. Blend until fully combined and smooth.

Carefully and slowly pour the flan mixture over the cake batter in the Bundt pan. Place the Bundt pan in a larger baking dish. Fill the larger dish with hot water until it reaches halfway up the sides of the Bundt pan, creating a water bath, or bain-marie.

Bake the flancocho for 1 hour 15 minutes—the flan and cake batter will switch positions, so the cake ends up on top, and a toothpick inserted into the cake should come out clean.

Remove the Bundt pan from the water bath and let the flancocho cool to room temperature. Transfer to the refrigerator to chill for at least 8 hours, or overnight, so the flan can set.

Run a knife around the edges of the flancocho to loosen it. Invert onto a serving plate so the caramel is on top, slice, and enjoy.

Omi Tip: I encourage you to play around with different variations and try other flavors that go well with dulce de leche. Try a spiced cake mix or carrot cake to replace the chocolate. YUM!

Coconut banana pudding

Makes 10 to 12 servings

Pudding

One (3.4-ounce/96g) package instant vanilla pudding mix

2 cups/480ml coconut milk

One (7.25-ounce/206g) package Pepperidge Farm Chessmen butter cookies

4 to 5 ripe bananas, sliced

Whipped Cream

1 cup/240ml heavy cream

2 tablespoons powdered sugar

1 teaspoon coconut extract

Toasted coconut flakes, for garnish (optional)

Omi Tip: I sometimes like using a mixture of Chessmen cookies and Nilla wafers, which are traditionally used to make banana pudding. I also love to crumble the Nilla wafers and sprinkle them on top.

Coconut banana pudding is an American dessert that I adapted to my family's favorite flavors. I know it's not Puerto Rican—though I would argue that some of the ingredients fit the bill—but listen, it's made by a Boricua, and it's become one of my summer classics. I get asked to bring this pudding to gatherings, events, and cookouts so often that I have extra aluminum pans and a shelf in my pantry dedicated to coconut milk and Chessmen cookies just for this recipe. You probably won't find this one at your local panadería, but I know you'll love the tropical flavors in every bite.

Make the pudding: In a large bowl, whisk together the instant pudding mix and coconut milk until smooth and thickened, about 2 minutes. Let the pudding sit for a few minutes to set.

In an 8 by 8-inch casserole dish (or 4- or 6-ounce individual cups), layer the puddings, starting with Chessmen cookies at the bottom, then banana slices, then coconut pudding. Repeat the layering until all ingredients are used, making sure to end with a layer of pudding on top.

Make the whipped cream: In a large bowl, beat the heavy cream, powdered sugar, and coconut extract until stiff peaks form.

Spread or pipe the whipped cream over the top of the pudding. Sprinkle toasted coconut flakes on top, if using.

Refrigerate the pudding for at least 2 hours before serving to allow the flavors to meld. Serve chilled.

Buñuelos sorpresa

Next level *buñuelos with coconut cream*

Buñuelos are fried balls of dough, similar to donut holes, that are tossed in cinnamon and powdered sugar. My abuela used to make these all the time, and when my kids were little, I'd fry some up for them as a treat, too. So when the baking challenge came along on *Next Level Chef*, I immediately thought of this dessert. Most of them I fried, but I also baked a few in order to stick to the rules of the challenge. That meant I had to keep a careful eye on the oven, because I had never made baked buñuelos before that day! Even though our traditional buñuelos are not filled, I decided to add a coconut cream filling to the center of my baked buñuelos to give them a *next-level* touch of sweet decadence. They came together like a dream—and turned me into a top dish winner. Chef Ramsay liked them so much, he asked me for the recipe. Hey, Chef, here it is!

Makes 10 to 12 servings

Choux Pastry

½ cup/110g unsalted butter

¼ teaspoon salt

1 cup/140g all-purpose flour

4 large eggs

Coconut Cream Filling

¼ cup/35g cornstarch

2 cups/480ml coconut milk

½ cup/100g granulated sugar

1 teaspoon vanilla extract

½ teaspoon ground cinnamon

¼ teaspoon ground nutmeg

¼ teaspoon ground cloves

¼ teaspoon ground allspice

For Serving

Nutella

Powdered sugar

Make the choux pastry: Preheat the oven to 400°F/200°C. Line an 18 by 13-inch baking sheet with parchment paper.

In a medium saucepan over medium heat, add 1 cup/240ml of water, the butter, and salt and bring to a boil.

Add the flour to the saucepan all at once and stir vigorously until the mixture forms a ball and pulls away from the sides of the pan. Remove from the heat and let cool for about 5 minutes.

Add the eggs to the mixture one at a time, stirring well after each addition, until you have a smooth and glossy dough.

Transfer the dough to a piping bag fitted with a large round tip. Pipe nickel-size mounds onto the prepared baking sheet, spaced about 2 inches apart.

Bake the choux pastry for 20 to 25 minutes, until puffed and golden brown. Turn off the oven, but let the pastries sit in the oven for another 10 minutes to dry out. Then remove from the oven and set aside to cool.

Make the coconut cream filling: Add the cornstarch to a small bowl and set aside.

In a medium saucepan over medium heat, combine the coconut milk and sugar. Cook until the mixture is hot but not boiling.

Add a little bit of the hot coconut milk mixture to the bowl with the cornstarch and whisk together to make a slurry. Add the slurry back to the saucepan with the coconut milk mixture and stir to combine—this will help the mixture thicken.

Add the vanilla extract, cinnamon, nutmeg, cloves, and allspice to the saucepan and continue to cook, stirring continuously, until the mixture thickens and coats the back of a spoon, 5 to 7 minutes. Remove from the heat and let cool completely.

Assemble the buñuelos: Once the pastries are completely cool, cut a small slit on the bottom of each one. Fill a piping bag with the cooled coconut cream and pipe the filling into each pastry.

To serve, drizzle warm Nutella over the top of each filled buñuelo, dust with powdered sugar, and get ready to go to buñuelo heaven.

Omi Tip: If you want to keep it tradish, you can fry these instead—pipe golf-size balls of the choux pastry straight into 350°F/175°C hot oil. Fry until golden, then toss with cinnamon and powdered sugar and you're good to go!

Arroz con dulce

Sweet rice pudding

Makes 10 to 12 servings

Spiced Tea

2 cinnamon sticks

1-inch piece fresh ginger, peeled and sliced

6 whole cloves

6 or 7 allspice berries

1 star anise

½ teaspoon kosher salt

Arroz con dulce

2 cups/400g short- or medium-grain white rice

Two (13.5-ounce/400ml) cans coconut milk

Two (12-ounce/350ml) cans evaporated milk

¼ cup/55g unsalted butter

1 teaspoon vanilla bean paste

½ teaspoon ground cinnamon, plus more for garnish

¼ teaspoon ground nutmeg

¼ teaspoon ground cloves

¼ teaspoon lime zest

One (14-ounce/415ml) can sweetened condensed milk

½ cup/100g granulated sugar

½ cup/100g brown sugar

½ cup/70g raisins, soaked in rum for 10 minutes (optional)

Omi Tip: Allowing the rice to cook all the way through before you add the sugars will result in a super-smooth and creamy arroz con dulce. It's my cheat code! This is a great dessert to put in jars and give away to your guests as adult party favors. If you have leftover arroz con dulce, turn to the recipe on the next page.

Even though my own abuela was the queen of arroz con dulce, it took me forever to get this recipe right—at least seven tries before I got here, and I figured it out only a couple of years ago. There are so many variables that can go wrong with this dessert, so you have to be patient when making it. Many people prefer to buy arroz con dulce from the local señora who has been making it for years to guarantee they'll be serving a delicious dessert at their party, but some of us don't have that luxury—especially those of us who live in the diaspora. I like to think I've come up with a bulletproof recipe, if you follow it to a tee. Instead of soaking the rice overnight, I precook it in the spiced tea to soften it and cut down on prep time. A great playlist will help you endure the stirring and focus necessary to perfect the consistency of your arroz con dulce. I know I say the rum is optional, but adding it in with the soaked raisins will provide depth of flavor that really enhances this nostalgic dessert.

Make the spiced tea: In a large pot over medium-high heat, bring 4 cups/950ml of water to a boil. Add the cinnamon sticks, ginger, cloves, allspice, star anise, and salt. Reduce the heat to medium-low and simmer for about 10 minutes to infuse the water with the spices.

Make the arroz con dulce: Add the rice to the same pot with the spiced tea and increase the heat to medium. Cook until the rice has absorbed most of the liquid, about 15 minutes. Discard all the spices except the cinnamon sticks and ginger.

In the same pot, still over medium heat, stir in the coconut milk, evaporated milk, butter, vanilla bean paste, ground cinnamon, ground nutmeg, ground cloves, and lime zest. Stir continuously—do not stop stirring or the rice will stick to the bottom of the pot. You'll need to babysit this one for 20 minutes until the rice resembles tapioca. At this point, the rice should be fully cooked.

After 20 minutes, reduce the heat to medium-low and add the sweetened condensed milk, granulated sugar, and brown sugar. Cook, stirring frequently but not continuously, until the mixture has thickened to a creamy consistency, 20 to 25 minutes. If using, add the rum-soaked raisins, along with the rum they were soaking in.

Remove the arroz con dulce from the heat and let cool slightly. Discard the cinnamon sticks and ginger slices and serve warm or chilled, garnished with a sprinkle of cinnamon, if desired.

Croquetas de arroz con dulce

Rice pudding croquettes

Makes 6 to 8 servings

- 1 recipe Arroz con dulce (page 199), fully set and firm
- 1 cup/140g all-purpose flour
- 2 large eggs, beaten
- 2 cups/240g plain breadcrumbs
- Vegetable oil, for frying
- Powdered sugar, for topping
- Ground cinnamon, for topping

One year, I made too much arroz con dulce during the holidays, and I didn't have enough people over to eat it all. By the new year, everyone at home was ready to call it quits on that dessert, but I didn't want to let it go to waste. After staring into the bowl for a few minutes, a lightbulb went off in my head: Why not try to turn that leftover into croquetas? I breaded and fried them until they were extra crunchy on the outside but still gooey on the inside, then I sprinkled them with powdered sugar and cinnamon, and my boys ate them up without a second thought—another Omified recipe for the win!

Shape golf ball–size scoops of arroz con dulce into 12 to 15 croquettes, about 2 inches long each.

Set up a breading station with three shallow bowls: one with the flour, one with the beaten eggs, and one with the breadcrumbs.

Dredge each croquette in the flour, then dip it in the eggs, and coat with the breadcrumbs. Place the breaded croquettes on a baking sheet for easy access.

In a large skillet over medium-high heat, add about 1 inch of vegetable oil and heat until it shimmers.

Add the croquettes to the oil and fry them in batches until golden brown and crispy, 2 to 3 minutes per side. Use a slotted spoon to remove the croquettes from the skillet and set on paper towels to drain excess oil.

Dust the croquettes with powdered sugar and a sprinkle of cinnamon and serve hot.

Bizcocho volteado de coco, ron y piña

Coconut-pineapple-rum upside-down cake

I'm a very visual eater—give me something with vibrant colors, and it will immediately speak to my tropical soul. That's one of the reasons I love this cake so much. The pineapples on top look like little umbrellas next to the bright-red maraschino cherries, which if you ask me have beach-ball vibes. I like to evenly intersperse the fruits in this cake, but feel free to dress it up anyway you like: add more shredded coconut, fewer cherries, lo que te diga tu corazón. Pero hazme caso—don't skip the rum. That's the secret ingredient that elevates this dessert into an explosion of all our favorite tropical flavors in one beautiful slice.

Makes 6 to 8 servings

Topping

½ cup/110g unsalted butter

1 cup/220g packed brown sugar

1 tablespoon pineapple juice

9 pineapple slices (fresh or canned), cut in half

9 maraschino cherries

Cake

Cooking spray or butter, for greasing

1 box yellow cake mix

One (3.4-ounce/96g) packet instant vanilla pudding mix (optional)

4 large eggs

½ cup/120ml vegetable oil

1 cup/240ml pineapple juice

½ cup/120ml coconut rum

1 teaspoon vanilla extract

½ cup/40g shredded toasted coconut (optional)

Omi Tip: Before inverting the cake, while it's still hot, add an additional ½ cup/120ml of coconut rum, allow it to fully absorb, then flip the cake onto the plate. De nada.

Preheat the oven to 350°F/175°C. Grease a Bundt pan with cooking spray or butter.

Prepare the topping: In a small saucepan over medium heat, melt the butter. Add the brown sugar and pineapple juice to the saucepan and stir until the sugar is melted and the mixture starts to bubble, 3 to 5 minutes.

Pour the brown sugar mixture into the bottom of the greased Bundt pan. Then, arrange the halved pineapple slices and maraschino cherries alternately around the bottom of the Bundt pan, on top of the brown sugar mixture. Set aside.

Make the cake: In a large bowl, combine the cake mix, instant pudding mix (if using—it helps add moisture), eggs, oil, pineapple juice, coconut rum, and vanilla extract. With a handheld electric mixer, beat the mixture on low speed for 30 seconds, then on medium speed for 2 minutes, until well combined. Fold the shredded coconut into the batter, if using.

Carefully pour the cake batter over the pineapple and cherries in the Bundt pan. Bake the cake for 50 to 60 minutes, until a toothpick inserted into the center comes out clean.

Let the cake cool in the pan for 10 minutes, then invert it onto a serving plate. Allow the cake to cool completely before serving.

Brazo gitano de especias de calabaza

Pumpkin spice Swiss roll cake

The brazo gitano, which is like a Swiss roll cake but translates to "gypsy's arm," is so popular in Puerto Rico that it can be found in almost every panadería. Inspired by the fall pumpkin spice craze here in the States, I added pumpkin purée and infused it with the classic pumpkin spice flavor we've all grown to crave. If you're not a baker, like me, make sure to set aside a morning or an afternoon so you can take your time with each step to get it right. You won't regret it, and neither will your friends and family!

Makes 6 to 8 servings

Cake

- Cooking spray, for greasing
- 1 cup/140g all-purpose flour
- 1 teaspoon baking powder
- ½ teaspoon ground cinnamon
- ¼ teaspoon ground nutmeg
- ¼ teaspoon ground ginger
- ¼ teaspoon kosher salt
- 4 large eggs
- 1 cup/200g granulated sugar
- 1 cup/225g pumpkin purée
- 1 teaspoon vanilla extract
- Powdered sugar, for dusting, plus more for topping
- 1 cup/60g sweetened shredded coconut, toasted, for topping

Filling

- 1 cup/240ml heavy cream
- 4 ounces/115g cream cheese, softened
- ½ cup/60g powdered sugar
- 1 teaspoon coconut extract

Make the cake: Preheat the oven to 375°F/190°C. Line a 15 by 10-inch jelly roll baking pan with parchment paper and grease it lightly with cooking spray.

In a large bowl, sift together the flour, baking powder, cinnamon, nutmeg, ginger, and salt.

In a separate large bowl, beat the eggs with the sugar until fluffy and pale. Add the pumpkin purée and vanilla extract and mix until well combined.

Gradually add the dry ingredients to the pumpkin mixture, mixing until just combined.

Spread the batter evenly in the prepared pan. Bake for 14 to 18 minutes, until the cake springs back when lightly touched.

While the cake is baking, lay a clean kitchen towel on a flat surface and dust it generously with powdered sugar.

When the cake is done, immediately turn it out of the pan onto the prepared towel. Carefully peel off the parchment paper.

Starting from a short end, roll the cake up in the towel while still warm—this will help it keep its shape later. Leave the cake rolled up with the towel and let cool completely.

Make the filling: In a large bowl, with an electric hand or stand mixer, beat the heavy cream, cream cheese, powdered sugar, and coconut extract until stiff peaks form.

Assemble the brazo gitano: Once the cake is completely cool, unroll it gently from the tea towel. Spread the coconut cream filling evenly over the cake. Carefully re-roll the cake, this time without the towel, of course. When you finish rolling, make sure the open edge/seam is on the bottom.

Spread the toasted coconut flakes on a large plate or baking sheet. Carefully roll the cake in the coconut flakes, pressing gently to adhere. Transfer the cake to a serving plate, dust with powdered sugar, and serve.

Omi Tip: I'm sure all my chocolate lovers out there will fall for this cake filled with Nutella instead of the cream cheese filling. Anuncio no pagado.

Guavalaítos

Guava fritters

This recipe was born after a couple of chef friends came over one weekend and suggested we make bacalaítos con guineos maduros (ripe bananas), which are a sweet-and-savory treat in rural Puerto Rico. I definitely looked at them sideways, but I never say no to a challenge, and I must say, it was surprisingly good. That dish immediately got my wheels turning. If we can add banana to a Bacalaíto (page 153), what else is possible? Well, I love guayaba in any shape, size, or form—if guava's there, I'm there. So, a few days later, I decided to experiment again, but I took out the bacalao and the guineos and replaced them with guava and cheese. When you eat this guavalaíto, you'll get the crunch from the original bacalaíto with the ooey-gooey goodness of the melted cheese and warm guava paste. When my mom tried my invention, she looked at me and said, "Esto es un disparate, pero un disparate bien bueno," and she was right: This is crazy, but really good crazy.

Makes 6 to 8 servings

- 1 cup/140g all-purpose flour
- 1 teaspoon baking powder
- ½ teaspoon kosher salt
- ½ teaspoon ground cinnamon, plus more for topping
- ¼ teaspoon ground nutmeg
- ¼ cup/50g granulated sugar
- ½ cup/155g guava paste, cut into small cubes
- ½ cup/65g queso de freír (frying cheese), cut into small cubes
- Vegetable oil, for frying
- Powdered sugar, for topping

In a large bowl, whisk together the flour, baking powder, salt, cinnamon, nutmeg, and sugar. Gradually add ½ cup/120ml of water to the dry mixture, stirring after each addition, until you have a smooth batter. Gently fold the cubed guava paste and cheese into the batter until evenly distributed.

In a large skillet over medium-high heat, add about 1 inch of oil and heat until it shimmers.

With a ladle, add spoonfuls of the batter into the hot oil, using the back of the ladle to flatten them slightly once they hit the oil so they have the same platelike shape as bacalaítos. Work in batches to avoid crowding the pan.

Fry the guavalaítos until golden brown and crispy, 2 to 3 minutes per side. Use a slotted spoon to remove the fritters from the skillet and set on paper towels to remove excess oil.

Dust the fritters with powdered sugar and a sprinkle of cinnamon and serve hot!

Omi Tip: To make sure each fritter has the perfect ratio of cheese to guava, add the cubed guava paste and cheese to the ladle with the batter mixture instead.

Bizcocho nube de parcha

Passion fruit cloud cake

Makes 10 to 12 servings

Cake and Filling

1 box angel food cake mix, plus any ingredients listed on the cake mix box (usually just water)

1 cup/240g frozen or fresh passion fruit purée with seeds

¼ cup/50g granulated sugar

2 tablespoons cornstarch

Frosting

4 ounces/115g cream cheese, softened

1 cup/240ml heavy cream

2 tablespoons powdered sugar

2 tablespoons passion fruit purée

1 teaspoon vanilla extract

Omi Tip: If you need to save time, you can also buy angel food cake from your local bakery, and all you'll have left to do is prepare the passion fruit filling and make the frosting. Shortcuts are made to be used!

Yes . . . I Omified the cloud cake. The classic cloud cake, or nube de parcha, recipe usually uses different flavors, such as vanilla, chocolate, strawberry, and coconut, but I wanted to give it my own twist, so I decided to try using passion fruit. I knew the flavors would get along—my challenge was to find the right consistency. The secret lies in balancing the lightness of the angel food cake with the strong punch of flavor from the passion fruit. The flavors came together beautifully and taste as soothing yet showstopping as a tropical sunset.

Make the cake: Preheat the oven according to the cake mix instructions (usually 350°F/175°C). Prepare the cake batter according to the package instructions. Pour the batter into an ungreased angel food cake pan.

Bake the cake according to the package instructions. Once done, invert the pan onto a cooling rack and let the cake cool completely, still in the pan.

Make the passion fruit filling: In a small saucepan over medium heat, combine the passion fruit purée and sugar and cook, stirring often, until the sugar dissolves.

In a separate bowl, mix the cornstarch with ¼ cup/60ml of water to create a slurry.

Gradually add the cornstarch slurry to the passion fruit mixture, stirring continuously.

Cook, stirring continuously, until the mixture thickens and becomes glossy. Remove from the heat and let cool completely.

Make the passion fruit frosting: In a large bowl, beat the cream cheese until smooth. Add the heavy cream, powdered sugar, passion fruit purée, and vanilla extract and beat until stiff peaks form.

To assemble: Slice the completely cooled angel food cake horizontally into two or three layers. Spread a layer of the cooled passion fruit filling between each layer of cake. Then frost the entire cake with the passion fruit frosting.

Refrigerate the cake for at least 1 hour to allow the flavors to meld. If desired, garnish the cake with fresh passion fruit pulp or whipped cream before serving.

Budín de coco

Coconut bread pudding

This is a Doña Connie special, from here till eternity. She makes the best budín de coco I have ever tried in my life. It's so good that when she started selling them, she could hardly keep up with demand. This recipe also has a special place in my heart because it was the first dessert Mami taught me to make, and now it's become my go-to budín anytime I have family or guests over. I did not dare change any measurements or Omify this in any way because it's perfect just the way it is.

Makes 10 to 12 servings

- 1 cup/200g granulated sugar
- One (13.5-ounce/400ml) can coconut milk
- One (12-ounce/350ml) can evaporated milk
- One (14-ounce/400ml) can sweetened condensed milk
- 4 large eggs
- 1 teaspoon vanilla extract
- ½ teaspoon ground cinnamon
- ¼ teaspoon ground nutmeg
- ¼ teaspoon ground cloves
- 1 loaf (about 1 pound/450g) day-old bread, cut into 1-inch cubes
- ½ cup/40g shredded coconut
- ½ cup/70g raisins

Preheat the oven to 350°F/175°C.

In a small saucepan over medium heat, combine the sugar and ¼ cup/60ml of water. Cook, stirring occasionally, until the sugar dissolves and turns a deep amber color.

Quickly pour the caramel into a 9 by 13-inch baking dish or a 9-inch round pan, swirling to coat the bottom evenly. Set aside to cool so the caramel can harden.

In a large bowl, whisk together the coconut milk, evaporated milk, sweetened condensed milk, eggs, vanilla extract, cinnamon, nutmeg, and cloves until well combined.

Add the bread cubes and shredded coconut to the milk mixture, stirring to ensure all the bread is soaked. Let it sit for about 10 minutes to absorb the liquid, then fold in the raisins.

Pour the bread pudding mixture over the hardened caramel in the baking dish.

Place the baking dish in a larger pan. Fill the larger dish with hot water until it reaches halfway up the sides of the baking dish, creating a water bath, or bain-marie.

Bake for about 1 hour, or until a knife inserted in the center of the bread pudding comes out clean. Remove the baking dish from the water bath and let it cool to room temperature.

Refrigerate the budín for at least 2 hours, or overnight, to fully set.

To serve, run a knife around the edges of the budín to loosen it. Invert onto a serving plate, so the caramel is on top, and enjoy.

Omi Tip: Any bread you have on hand is acceptable here, but if you have access to an enriched bread like pan sobao (that you haven't gobbled up yet) or brioche, do yourself that favor.

Barriguitas de vieja

Pumpkin dough fritters

Barriguitas de vieja, also known as tortitas de calabaza, were a Doña Gloria special. She used to make these all the time when I was a little girl and she and my abuelo were living in Loíza. Usually, it was a treat she'd serve us after dinner. When you bite into a barriguita, the flavors that burst on your palate are similar to those of a fresh-out-of-the-fryer pumpkin spice donut. Anytime I see these fritters, they spark a core memory: my abuelita in her beloved kitchen, tossing the warm barriguitas in sugar and cinnamon before bringing them out to the table with a smile on her face and warmth in her eyes.

Makes 10 to 12 servings

- 2 cups/450g pumpkin purée (fresh or canned)
- ½ cup/100g granulated sugar
- 1 teaspoon vanilla extract
- 2 large eggs, beaten
- 1 cup/140g all-purpose flour
- 1 teaspoon baking powder
- 1 teaspoon ground cinnamon
- ½ teaspoon ground ginger
- ¼ teaspoon ground cloves
- ¼ teaspoon ground nutmeg
- ¼ teaspoon kosher salt
- Vegetable oil, for frying
- Powdered sugar, for dusting (optional)

In a large bowl, combine the pumpkin purée, sugar, vanilla extract, and beaten eggs. Mix well and set aside. In another large bowl, whisk together the flour, baking powder, cinnamon, ginger, cloves, nutmeg, and salt. Gradually add the dry ingredients to the pumpkin mixture, stirring until well combined. The batter should be thick but scoopable.

In a deep skillet or deep-fryer over medium-high heat, add 2 inches of oil and heat to 325°F/165°C (use an instant-read thermometer to monitor the temperature of the oil). Drop tablespoons of the batter into the hot oil, working in batches to avoid overcrowding. Fry until the fritters are golden brown and cooked through, 3 to 4 minutes per side. Use a slotted spoon to remove the fritters from the skillet and set on paper towels to drain excess oil.

Dust the fritters with powdered sugar, if desired. Serve warm and enjoy!

Omi Tip: Instead of powdered sugar, you can also dust the fritters with a mix of granulated sugar and cinnamon to add an extra layer of flavor.

7

Que venga de to'
Puerto Rican party staples

Puerto Rico loves a good party. Whether it's a birthday, a wedding, or a holiday, we'll turn it up and make it a rumbón. No matter where we are, there will be music, dancing, and most important of all, fooood! Special occasions are our excuse to get together with family and friends, forget all our cares, live in the present, and have a good time, or as El Gran Combo wisely sings in "La fiesta de 'Pilito'," our holiday anthem, "¡A gozarlo to'!"

Back in my day, birthday parties were held in the house's marquesina (outdoor garage), and holidays were celebrated on the terraza (terrace) or the glorieta, the covered outdoor space where we had the yellow cement table and benches as well as my beloved hammock (see page 69). The only celebration that was ever held in a formal event space was a wedding—even our quinceañeros were held in the marquesina!

As you may or may not know, if you tell a Boricua that your party starts at 4 p.m., they won't show up until 5 or 6, which means that anyone who does show up on time is usually recruited to the decorating committee. I vividly remember the paper chains looped together and hung from the decorative fence, las verjas, using kitchen string left over from pasteles, and balloons taped to the ceilings and walls (as kids, we hoped the balloons would drift down to the ground so we could play with them). The decor colors varied depending on the birthday's theme, but I recall peach, mint green, and pastel yellow being the "it" colors back then.

Holiday decorations were a whole other story—those involved the indoor Christmas tree and the all-important Christmas lights out front, strung across the houses, balconies, bushes, and even the palm trees, turning them into twinkling beams. And who can forget the famous freestanding arches made of PVC pipes and decorated with lights in the front fence? It was a vibrant and joyful tradition, and an unspoken competition to see who did it best.

No matter the occasion, we always had music, oftentimes accompanied by Tío Pello playing his beloved congas or timbales, and dancing, which was always kicked off by Titi Marta. Kids played hide-and-seek or tag, and those adults who weren't dancing could be found huddled around the ever-present dominoes table watching the game unfold or playing cards at a nearby table. Eventually, the tías would head to the sala to squeeze in some juicy chisme time, and the tíos would stand in a corner and chat or grab a cafecito and smoke their cigars.

The party always stayed outside so that my abuelito could take refuge in his room when he got tired, or just overwhelmed by the noise. He liked to stick to his regular 9 p.m. bedtime regardless of the celebration, even on Christmas. Sometimes he'd fall asleep; other nights, Mami and her siblings would knock and ask if they could sneak in to give him a Happy New Year's kiss, and find him sitting up in bed praying. Abuela, on the other hand, couldn't get enough of us. She thrived when her house was full, and she whipped up feast after feast to keep us all fed, happy, and coming back for more.

Special-occasion food on the island varies somewhat depending on the celebration, but there are certain Puerto Rican party staples that must be present at every fiesta, no matter what. For our birthday parties in the marquesina, there were always sandwichitos de mezcla, pasta de guayaba con queso, salame con queso, salchichón, ensalada de coditos, ensalada de papas, and arroz con gandules, just to name a few. The main dishes were usually some kind of meat, either barbecued chicken, fricasé de pollo, ham, or pernil. Everything was served buffet-style on a long table so guests could choose what to try first (and what to save for their second helping). The star of the birthday party food show was always the bizcocho, the cake, which usually featured a guava or pineapple filling and a frosting that was so sweet it left a coating of sugar on our tongues.

Many of the same sides made an appearance during the holidays, but the main attractions were the pavochón at Thanksgiving; the pasteles, pernil, and arroz con gandules at Christmas; and anything seafood—such as an ensalada de mariscos or an asopao de mariscos—for New Year's Eve, which was said to bring prosperity in the new year. When my abuelos lived in Loíza, they usually cooked un lechón a la varita (a pig roast) and homemade morcillas (blood sausages), all from the pigs they raised on their farm.

During the 1940s and '50s, many of my abuelo's family members moved to New York, but they always made a point to come back to Puerto Rico for the holidays. And when they did, they always stayed at the Loíza house, so everything had to be ready for their big arrival. Abuelo would dig out his bottles of pitorro so that abuela could make coquito, Abuela would prepare and freeze the pasteles ahead of time, and the house would be spick-and-span for their guests.

My Christmas memories in Puerto Rico are all in that first house in Loíza because, once we moved to Rhode Island, Mami sent me back to visit every summer, but we couldn't afford to also return for the holidays. But that didn't

stop us from keeping our traditions alive in our new home away from home. Mami continued making our holiday staples, and we'd have Christmas dinner with her church friends instead of with family. We'd set up a long table in one of the halls and everyone would bring their traditional food, which meant I got to try holiday dishes from the Dominican Republic, El Salvador, and Guatemala—that's how I became a fan of tamales at a young age. These heartwarming gatherings helped ease the melancholy of being away from our own families during this special time of the year.

Aside from our traditional main and side dishes, I've also included a few recipes in this chapter that I believe will speak to many of my fellow Boricuas living in the States, who may be looking to incorporate some American classics in their holiday spread. It's a beautiful way to create an inviting table that embraces the friends and families who opened their doors to us when we were newcomers. As for the desserts table, I've got you covered with classics like Tembleque (page 242) and Flan de 5 ingredientes (page 247), as well as one of my own Christmas morning breakfast staples, Tostadas francesas con coquito (page 243), which my boys wish they could have year-round. And if you're looking for drinks to complement your fiesta, choose your favorites from chapter 5 (page 161), such as Coquito (page 169), our traditional Christmas drink.

Now it's time for you to play mix-and-match and choose the dishes that sing to you to turn your next party or holiday gathering into an unforgettable culinary journey. Remember, mi gente, there are no rules, ¡en tu cocina tú mandas!

La Navidad más larga del mundo
The longest Christmas in the world

Puerto Rico has one of the longest Christmas seasons in the world, second only to the Philippines, who start celebrating in September and end on January 6, Three Kings Day. Okay, Philippines, we see you, and we're right behind you. Some say we begin our Christmas season on Thanksgiving, but any good Boricua knows that as soon as Halloween is over, Christmas takes the reins.

Like clockwork, on November 1, everyone starts rummaging through their boxes of Christmas decorations and begins dressing their homes with string lights and all things red and green, including festive wreaths, garlands, Santas, and Feliz Navidad signs. The stores start playing traditional aguinaldos and classic Christmas songs, including José Feliciano's "Feliz Navidad," Richie Ray and Bobby Cruz's "Seis chorreao," Willie Colón and Héctor Lavoe's "Asalto navideño," El Gran Combo's "La fiesta de 'Pilito'," and many more. You can't help but shimmy your way down the aisles while searching for decorations and ingredients for holiday dishes. I love the excitement that comes with those preparation weeks. The energy is contagious.

By the time Thanksgiving comes along, our homes are decorated; our trees are adorned with dangling ornaments, baubles, tinsels, lights, ribbon bows, and tree toppers in all their glory; and many of us have already started the process of making coquito and pasteles. (This is when the illicit side hustle of selling pasteles and coquito takes place.) We also begin to plan what we're going to keep in the fridge in case we're sent parranderos in the middle of the night.

Las parrandas are a Puerto Rican–style Christmas carol tradition, but the parranderos don't just sing aguinaldos—they also play several instruments, such as cuatros, güiros, maracas, panderos, and guitars. And they're not a group of five to ten people—it's more like twenty people who are asked to go to specific homes to spread their joy. Parrandas are not paid; they're done out of love. It's all about sharing the joy of the holiday season within the community. Instead of singing house to house around a neighborhood in the early evening, they quietly arrive at the first house after midnight and burst into joyful music and song right outside the family's front door. That's why it's called un "asalto navideño"—a "Christmas ambush"—because you're taking the family by surprise to shake them from their slumber, calling them to celebrate.

If someone surprises you by sending a parranda to your house, no matter what time of night, you must let them *all* in. While they continue to sing and play, you pull out whatever food and drinks you've kept in the fridge for this very occasion to feed them and quench their thirst before they leave for the next house. They're usually only able to hit a few houses per night, and if yours happens to be the last one, expect to stay up until dawn, which signals the end of that night's rumba. People have the green light to start sending their friends and family parrandas right after Thanksgiving and through early January, so you best be ready to have some fun, either as a receiver or as a parrandero yourself—because anyone can be a part of a parranda, and anyone can get one when they least expect it.

When I was a kid, on the day of Christmas Eve, neighbors would come out of their homes and exchange dishes: You'd give someone a few pasteles, and they'd give you some of their arroz con gandules. It was a beautiful community event where the entire town was like family for a day. That no longer happens, but Nochebuena, what we call Christmas Eve, continues to be the night we celebrate Christmas with our nearest and dearest, when we eat the pasteles we prepared weeks earlier, the arroz con gandules, morcilla, pernil, ensalada de papas, arroz con dulce, tembleque, and coquito. It is the biggest feast of the year. My abuela liked to set a basket filled with grapes at the center of the buffet table so that there would always be food in the home and blessings for the family.

The following morning, we'd stagger into the living room to open gifts, and my abuela would greet us with an "Ahí está, sírvanse," urging us to head into the kitchen to help ourselves to a plate of the revoltillo (scrambled eggs) she'd just made, together with salchichón, fresh bread and butter, and a much-needed cafecito.

After a few days off comes New Year's Eve, when everyone gathers once again to eat, drink, dance, and ring in the new year, but not without first thoroughly cleaning every nook and cranny of our homes to rid the house of negativity. Clothes must be washed, and bedsheets changed to attract prosperity in the new year. Even the outside needs to be hosed down to get rid of any negative energy. I used to love that part when I was a little girl, because as soon as my abuela and Mami poured that soapy water outside on the smooth tile floor, I'd turn it into my very own Slip 'N Slide, which made them burst into laughter. But I also paid attention—now, I can't start the new year without cleaning up every last speck of dust in my house.

The other tradition I saw the adults take part in was eating twelve grapes during the last twelve seconds before the stroke of midnight, one for each month of the upcoming year, to bring them good luck—half choking while they giggled through this almost impossible task. There are even more traditions now, like putting on red underwear to attract love (or a yellow pair to attract prosperity), throwing a bucket of water out the door to keep evil spirits away, or walking around the block with a suitcase if you wish to travel more. That's one too many things for me to worry about while ringing in the new year, so I stick to the cleaning and the grapes. But you do you!

You'd think that after so many celebrations, we'd call it after New Year's, but oh no, there's more. On January 6 we have El Día de los Reyes, Three Kings Day, which commemorates the day the Three Wise Men visited baby Jesus and brought him gifts. That's why only children receive gifts on this day. On the night of January 5, the kids grab an empty shoebox and fill it with grass, for the kings' camels. Usually, the box is placed under the bed, but I always liked to place mine outside—how would the camels reach it otherwise? While us kids slept, my family would hide our gifts around the outside of our home, and the next morning, we'd set off on a treasure hunt to find the gifts the Three Kings had left us. Thankfully for my abuela, that was a day when she got a break from cooking and hosting, as we'd head out to visit family members and friends.

Then come las Octavitas (I wasn't joking when I said this keeps going way past New Year's Day). This is a newer tradition, so I didn't experience it when I was a little girl. Initially, it was a way of honoring the Three Kings and Jesus, but as good Boricuas, we also found it to be the perfect reason to keep the party going a little longer. Las Octavitas are celebrated during the eight days following Three Kings Day.

That brings us to January 14. Is it over yet? No. The end of one of the longest Christmas seasons in the world arrives with La Fiesta de San Sebastián, aka La SanSe, held on the third weekend in January in El Viejo San Juan. It's a Thursday-through-Sunday festival where the streets come alive with live music, another round of amazing food and drinks, and no small amount of dancing—everything from bomba and plena to salsa and reggaeton. On that third Sunday in January, as the fiesta dies down and everyone heads home, our holiday season is officially over.

Pavochón

Puerto Rican Thanksgiving turkey

Makes 1 turkey, 8 to 10 servings

One 12- to 14-pound/5.4kg to 6.3kg whole turkey, thawed

½ cup/110g Mantequilla criolla (page 42), at room temperature, plus more for basting

1 large onion, finely chopped

3 tablespoons Garlic paste (page 39)

¼ cup/60ml extra-virgin olive oil

¼ cup/60ml Mojo de Omi (page 37), or a mix of orange and lime juice

2 tablespoons dried oregano

2 tablespoons ground cumin

2 tablespoons kosher salt

1 tablespoon freshly ground black pepper

1 tablespoon paprika (optional, for color)

1 tablespoon dried thyme

1 teaspoon Sazón (page 43)

¼ cup/60ml Achiote oil (page 39), plus more for basting

¼ cup/10g chopped cilantro (optional)

3 to 4 cups cooked Arroz con gandules (page 241), for stuffing

1 or 2 bay leaves

Much like turkey in the United States, our pavochón is the star of Puerto Rican Thanksgiving. If you're honored with the task of making the turkey, you have just received an enormous responsibility, so let me give you some advice. First and foremost, NEVER poke holes in the turkey. That technique may work on other meats to help the marinade penetrate the flesh, but with a turkey, all those holes will make it lose its moisture even faster in the oven, resulting in a dry pavochón—and your family likely disowning you. Instead, follow the instructions below and bathe the turkey in Mantequilla criolla (page 42), the marinade paste, and Achiote oil (page 39), and make sure to baste it while it is cooking. Last but not least, my recipe calls for Arroz con gandules (page 241) as the stuffing, porque eso es lo que dice mi corazón, but you can choose whatever stuffing you prefer. Classic American stuffing will work, but if you want to give your pavochón a Puerto Rican twist, consider stuffing it with mofongo, yuca en escabeche, or my tried-and-true arroz con gandules.

Remove the giblets and neck from the turkey. Rinse the turkey inside and out and pat dry with paper towels.

Using a rubber pastry spatula, gently lift the skin from the turkey breast and pull to separate it from the meat without tearing it.

Rub the mantequilla criolla under the skin of the turkey breast and all over the outside of the turkey.

In a bowl, combine the onion, garlic paste, olive oil, mojo, oregano, cumin, salt, pepper, paprika (if using), thyme, and sazón and mix well to form a paste.

Rub the marinade paste all over the turkey, making sure to get it under the skin and inside the cavity.

Rub the achiote oil all over the turkey, ensuring it is evenly coated. Sprinkle the cilantro over the turkey, if using.

Cover the turkey with plastic wrap or place it in a large resealable bag and refrigerate for at least 12 hours, preferably 24 to 48 hours, to allow the flavors to penetrate the meat.

When ready to cook, preheat the oven to 325°F/165°C.

Place the turkey on a rack in a roasting pan and spoon the arroz con gandules into the cavity, making sure to pack it loosely to allow for expansion during cooking. Add the bay leaves to the cavity, then tie the turkey legs with kitchen twine.

Roast the turkey, basting with the pan juices (or a mixture of melted mantequilla criolla and achiote oil) every 30 to 45 minutes to keep the meat moist and flavorful, until the internal temperature reaches 165°F/75°C in the thickest part of the thigh—about 4 hours, depending on the size of the turkey. If the turkey skin starts to brown too quickly, tent it loosely with aluminum foil. This prevents the skin from burning while allowing the meat to continue cooking evenly.

Remove the turkey from the oven and let it rest for 20 to 30 minutes before carving. This allows the juices to redistribute throughout the meat, making it juicier and more tender. Carve and serve your pavochón with your favorite sides.

Omi Tip: If you have the time, you can roast the turkey at a lower temperature (300°F/150°C) for a longer period, 5 to 6 hours. I prefer this slow-cooking method because it helps break down the meat fibers, resulting in more tender meat. Aquí no hay prisa.

Pernil

Roasted pork shoulder

Sin pernil, no hay fiesta. And if the pernil isn't cooked right, the party will be a flop. Like pavochón, when you are entrusted to make this crown jewel for a special occasion or the holidays, the pressure is on. Everyone will be checking on you to make sure your pernil is at the very least acceptable, so take your time with this recipe, and follow the instructions carefully. Don't get frustrated if you aren't able to master the perfect meat tenderness-to-skin crunchiness ratio right off the bat. It took me a very long time and many disappointing attempts before I was able to get it just right, but now I can make it with my eyes closed. You'll know you've cooked it perfectly when the meat is soft and succulent, and the skin is so crispy you can play it like a güiro, aka the sound machine, and the bone can be easily pulled out. This is my bulletproof, party-ready pernil.

Makes 10 or 11 servings

- ¼ cup/60ml Achiote oil (page 39)
- 1 tablespoon Mi Sofrito Fresquecito (page 37)
- 8 to 10 garlic cloves, mashed in a pilón
- 1 tablespoon dried oregano
- 1 teaspoon kosher salt
- 1 teaspoon freshly ground black pepper
- 1 tablespoon Adobo (page 38)
- 3 or 4 limes, juiced
- 1 teaspoon cumin
- 10 to 11 pounds/4.5kg to 5kg pork picnic shoulder

In a medium bowl, mix together the achiote oil, sofrito, garlic, oregano, salt, pepper, adobo, lime juice, and cumin to form a paste.

Use a sharp knife to score the skin of the pork shoulder in a crosshatch pattern without breaking through the fat cap. Carefully detach the fat from most of the meat, making sure it is attached at the edges.

Make deep X-shaped cuts all over the meat to allow the marinade paste to penetrate it. Rub the paste generously all over the pork, making sure to get it into the incisions and under the fat cap.

Cover the pork and let it marinate in the refrigerator for at least 4 hours, preferably overnight.

Preheat the oven to 300°F/150°C.

Place the pork shoulder in a roasting pan, skin side up, tented with aluminum foil. Roast for 4 to 6 hours, until the internal temperature reaches at least 145°F/63°C and the meat is tender and pulls apart easily.

If the skin isn't getting crispy enough, remove the foil and increase the oven temperature to 450°F/230°C for the last 20 to 30 minutes of cooking, until the skin is crispy and golden brown.

Remove the pork from the oven and let it rest for about 20 minutes before carving (it should be falling off the bone at this point). I love my pernil with a side of Arroz con gandules (page 241), Ensalada de papas (page 230), y Guineos en escabeche (page 235) . . . ¡no me mires con ese tono de voz!

Omi Tip: To get the crispiest possible skin on the pork shoulder, make sure to pat the top dry with a paper towel before placing it in the oven.

Pasteles

Steamed green banana and meat pies

Those who have the know-how make their own pasteles; those who don't know buy them—but most, if not all, Puerto Ricans eat them. Pasteles are the star, the crown jewel, the heart of our Christmas dinners, so mastering this recipe will earn you endless boricua brownie points. I come from a long lineage of pasteleras, pastel-making women. My great-grandmother passed down her recipe to my abuela Gloria, who was able to make a living as a newlywed by selling them. They were so good, people said her hands were sacred, and they'd place their orders in June and July to ensure they could get their batch by the holidays. With time, she and Abuelo began to start each year planning how many pigs, bananas, and vegetables they would need to grow to fulfill the next holiday's orders. When we moved to the States, Mami continued the pastel-making and -selling tradition in Rhode Island, with the recipe her mother had passed down to her. At long last, eight years ago, it was my turn. I had never paid attention to the process growing up, but I'd learned a lot through osmosis, so I was familiar with the recipe. I still called my mom for help, and she patiently guided me through each step. My first round of pasteles actually tasted great, but they stuck to the banana leaves, which meant they were too soft. Mami then passed down her secret trick: She uses malanga de coco instead of milk to soften the masa. After a few more tries, I hit my stride and got my pasteles to come out just right.

Makes 1 dozen pasteles

Filling

2 pounds/900g pork shoulder

2 tablespoons kosher salt

2 or 3 bay leaves

½ cup/120ml Mi Sofrito Fresquecito (page 37)

¼ cup/60ml canned tomato sauce

¼ cup/30g diced roasted red peppers

¼ cup/40g green olives, pitted and chopped

½ cup/80g chickpeas, liquid reserved

1 tablespoon Adobo (page 38)

½ tablespoon ground cumin

½ tablespoon dried oregano

1 cup/240g Achiote oil (page 39)

1 teaspoon freshly ground black pepper

Masa (dough)

5 pounds/2kg green cooking bananas (guineos verdes), peeled

2 pounds/900g yautía, peeled

1 pound/450g pumpkin (calabaza), peeled

1 pound/450g taro root (malanga de coco), peeled

½ cup/120ml Achiote oil (page 39)

1 cup/240ml of the strained pork shoulder water

1 tablespoon kosher salt

Wrapping

One (16-ounce/450g) package banana leaves, cut into 10-inch squares

Parchment paper sheets (or papel para pasteles)

Achiote oil (page 39), for brushing

Kitchen twine, cut into six 3-foot-long pieces

Make the pork filling: Cut the pork shoulder into 1-inch chunks, making sure to cut around the bone.

In a large pot over medium heat, add the pork shoulder chunks and cover with water. Add the salt and bay leaves and boil for 1 hour.

Once the meat is boiled, remove from the heat and allow to cool for 15 minutes. Once cooled, strain and reserve all the water—eso es oro. Cut the meat into bite-size pieces and set aside.

In the same pot over medium heat, add ½ cup/120ml of the pork shoulder water, the sofrito, tomato sauce, roasted red peppers, olives, chickpeas (with their liquid), adobo, cumin, and oregano and simmer for 10 to 12 minutes to create a guiso.

Set aside 1 cup/240ml of the pork shoulder water for the masa. Add the meat back into the pot along with the remaining strained pork shoulder water and set over medium heat. Make sure the water covers the meat. Add the achiote oil and pepper to the pot and allow the mixture to come to a simmer. Reduce the heat to low and cook for another 25 to 30 minutes, until the meat is fork-tender. Remove from the heat and set aside.

Make the masa: Using the finest part of a grater (or a food processor), grate the green bananas, yautía, pumpkin, and taro root. Mix the grated ingredients in a large bowl until well combined. Add the achiote oil, the reserved strained pork shoulder water, and the salt to the mixture and stir to incorporate. Transfer the mixture to a food processor and process until you have a smooth, consistent dough with no clumps. Set aside.

Assemble the pasteles: Soften the banana leaves by passing them over an open flame or dipping them in hot water.

Place a sheet of parchment paper on a flat surface and a banana leaf square on top of the paper. Brush a small amount of achiote oil on the banana leaf and spread about ¼ cup/30g of masa in the center.

Add 2 to 3 tablespoons of the pork shoulder filling on top of the masa.

Fold the parchment sheet and banana leaf in half, starting with the edge closest to you and folding over to the edge farthest from you, so the masa folds over the filling. Press down on the edge to seal. Fold the top/open edge of the parchment and banana leaf back down over itself a couple of times until it is flush with the pastel. Then fold both open ends inward, like a burrito, to form a rectangular package. Repeat to assemble a second pastel.

Once you have two pasteles shaped into rectangular packages, place one on a flat surface, seam side up, and stack the other one on top, seam side down. Grab a piece of kitchen twine, fold it in half, wrap it around the center of the pasteles, and pull the ends through the loop. Then grab the ends, cross them over, and secure the pasteles lengthwise, then tie the kitchen twine in a knot. The two pasteles should be securely tied together, like a perfectly wrapped present. Set aside on a large plate.

Repeat these steps to make pairs of pasteles until the masa and filling are used up.

continued

Pasteles, *continued*

Omi Tip: Pasteles are a labor of love, so I highly recommend you give yourself 2 days to make them. Mami and I like to make the filling and the masa on a Saturday (that alone takes about 8 hours). We store everything in the fridge overnight and spend Sunday assembling the pasteles, which becomes another all-day affair, because we usually make about seven and a half dozen. Even if you make just one recipe's worth, it will take time to assemble. I always encourage everyone to make it a friend-and-family weekend event with music, easy bites, and drinks to ease the ride—the more hands helping, the better!

Cook the pasteles: Bring a large pot of salted water to a boil over medium heat. Carefully add the pasteles to the boiling water, making sure they are fully submerged. Boil the pasteles for 1 hour.

After an hour, remove one package, let it cool slightly, then unwrap a pastel and check to make sure the masa is firm and cooked through. If not, continue to cook the rest of the pasteles for another 5 to 10 minutes. You probably won't need more than 1 hour of cooking time.

Remove the pasteles from the pot, place them on a large plate, and let them cool slightly for 5 to 7 minutes before unwrapping.

If you have extra pasteles, place them in gallon-size ziplock bags, seal them tightly, and freeze for up to 6 months. To reheat frozen pasteles, bring a pot of water to a rolling boil over medium-high heat and cook the frozen pasteles for 1 hour 15 minutes, making sure the water is fully covering them.

Once you're ready to serve them, the real debate will be: Will you eat them with ketchup or hot sauce?

Ensalada de papas

Puerto Rican potato salad with apples

As a kid, when I thought of potato salad, this is the one that came to mind. I had no idea there were other versions of potato salad until I moved to the States, and the American ones just didn't cut it for me. I always do a happy dance when I see ensalada de papas on the table because it's not an everyday side—it only makes an appearance on special occasions or during the holidays. An ensalada de papas without apples is not an ensalada de papas in my book. I like to use a green apple for just the right amount of sweet and tangy crunch that doesn't overpower the rest of the ingredients. I've added my own twist with the sweet relish and celery, but if you want a more classic Puerto Rican ensalada de papas, you can leave those out.

Makes 6 to 8 servings

- 4 or 5 large russet potatoes, peeled and cubed
- 3 large eggs
- 1 green apple, peeled, cored, and diced
- 1 thin carrot, diced
- ½ cup/120g mayonnaise
- 2 tablespoons mustard
- 2 tablespoons sweet pickle relish
- ½ cup/70g finely chopped red onion
- ½ cup/55g finely chopped celery
- ½ cup/75g finely chopped red bell pepper
- Kosher salt and freshly ground black pepper to taste, *LQTDT*♥
- Paprika, for garnish

In a large pot over medium heat, add the potatoes and cover with water. Bring to a boil and cook for 5 minutes. Then, to the same pot, add the eggs and boil everything for about 10 minutes. Once the potatoes are fork-tender, drain and let cool. Peel and dice the boiled eggs.

In a large bowl, add the diced eggs, apple, carrot, mayonnaise, mustard, relish, onion, celery, and bell pepper and toss gently to combine. Then add the cooled potatoes to the bowl and gently mix everything together until well combined. Season with salt and pepper; ¡sal y pimienta se quieren casar!

Cover the bowl and refrigerate the potato salad for at least 1 hour before serving to allow the flavors to meld. Garnish with a sprinkle of paprika and enjoy with your party guests.

Omi Tip: Do not let your potatoes sit in the hot water for too long after boiling. Remove them immediately and shock them with cold water—this will ensure they don't get mushy.

Sandwichitos de mezcla

Mezcla sandwiches

The first plate on the table—and the first one that is wiped clean at a Puerto Rican party—is the one that has these sandwichitos de mezcla. These are also the go-to snack to take to the beach or keep handy in the fridge in case someone sends you a parranda (see page 216). They are so popular on the island that they even show up at funerals. Since they're easy, inexpensive, and can be made earlier in the day and stored in the fridge, they're a great choice when you're having a lot of people over. These matahambre (hunger-killer) bites taste even better cut into triangles, so don't skip that crucial step to put a smile on the faces of your fellow Boricuas.

Makes 30 servings (and it's never enough!)

One (12-ounce/340g) can Spam or other luncheon meat, cubed

One (15-ounce/425g) jar Cheese Whiz

4 ounces/115g cream cheese, softened

½ cup/125g jarred roasted red peppers or pimientos

¼ cup/60g mayonnaise

1 teaspoon garlic powder

1 teaspoon onion powder

1 loaf sliced white sandwich bread, crusts removed

In a food processor, combine the Spam, Cheese Whiz, cream cheese, roasted red peppers, mayonnaise, garlic powder, and onion powder. Blend until smooth and creamy.

Spread a generous amount of the filling onto a slice of bread. Top with another slice of bread to form a sandwich. Repeat until all the bread and filling are used up.

Cut each sandwich into triangles or squares. Arrange on a platter and serve immediately, or cover and refrigerate until ready to serve.

Omi Tip: For a healthier version, you can substitute the Spam with low-sodium turkey or chicken luncheon meat, and swap the Cheese Whiz for Greek yogurt.

Ensalada de coditos

Macaroni salad with ham and hard-boiled eggs

Ensalada de coditos is similar to an American macaroni salad, but with a different take on flavor and some different ingredients. My dressing isn't mayonnaise-based; it's more like a vinaigrette. And we add ham to this version for added texture. The type of ham you want to use and how you want to cut it—sliced, diced, cubed—is totally up to you. I encourage you to play around with this party staple until you find your ideal texture and flavor.

Makes 10 to 12 servings

Ensalada de coditos (Macaroni Salad)

- Kosher salt to taste, *LQTDT*♥
- 1 pound/450g elbow macaroni
- 1 cup/145g diced cooked ham
- 2 hard-boiled eggs, diced
- ½ cup/75g finely chopped red bell pepper
- ½ cup/75g finely chopped green bell pepper
- ½ cup/70g finely chopped red onion
- ½ cup/55g finely chopped celery
- ½ cup/80g sweet peas

Vinaigrette

- ¼ cup/60ml extra-virgin olive oil
- 2 tablespoons apple cider vinegar
- 1 tablespoon Dijon mustard
- 1 teaspoon honey
- Kosher salt and freshly ground black pepper to taste, *LQTDT*♥

Make the macaroni salad: Fill a large pot with water, add a pinch of salt, and bring to a boil over medium-high heat. Cook the elbow macaroni according to the package instructions until al dente. Drain and run under cold water to stop the cooking process. Set aside to cool.

Make the vinaigrette: In a small bowl, whisk together the olive oil, vinegar, mustard, honey, salt, and pepper, until well combined.

Assemble and serve: In a large bowl, add the cooled macaroni, the ham, hard-boiled eggs, bell peppers, onion, celery, and peas and gently mix.

Pour the vinaigrette into the bowl and toss gently until everything is well coated. Adjust the seasoning as needed.

Cover the bowl and refrigerate the macaroni salad for at least 1 hour before serving to allow the flavors to meld.

Serve the macaroni salad on your party table and let your guests combine it with other delicious dishes. I personally love my ensalada de coditos as a side for Arroz con gandules (page 241) or Pernil (page 224).

Omi Tip: This salad is always better the next day, so feel free to prep ahead of time and let it marinate in the fridge for the day (or overnight) before serving.

Bola de fuego

Ball-of-fire cheese and ham dip

Makes 10 to 12 servings

- One (12-ounce/340g) can cooked ham, finely chopped
- One (8-ounce/225g) package cream cheese, softened
- 1 cup/330g pineapple preserves
- ½ cup/125g crushed pineapple, drained
- ¼ cup/40g finely chopped red bell pepper
- 1 jalapeño, finely diced
- 1 habanero (preferably yellow), finely diced
- ¼ cup/10g finely chopped cilantro, plus more for garnish
- 1 teaspoon hot sauce (optional, for a spicy twist)
- Kosher salt and freshly ground black pepper to taste, *LQTDT*♥

I consider this classic Puerto Rican party essential a *refined* dip, because rather than being served in a bowl like other dips, it's packed into a bowl and then unmolded onto a plate to give it a half-ball shape. A drizzle of pineapple glaze on top gives the bola de fuego its signature fiery color, which, as the name suggests, resembles a ball of fire, or even the sun. My twist in this recipe is to add hot sauce to the mix to pay homage to the *fuego* in its name, but you can leave that out if spicy notes are not your thing. As you can imagine, this is a hit with kids, so it mostly shows up at birthday parties. Serve it with crackers, tortilla chips, or vegetable sticks for dipping.

In a large bowl, combine the ham, cream cheese, and ½ cup of the pineapple preserves. Mix until well combined.

Make the pineapple glaze: In a separate bowl, stir in the remaining ½ cup of pineapple preserves, the crushed pineapple, bell pepper, jalapeño, habanero, cilantro, and hot sauce, if using. Mix until all the ingredients are evenly incorporated. Season with salt and pepper and set the glaze aside.

Line a medium bowl with plastic wrap and transfer the cream cheese mixture to the bowl, packing it in firmly to turn it into a ball. Cover and refrigerate in the bowl for at least 1 hour to allow the flavors to meld and the dip to firm up.

Unmold the ball onto a serving platter and remove the plastic wrap. Drizzle the pineapple glaze evenly over the ball and spread to cover. Garnish with more cilantro and serve with galletitas, tortilla chips, or sliced vegetables.

Guineos en escabeche

Pickled green bananas

When the tías start throwing down during the holiday, the competition is usually about who makes the best pernil, the best rice, and the best guineos en escabeche. The secret ingredient to this seemingly simple pickled green banana is the chicken gizzards, aka mollejas de pollo. And how you prepare those gizzards before adding them to the escabeche sauce is more than half the battle. I can't imagine my plate of pernil on Christmas without a side of guineos en escabeche, sitting next to arroz con gandules and ensalada de papas.

Makes 8 to 10 servings

- 1 pound/450g chicken gizzards
- ½ cup/120ml white vinegar, plus a splash for cooking the gizzards
- 2 bay leaves
- ½ green bell pepper, cut into chunks
- ¼ onion, cut into chunks
- 4 garlic cloves, 2 whole and 2 mashed
- 6 to 8 green cooking bananas (guineos verdes)
- ½ cup/120ml whole milk
- ½ cup/120ml extra-virgin olive oil
- 1 large red onion, thinly sliced
- ½ cup/85g green olives, sliced
- ½ cup/125g sliced jarred roasted red peppers
- 1 teaspoon black peppercorns
- 1 teaspoon dried oregano
- Kosher salt and freshly ground black pepper to taste, *LQTDT♥*

Prepare the gizzards: Using a sharp knife, peel the yellow skin off each chicken gizzard and discard. Rinse the gizzards under cold running water, place them in a bowl of fresh water with a splash of vinegar, and let them soak for 5 to 10 minutes. Cut any yellow nerves or hard tendons off the gizzards and discard. Then rinse them again under cold running water and pat dry with paper towels.

Transfer the cleaned, trimmed gizzards to a pressure cooker. Add 1 bay leaf, the green bell pepper, onion, and the 2 whole garlic cloves. Cover with water and pressure cook on high for about 40 minutes, or until the gizzards are tender. Once done, drain and set aside. (See Tip for stovetop cooking.)

Prepare the bananas: Cut both ends off the green bananas and slice the skins straight down the middle. Set a large pot over medium heat and add enough water to cover the bananas. Add the milk and bring to a boil. Once boiling, add the bananas and cook until they are tender but not mushy, 10 to 15 minutes. Drain and set aside to cool to room temperature. Once the bananas are cool, peel them. Cut into ½-inch rounds and set aside.

Make the escabeche sauce: In a large skillet over low heat, add the olive oil and the ½ cup of vinegar. Then add the red onion, olives, the remaining bay leaf, the roasted red peppers, the 2 mashed garlic cloves, the black peppercorns, and oregano. Cook for 10 minutes, until the onion becomes translucent and the garlic is fragrant. Remove from the heat.

Add the cooked chicken gizzards and boiled green bananas to the escabeche sauce and gently toss to coat everything evenly.

Place the mixture in a large bowl and season with salt and pepper. Cover the bowl and refrigerate for at least 2 hours, preferably overnight, to allow the flavors to meld. Serve at room temperature.

Omi Tip: Make sure to clean and cook the chicken gizzards well to rid them of their gaminess and give them a tender bite. If cooking them in a regular large pot on the stovetop, follow the same directions in the main recipe, but cook over medium-low heat for about 2 hours. The chicken gizzards should be very tender once they're done.

Pasteles al caldero

Plantain and meat pie soup

A relatively newer recipe to hit the Puerto Rican food scene, this is basically a deconstructed pastel turned into a hearty soup. If you happen to have a surplus of masa and filling from your pastel-making weekend (page 226), don't let them go to waste—turn them into this beloved dish. The end result looks like a plantain soup with pieces of meat and tastes like a pastel. If you have a big family to feed, this is the perfect recipe. It's become so popular that you can now order pasteles al caldero at many restaurants in Puerto Rico.

Makes 8 to 10 servings

1 pound/450g boneless pork stew meat or boneless pork shoulder roast, cut into 1-inch cubes

¼ cup/60ml Achiote oil (page 39)

2 tablespoons Mi Sofrito Fresquecito (page 37)

6 garlic cloves, minced

Kosher salt and freshly ground black pepper to taste, *LQTDT*♥

1 teaspoon ground cumin

1 teaspoon Better Than Bouillon or 1 chicken bouillon cube

½ cup/120ml tomato sauce

8 green olives, sliced

5 or 6 green plantains, peeled

½ cup/90g yautía, peeled

½ cup/120g pumpkin (calabaza), peeled

Chopped cilantro, for garnish

Hot sauce, for serving

In a bowl, combine the pork with 3 tablespoons of the achiote oil, 1 tablespoon of the sofrito, 1 minced garlic clove, and a pinch of salt and pepper. Mix well and set aside to marinate for at least 30 minutes.

In a large caldero or heavy pot over medium heat, add the remaining tablespoon of achiote oil and heat until it shimmers. Add the marinated pork and cook until browned on all sides, 7 to 8 minutes.

Add the remaining tablespoon of sofrito, the cumin, bouillon, tomato sauce, olives, and the remaining 5 garlic cloves. Stir well and continue to cook for 7 to 8 minutes.

Add 8 cups/1.9L of water and bring the mixture to a boil.

Grate the plantains, yautía, and pumpkin to a paste using the finest side of a grater or a food processor (see Tip). Combine in a large bowl and mix well to form a masa.

Gradually add the masa mixture to the pot with the pork and vegetables, stirring continuously to avoid lumps. Reduce the heat to medium-low, cover, and simmer for 45 minutes to 1 hour, until the masa is fully cooked and the stew has thickened.

Adjust the seasoning. Serve hot, garnished with cilantro and with drizzled with hot sauce, if desired.

Omi Tip: Make your life a little easier by placing the root vegetables in a food processor and blending instead of grating. Feel free to also substitute chicken thighs for the pork. Remember, ¡en tu cocina tú mandas!

Yuca en escabeche

Pickled cassava

Unlike Guineos en escabeche (page 235), no meat is involved in this pickled dish. Here, we use la yuca y más na'. Although it's a little easier to make, this is still considered a special-occasion dish, and it's perfect for those of you who aren't into its brother recipe's gizzards. I usually make this dish for Thanksgiving and Christmas, and I love to bring it along when invited to a friend or family gathering. It's a great gift for a foodie or a Boricua who misses home.

Makes 6 to 8 servings

1 tablespoon kosher salt, plus more to taste, *LQTDT*♥

2 pounds/900g yuca (cassava), peeled

½ cup/120ml extra-virgin olive oil

1 large red onion, thinly sliced

4 garlic cloves, mashed in a pilón

½ cup/120ml white wine vinegar

½ cup/85g green olives, sliced

½ cup/125g sliced jarred roasted red peppers

¼ cup/40g capers

2 bay leaves

1 teaspoon black peppercorns

¼ cup/10g chopped cilantro

Fill a large pot with water and bring to a boil over medium heat. Add the salt and yuca and cook until tender, 20 to 25 minutes. Drain and let cool slightly. Once cool enough to handle, remove and discard the tough, fibrous core from the center of each piece of yuca. Cut the remaining yuca into 2-inch chunks and set aside to cool.

In a large skillet over medium heat, add the olive oil and heat until it shimmers. Add the onion and sauté until softened, about 5 minutes. Add the garlic and cook for another minute, until fragrant.

Stir in the vinegar, olives, roasted red peppers, capers, bay leaves, and black peppercorns. Cook for another 2 to 3 minutes, allowing the flavors of the escabeche sauce to meld.

In a large bowl, combine the chunks of yuca with the escabeche sauce. Gently toss to coat the yuca evenly with the sauce. Stir in the cilantro for a vibrant finish.

Cover the bowl and refrigerate for at least 1 hour, preferably overnight, to allow the flavors to develop. Serve at room temperature with Arroz con gandules (page 241) and Pernil (page 224), or ¡lo que te diga tu corazón!

Omi Tip: If you have leftovers, you can store this in a container with a lid in your fridge for up to a week.

May's baked mac and cheese

Makes 10 to 12 servings

1 cup/220g (2 sticks) salted butter, plus more for greasing

Kosher salt and freshly ground black pepper to taste, *LQTDT*♥

1 pound/450g elbow macaroni

¼ cup/35g all-purpose flour

Three (12-ounce/350ml) cans evaporated milk

2 cups/200g shredded sharp Cheddar cheese

1 cup/100g shredded Monterey Jack cheese

1 cup/100g shredded Colby cheese

1 teaspoon mustard powder

1 teaspoon garlic powder

½ teaspoon smoked paprika, plus more for dusting

By the time I started dating my now-husband, Kradin, Mami had already moved back to Puerto Rico—so his family opened their doors and took me in as their own. After my first Thanksgiving at the Hopper house, I was so in awe of the food that I asked Kradin to please let me come earlier the following year, because I wanted to be by his mom's side while she was making dinner. The depth of flavor in my mother-in-law May's Southern dishes, plus the way she saw food as a connection to love, immediately evoked memories of my abuela in her kitchen—it made me feel right at home. May's mac and cheese was such a big hit with my husband that I asked May if she'd teach me the recipe, and, recognizing my budding passion for cooking, she immediately let me into her kitchen and took me under her wing. It was more than just sharing recipes and cooking together between May and me; she became my second mom. Once she passed away, this recipe became a way to always keep her close to us, a nostalgic hug in a dish. The quantities and technique are perfect as is, so I did not dare to Omify this dish. It's all May on a plate.

Preheat the oven to 350°F/175°C. Grease a 13 by 9-inch baking dish with butter. Fill a large pot with water, add a pinch of salt, and bring to a boil over medium-high heat. Cook the elbow macaroni according to the package instructions until al dente. Drain and set aside.

In a large saucepan over medium heat, melt 1½ sticks of the butter. Then whisk in the flour to create a roux. Cook the roux, whisking continuously, for 2 to 3 minutes, until it turns a light golden color.

Gradually whisk in the evaporated milk, ensuring there are no lumps of roux. Cook, whisking continuously, until the mixture thickens and starts to bubble, about 10 minutes.

Reduce the heat to low and stir in the cheeses until melted and smooth. Add the mustard powder, garlic powder, and smoked paprika and season with salt and pepper. Stir until well combined.

Add the cooked macaroni to the saucepan with the cheese sauce, along with the remaining ½ stick of butter. Stir until the pasta is fully coated.

Transfer the macaroni and cheese to the prepared baking dish. Dust a little more smoked paprika over the top. Bake the macaroni in the oven for 25 to 30 minutes, until the top is golden and bubbly.

Let the mac and cheese rest for a few minutes, then serve hot.

Omi Tip: When May first taught me this recipe, I didn't quite understand the patience that the roux required, but she showed me how to get it just right. You have to whisk continuously to break down any lumps that may form and keep an eye out for that light golden color that will tell you it is ready for the next ingredient. Practice makes perfect!

May's sweet potatoes

Makes 6 to 8 servings

4 large sweet potatoes, peeled and cut into ½-inch-thick rounds

½ cup/100g brown sugar

¼ cup/55g salted butter

1 teaspoon ground cinnamon

¼ teaspoon ground cloves

1 teaspoon orange zest

½ cup/120ml orange juice

Pinch of kosher salt

1 teaspoon vanilla bean paste

¼ teaspoon ground nutmeg

Many people like to roast their sweet potatoes, but I make them on the stovetop, just like my mother-in-law, May, taught me. Rather than boiling and then adding sauce to them, she cooked them directly in their sauce, which infused them with a depth of flavor that's hard to beat—plus, you'll end up with the most amazing brown-sugary syrup. I did Omify this recipe just a little bit by adding the juice and zest of an orange and a few more spices, but May's essence still permeates this dish. If you have May's baked mac and cheese (opposite) on your plate together with this dish, take a forkful of the macaroni with some of these sweet potatoes in the same bite—and thank me later!

In a large pot or deep skillet over medium heat, add the sweet potato rounds, brown sugar, butter, cinnamon, cloves, orange zest and juice, salt, vanilla bean paste, nutmeg, and ¼ cup/60ml of water. Stir until the sugar is dissolved and the spices are evenly distributed.

Cover the pot and cook, stirring occasionally, until the sweet potatoes are tender and the sauce has thickened, 30 to 35 minutes. If the sauce reduces too much, add a little more water as needed to prevent scorching (see Tip). Once the sweet potatoes are tender and the sauce is thick and glossy, remove from the heat. Serve hot.

Omi Tip: I learned from May that sweet potatoes naturally release water when cooked, but if the sauce feels like it's drying up, add a touch of water to keep it from burning. To ensure a velvety sauce, resist the urge to add more water to the pot unless absolutely necessary!

May's collard greens

I'll never forget the care with which my mother-in-law, May, handled such a simple and unassuming vegetable. She'd take her time to thoroughly wash her collard greens to rid them of all specks of dirt and sand, moving around the kitchen as if she were performing a well-choreographed dance. Then she'd carefully roll the leaves and chop them with such grace, I just couldn't take my eyes off her work. Instead of cooking her collards with bacon, she used smoked turkey, which infused the greens with a flavor that took them to another level. This is another favorite of my husband, Kradin, and a staple on my holiday table in honor of May and her big heart, kind soul, and beautiful presence. These also go well with many of our Puerto Rican classics—I encourage you to serve them as a side to your Pernil (page 224) or Pavochón (page 220), or revel in the collard greens' flavorful juices mixed with Arroz con gandules (page 241).

Makes 6 to 8 servings

2 pounds/1kg collard greens, washed, stems removed

1 tablespoon vegetable oil

1 large onion, chopped

4 garlic cloves, minced

1 pound/450g smoked turkey, dark meat (such as legs or wings)

6 cups/1.4L chicken broth

1 teaspoon garlic powder

1 teaspoon onion powder

1 teaspoon paprika

½ teaspoon white pepper

1 teaspoon Better Than Bouillon or 1 chicken bouillon cube

¼ cup/60ml apple cider vinegar

1 teaspoon red pepper flakes (optional, for a bit of heat)

Kosher salt and freshly ground black pepper to taste, *LQTDT*♥

Make stacks of the collard greens, up to 15 leaves at a time. Tightly roll up each stack into a log, then thinly slice into ½-inch rounds. Place the sliced collards in a bowl and rinse under water 2 to 3 times, to make sure all remaining dirt has been removed.

In a large pot over medium heat, add the oil and heat until it shimmers. Add the onion and sauté until translucent, about 5 minutes. Add the garlic and sauté for an additional minute, until fragrant.

Add the smoked turkey to the pot, pour in the broth, and bring to a boil. Then reduce the heat to low, cover the pot, and simmer for about 30 minutes, until the turkey is tender. Remove the turkey meat from the pot, shred into smaller pieces, and set aside.

Add the sliced collard greens to the pot and stir to combine, making sure the greens are submerged in the broth. Stir in the garlic powder, onion powder, paprika, white pepper, and bouillon. Add the shredded turkey meat back to the pot, followed by the vinegar and red pepper flakes (if using). Cover and simmer until collard greens are tender, 45 minutes to 1 hour. Remove the pot from the heat, season with salt and pepper, and serve hot.

Omi Tip: If it seems like you have too many collard greens at the start of this recipe, trust me, you do not. They cook down significantly, and there will be plenty of room in the pot.

Arroz con gandules

Rice and pigeon peas

¡Más que un arroz, es una tradición! Arroz con gandules is how you know we're celebrating something special in Puerto Rico, because it only shows up at parties, events, or during the holidays. My mom had this side dish with main-character vibes at her wedding, it made an appearance at my quinceañera, and it's always on the table during the holidays. Nowadays, it's easier to make this recipe because pigeon peas are easily found at grocery stores in dried or canned form. But when I was a kid, I'd sit outside with my abuelo and we'd patiently pick the individual peas from each pod he'd harvested from our land. Then, my abuela would store them in the freezer, only pulling them out on special occasions. Arroz con gandules is so entrenched in our food culture, it's often considered Puerto Rico's national dish.

Makes 4 to 6 servings

¼ cup/60ml Achiote oil (page 39)

½ pound/225g salted cooking ham, cubed

1 tablespoon Mi Sofrito Fresquecito (page 37)

1 tablespoon Garlic paste (page 39)

8 to 10 pimiento-stuffed green olives, halved (optional—they're very controversial in this dish!)

1 tablespoon sliced jarred roasted red peppers

One (15-ounce/425g) can pigeon peas, rinsed

1 tablespoon Adobo (page 38)

1 teaspoon Better Than Bouillon or chicken bouillon cube

3 cups/600g medium-grain white rice

In a caldero or large pot over medium-high heat, add the achiote oil and heat until it shimmers. Add the cubed ham and cook until golden brown on all sides, 7 to 8 minutes. Add the sofrito and garlic paste and stir to combine. Add the olives (if using), roasted red peppers, pigeon peas, adobo, and bouillon, stir to incorporate, and cook for 5 to 7 minutes, until it looks like a paste.

Add 3 cups/720ml of water, stir, and continue to cook for another 5 minutes, until the water reaches a rapid boil. Add the rice, stir to incorporate into the mixture, and cook for 7 to 10 minutes, until most of the water has evaporated and the rice is peeking through the vegetables in the pot.

Reduce the heat to low and mix the rice by using a wooden spoon to reach the rice at the bottom of the pot, lift it to the surface, and fold it back into the mixture. Cover and cook for another 25 to 30 minutes. Resist the urge to remove the lid during this stage to allow the rice to fluff up in the steam!

Uncover the pot and mix the rice again from the bottom up. Cover again and cook for 5 more minutes. Then fluff the rice and serve warm.

Tembleque

Coconut custard

A Puerto Rican holiday classic if there ever was one, tembleque is a dessert we usually buy from a señora we know who makes it just the way we like it. But now, with this recipe, you can give it a shot and make your own. The list of ingredients is short and easy to find, and it's actually pretty simple to make, so don't be afraid to give it a try. The name "tembleque" comes from the word *temblar,* which means "to tremble or shake," and it couldn't be more appropriate. When you unmold this dessert, it jiggles like Jell-O, yet it tastes like a light and creamy coconut cloud.

Makes 6 to 8 servings

- Two (14-ounce/415ml) cans coconut milk
- ¾ cup/150g granulated sugar
- ½ cup/70g cornstarch
- ¼ teaspoon kosher salt
- 1 teaspoon vanilla extract
- Ground cinnamon, for garnish

In a medium saucepan off the heat, combine the coconut milk, sugar, cornstarch, and salt. Whisk until the cornstarch is fully dissolved and the mixture is smooth. Then, place the saucepan over medium heat and cook the mixture, stirring continuously, until it thickens and starts to boil, 5 to 7 minutes.

Once the mixture reaches a boil, reduce the heat to low. Cook for 2 to 3 minutes, stirring continuously, until the mixture is very thick, like a pudding. Remove from the heat and stir in the vanilla extract.

Pour the mixture into a round 8-inch cake pan and smooth out the top with a spatula. Let the tembleque cool to room temperature, then cover and refrigerate for at least 4 hours, or until fully set.

To serve the tembleque, run a knife around the edges of the pan to loosen it, then invert onto a serving plate. Sprinkle with cinnamon, serve, and enjoy.

Omi Tip: It's important to stir the cornstarch off the heat to avoid clumping; once the mixture is on the heat, never stop stirring.

Adding a slice of lime peel to the coconut milk while it's boiling will really enhance the flavor of your tembleque—remove and discard before serving.

Tostadas francesas con coquito

French toast with coconut and rum sauce

We're huge on breakfast in my house. My sons love their French toast, pancakes, sausage, and bacon on any given weekend. But these tostadas francesas con coquito are a Christmas morning special, so they wait for me to make them all year long. My secret ingredient is adding coquito to the custard mixture. It's a perfect way to use up any leftover coquito from the night before. And don't worry—the rum evaporates during the cooking process, so it's safe for kids to eat, too—they'll become your number one fans that morning. I'm hoping that when you make this, you'll have friends and family sleeping in your rooms, on the sofa, and on the floor—whatever the case, this is meant to be shared in a full house. Aquí sí hay cama pa' mucha gente. 😉

Makes 4 to 5 servings

- 1 cup/240ml coconut milk
- ½ cup/120ml Coquito (page 169), or see Tip
- ¼ cup/60ml spiced rum (optional)
- 4 large eggs
- 1 teaspoon vanilla bean paste
- 1 teaspoon ground cinnamon
- ½ teaspoon ground nutmeg
- ¼ teaspoon ground cloves
- ¼ teaspoon kosher salt
- 8 to 10 thick slices brioche or challah bread
- 2 to 3 tablespoons salted butter
- ¼ cup/10g toasted coconut flakes, for serving
- Powdered sugar, for serving
- Maple syrup, for serving

In a large bowl, whisk together the coconut milk, coquito, spiced rum (if using), eggs, vanilla bean paste, cinnamon, nutmeg, cloves, and salt until well combined.

Place the bread slices in a shallow dish in a single layer. Pour the custard mixture over the bread, making sure each slice is well soaked. Let the bread soak for 5 to 10 minutes, flipping halfway through to make sure the custard is evenly absorbed.

In a large skillet or griddle over medium heat, melt 1 tablespoon of the butter. Add 3 or 4 slices of the soaked bread and cook until golden brown and crispy, 3 to 4 minutes per side. Set aside and repeat this step with the remaining butter and slices of bread, working in multiple batches if needed.

Transfer the French toast to a serving platter. Sprinkle with the toasted coconut flakes and powdered sugar and serve immediately, with warm maple syrup on the side.

Omi Tip: If you don't have coquito on hand, you can replace it with ½ cup/120ml of cream of coconut (Coco López, por supuesto). Follow the rest of the recipe as described.

Dulce de papaya

Candied papaya

A bite of dulce de papaya immediately evokes a nostalgic sense of home—and Christmas—on my taste buds. Although this is usually served on special occasions, my abuela often had some in the fridge waiting for me when I visited during the summers, and I was twice as lucky, because Mami used to make dulce de papaya from time to time at home, too. This recipe takes time, patience, and love, but it is worth every second of dedication. The glistening orange color of this candied papaya is a delight to the senses, not to mention its sweet, syrupy flavor. Pair it with a slice of queso blanco, and you'll feel like you've touched the sky.

Makes 10 to 12 servings

2 tablespoons baking soda

1 medium green or semi-ripe papaya (2½ pounds/1.1kg), peeled, deseeded, and cut into ½-inch-thick strips

4 cups/800g granulated sugar

1 cinnamon stick

5 whole cloves

⅛ teaspoon kosher salt

In a large bowl, mix 8 cups/1.9L of water with the baking soda. Add the papaya strips and soak in the baking soda–water mixture for 20 minutes to soften. Drain and rinse the papaya strips thoroughly with fresh cold water.

In a wide saucepan off the heat, add the papaya strips to the pan in an even layer. Add the sugar, cinnamon stick, cloves, salt, and 1 cup/240ml of water.

Place the saucepan on the stove over medium-high heat. Allow the water to come to a boil, then reduce the heat to medium-low and gently simmer until the papaya is tender and the liquid thickens into a syrup, 1 to 2 hours, stirring occasionally to prevent sticking.

Let the dulce de papaya cool to room temperature before serving. Serve as a dessert, either on its own or with a slice of any white cheese of your choice, such as queso fresco or queso blanco.

Omi Tip: One way to check if the dulce de papaya is fully done is to dip a metal spoon in the syrup, wait a few seconds, and then touch the spoon with your thumb and middle finger. If your finger sticks to the syrup, it's ready!

Budín de queso y dulce de leche

Cheese and dulce de leche bread pudding

One day, as my mind wandered into the realm of desserts—as it often does—I started thinking of my favorite flavor combinations, and dulce de leche with cream cheese came to mind. That led me to imagine dulce de leche and cream cheese sandwiches, and thinking about the bread brought Mami's delicious, custardy budines (bread puddings) to mind. So, I decided to put all these wandering ideas together to see what would happen. When I tried it, I found each bite so decadently delicious I had to post the recipe to my social media, and it went viral immediately.

Makes 8 to 10 servings

One (8-ounce/225g) package cream cheese, softened

One 9 by 13-inch loaf day-old bread, sliced

1 cup/310g dulce de leche, plus more for drizzling

4 cups/950ml whole milk

1 cup/240ml heavy cream

1 cup/200g granulated sugar

4 large eggs

1 teaspoon vanilla extract

1 teaspoon ground cinnamon

½ teaspoon ground nutmeg

¼ teaspoon kosher salt

Butter, for greasing

Spread a layer of cream cheese on half of the slices of bread. Spread a layer of dulce de leche on the other half of the slices. Make sandwiches with cream cheese on one side, dulce de leche on the other. Then, cut the sandwiches into small squares/cubes and set aside.

In a large bowl, whisk together the milk, heavy cream, sugar, eggs, vanilla extract, cinnamon, nutmeg, and salt until well combined and set aside.

Preheat the oven to 350°F/175°C. Grease a 9 by 13-inch baking dish with butter.

Place the sandwich cubes in the prepared baking dish in an even layer. Pour the custard mixture over the baking dish, ensuring all the bread is soaked. Let the mixture sit for about 15 minutes to allow the bread to absorb the custard.

Bake the budín for 45 to 50 minutes, until the top is golden brown and a knife inserted in the center comes out clean.

Allow the budín to cool slightly before serving. Serve warm or at room temperature, with extra dulce de leche drizzled on top, if desired.

Omi Tip: For budines, stale bread is the best bread, so make sure the bread you use is a day old—this will ensure it can absorb the custard mixture well. Ya te lo dije.

Flan de 5 ingredientes

5-ingredient caramel custard

My titi Angie gave me this recipe during one of my visits to Puerto Rico. When she first made it for me, I couldn't believe how delicious and extra creamy it was, so, of course, I had to ask her for the recipe. "Ay, nena," she said, "this only takes five ingredients to make." As soon as I returned home I added it to my arsenal of flans. It's so simple yet decadent, I love to serve this flan alongside a chocolate dessert and another dessert featuring pineapple, to satisfy everyone's taste buds during the holidays.

Makes 6 to 8 servings

1½ cups/300g granulated sugar

6 large eggs

1 teaspoon vanilla extract

One (12-ounce/350ml) can evaporated milk

One (14-ounce/415ml) can sweetened condensed milk

In a small saucepan over medium heat, combine the sugar and ¼ cup/60ml of water and cook, stirring occasionally, until the sugar is dissolved.

Increase the heat to medium-high and continue to cook, this time without stirring, until the sugar completely dissolves and turns a golden color, 7 to 10 minutes. Begin gently swirling the dissolved sugar in the saucepan until the color turns amber, about 2 minutes.

Remove the saucepan from the heat and carefully add 2 tablespoons/30ml of warm water, swirling until fully combined—you should have deep amber-brown caramel.

Quickly pour the caramel into a flan mold or a 9-inch round baking dish, tilting the dish to coat the bottom and sides evenly with the caramel. Set aside to cool and allow the caramel to harden.

Preheat the oven to 350°F/175°C.

In a blender, combine the eggs, vanilla extract, evaporated milk, and sweetened condensed milk. Blend until fully combined and smooth.

Pour the flan mixture through a fine-mesh strainer directly on top of the hardened caramel in the mold.

Place the flan mold in a larger baking dish and fill the larger dish with hot water reaching halfway up the sides of the mold—this creates a water bath (bain-marie), or as we call it, un baño de María.

Bake the flan for 50 to 60 minutes, until the custard is set and a knife inserted in the center comes out clean.

Remove the flan mold from the water bath and let it cool to room temperature. Then transfer it to the refrigerator for at least 4 hours, or overnight.

To serve, run a knife around the inner edges of the flan mold to loosen it. Invert the flan onto a serving plate so the caramel is on top, slice, and enjoy.

Omi Tip: Pouring the custard through a fine-mesh strainer helps ensure there are no lumps, and you'll end up with an ultra-smooth flan.

Acknowledgments

I am filled with deep gratitude for every single person who walked with me through this journey. Writing this cookbook has been one of the most challenging and life-changing things I've ever done, because it's not just a collection of recipes—it's a love letter to my island, my family, and my people. This book exists because of community, because of love, because of you.

A mis padres, Doña Connie y Don Alberto, gracias por darme la base sobre la que he construido mi vida. Mami: Tu sazón, tus oraciones y tu fuerza están presentes en cada página de este libro. Papi: Tu apoyo silencioso y tus consejos siempre me han recordado que nunca estoy sola. Y a mis padrastros, Cooper y Maritza, gracias por llegar a mi vida y elegirme como suya. Nunca intentaron reemplazar a nadie, simplemente sumaron más amor, más alegría y más guía. A mi hermano, Carlos (Junior), te adoro. Gracias por tu apoyo y por siempre creer en mí. Soy quien soy porque cada uno de ustedes me ha moldeado a su manera. Llevo conmigo las lecciones, el cariño y el legado de todos ustedes con profunda gratitud.

To my husband, Kradin, thank you for your prayers, your patience, and your encouragement throughout this journey. You never asked for the spotlight, but you've been there every step of the way. You believed in the vision and stood beside me as it came to life, especially during the long days and early mornings. You have seen me in all forms, and you've been my number one fan since we met that day at the bank. This book reflects the season of perseverance we walked through together, and for that I am grateful. This book is yours too. Te amo.

To my boys, Lil' Kradin, Zekiah, X'Avian, and Isaiah, you are my greatest teachers, you are my daily dose of laughter and humility, you are my why. Thank you for giving me the space to chase this dream, through late nights, busy days, and meals that weren't made with the same hands-on love you're used to. Each of you carry a part of me, and I hope this book shows you

that our culture is a treasure worth protecting, that your roots are strong, rich, and beautiful. I hope that you'll hold this book in your hands and feel proud, not just of me, but of who we are as a family. I love you more than words could ever explain, My HopperBots.

To my chosen family, my sisterhood, Elizabeth Succart, my person and forever amiga, we're locked in for life. You made sure I never felt alone in this journey, encouraging every decision with unwavering support and love. Shelby "Bubbs" Malaska, all the way from the land of potatoes, your friendship has been a grounding force; you never missed a beat and always showed up with your whole heart. Dimaris Salgado, from day one, you've manifested this dream alongside me; your excitement and faith gave me the strength to keep going even when things felt overwhelming. Coach Nadia, your workouts became my refuge, helping me push through some of the most difficult moments during this project. You truly are a gift. To my tribe, Vironica Anderson, Jetzabel Mills, Candy Hall, Lisa Moody, Crystal Smith Johnston, and Rosalie Berrios, thank you for showing up with open arms, open hearts, and empty stomachs. You have been a steady source of strength, encouragement, and prayer. You reminded me that faith isn't just felt in pews, but also passed around in Tupperware after service, at potlucks filled with arroz con gandules. Every "I'm praying for you" was deeply felt and truly needed. Together, you all have made this journey not just possible, but joyful, and I am endlessly grateful for each of you.

To my colleagues turned RIO sisters, Ivelissa Rios and Rebeca Huffman, thank you for showing me that friendship can exist in adulthood, and that it can be powerful and deeply rooted. What began as a connection through social media blossomed into something real and lasting. I'm grateful our paths crossed and that we can enjoy one another's wins, big and small.

Las familias García-Castro, Hernández-Opio, Hopper, to every titi, tío, and cousin who ever shared their wisdom, memories, and recipes with me, thank you. You trusted me with your stories, and I carry them with care. This is our collective cocina, made with pride and deep reverence for all who came before us.

To my incredible community on Instagram, Facebook, TikTok, and YouTube, both online and offline, thank you for welcoming me into your homes and hearts. Your unwavering support, heartfelt comments, and encouraging messages have been my guiding light. Every time one of you shared, "That's how my abuela made it, too," you filled me with immense pride and joy, reaffirming that I was on the right path. And each in-person encounter has felt like a reunion with a long-lost family member; I cherish those moments deeply. Thank you for reminding me why this work matters and for being the incredible community that you are. Together, we are family.

To my literary agent, Johanna Castillo, your presence alone is inspiring, but the way you championed this project was so empowering for me. You saw me—and the heart of this book—before the first word was written. Your fierce guidance and commitment to representing our comunidad with such excellence has left an eternal imprint in my life.

To executive editor Cristina Garces, this book exists in the world because you stood in the gap and made sure it had a chance to be heard. As a fellow Puerto Rican woman in this space, you didn't just see a manuscript, you saw a legacy, and you helped me honor that. Thank you for holding my hand through this journey and for helping me bring this book into the world with the same love that lives on each page.

To the outstanding team at Ten Speed Press, who diligently worked their magic behind the scenes to design, produce, and market this project with all the care that it requires: thank you! I now know it takes much more than a village—this book wouldn't be in our hands without your invaluable contributions.

To Cecilia Molinari, "Mi Omi querida" will forever be my favorite greeting on our voice texts. From the very beginning, you approached my story with care and deep respect, listening intently and writing with a sensitivity that made every word feel like mine. What started as a professional collaboration has turned into a real friendship with a shared love of music, food, and cultura. I could not have worked with a better human. Eres lo máximo.

To my incredible photographer and culinary team, Beth Fuller and Joy Grant, the powerhouse women who brought their talent, expertise, and full hearts to this project: Thank you for embracing this cookbook—and my culture—with genuine curiosity, care, and appreciation. Watching you experience our culture sitting at my grandmother's table, tasting my mom's food for the first time in the home where so many of these meals were born, was magic you can't plan. Thank you for helping me honor my roots so beautifully through your lenses. This book carries your fingerprints, through more than just images, because you became part of the story.

Finally, to Puerto Rico, mi isla bella, mi tierra, mi orgullo, mi inspiración. You are the rhythm in my footsteps, the flavor in my food, and the fire in my heart. This book is for you. De aquí hasta el cielo.

Index

TEN SPEED PRESS
An imprint of the Crown Publishing Group
A division of Penguin Random House LLC
1745 Broadway
New York, NY 10019
tenspeed.com
penguinrandomhouse.com

Typefaces: Bretagne's Self Modern, Tipo Pèpel's Gina, and Tokotype's Stroma.

Library of Congress Cataloging-in-Publication Data
Names: Hopper, Omi author | Molinari, Cecilia author
Title: Cooking con Omi : a love letter to Puerto Rican cuisine / Omi Hopper with Cecilia Molinari.
Description: First edition. | New York, NY : Ten Speed Press, [2026] | Includes index.
Identifiers: LCCN 2025031679 (print) | LCCN 2025031680 (ebook) | ISBN 9780593837689 hardcover | ISBN 9780593837696 ebook
Subjects: LCSH: Cooking, Puerto Rican | LCGFT: Cookbooks
Classification: LCC TX716.P8 H677 2026 (print) | LCC TX716.P8 (ebook) |
DDC 614.59/27295—dc23/eng/20251113
LC record available at https://lccn.loc.gov/2025031679
LC ebook record available at https://lccn.loc.gov/2025031680

Hardcover ISBN 978-0-593-83768-9
Ebook ISBN 978-0-593-83769-6

Editor: Cristina Garces | Production editor: Joyce Wong
Editorial assistant: Kausaur Fahimuddin
Designer: Emma Campion | Production designers: Mari Gill and Faith Hague
Production and prepress color: Jane Chinn
Food stylist: Joy Howard | Food stylist assistants: Olivia Counter and Kayla Tabb
Prop stylist: Joy Howard | Prop assistant: Beth Fuller
Copy editor: Allie Kiekhofer | Proofreaders: Heather Rodino, Eldes Tran, Sigi Nacson
Indexer: Elizabeth Parson
Publicist: Natalie Yera-Campbell | Marketer: Brianne Sperber

Manufactured in Malaysia

10 9 8 7 6 5 4 3 2 1

First Edition